THE SINKING
OF THE BELGRANO

by

Arthur Gavshon

and

Desmond Rice

NEW ENGLISH LIBRARY

First published in Great Britain in 1984
by Martin Secker & Warburg Limited

First NEL Paperback Edition November 1984

NEL Books are published by
New English Library,
Mill Road, Dunton Green,
Sevenoaks, Kent.
Editorial office: 47 Bedford Square, London WC1B 3DP

Made and printed in Great Britain by Cox & Wyman Limited, Reading

British Library Cataloguing in Publication Data

Gavshon, Arthur
　Sinking of the Belgrano.
　1. General Belgrano (*ship*)　　2. Falkland Islands,
War, 1982—Naval operations
　1. Title　　II. Rice, Desmond
　997'.11　　F3031.5
　ISBN 0-450-05786-0

ABOUT THE AUTHORS

Arthur Gavshon was until 1981 diplomatic correspondent for Europe for Associated Press of America. Based in London, he worked in Washington, Moscow, Paris and Peking, building a network of contacts in the political and diplomatic world. He is the author of *The Last Days of Dag Hammarskjold* and *Crisis In Africa*. He is married, with three daughters.

Desmond Rice was born in Kenya, and has since travelled the world as an international oil executive. He was president of the Royal Dutch Shell Company in Argentina, and established wide contacts inside and outside the government there. He has written seven novels under the pen name Desmond Meiring. He is unmarried and lives on Hydra, Greece.

Contents

Maps

Illustrations

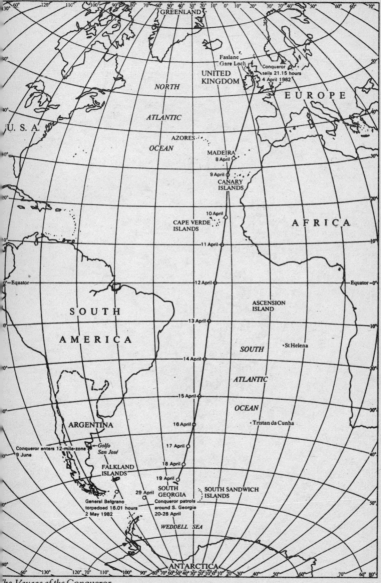

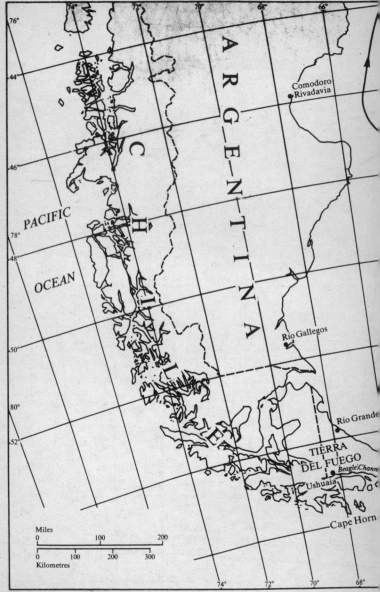

The South Atlantic Battle Ground

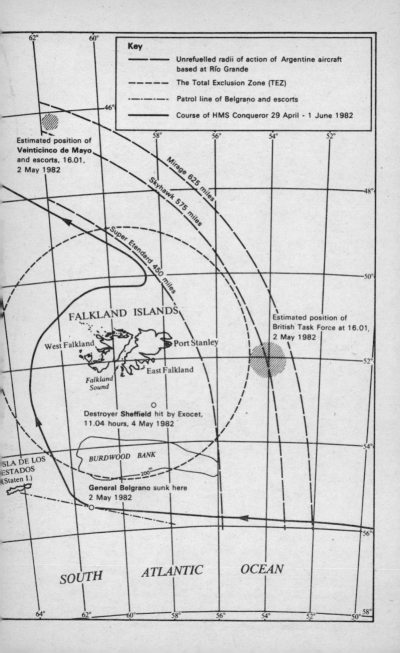

Key

————	Unrefuelled radii of action of Argentine aircraft based at Río Grande
– – – –	The Total Exclusion Zone (TEZ)
–·–·–	Patrol line of Belgrano and escorts
————	Course of HMS Conqueror 29 April - 1 June 1982

Estimated position of **Veinticinco de Mayo** and escorts, 16.01, 2 May 1982

Mirage 625 miles

Skyhawk 575 miles

Super Etendard 450 miles

FALKLAND ISLANDS

West Falkland

Port Stanley

Falkland Sound

East Falkland

Estimated position of British Task Force at 16.01, 2 May 1982

Destroyer **Sheffield** hit by Exocet, 11.04 hours, 4 May 1982

BURDWOOD BANK

200ᵐ

ISLA DE LOS ESTADOS (Staten I.)

General Belgrano sunk here 2 May 1982

SOUTH ATLANTIC OCEAN

AUTHORS' NOTE

Secrets are the currency of modern military and diplomatic exchange. Its goodwill is confidence. We have been helped in the writing of this book by authorities in several countries. Among them are past and present foreign ministers, ambassadors, military personnel from admirals to rank-and-file sailors, soldiers and airmen. Many requested anonymity. We acknowledge their cooperation without naming them, for to do so would be to debase the currency and destroy the goodwill.

Apart from original researches in Argentina, Britain, Peru and the United States we have made liberal use of information contained in a variety of governmental publications. These include the reports of Lord Franks' Committee of Privy Counsellors; the Commission headed by General Benjamín Rattenbach which investigated Argentina's entry into and conduct of the war; proceedings in the House of Commons; and UN Security Council and General Assembly debates and resolutions.

Desmond Rice, who speaks Spanish fluently, was based in Buenos Aires for several years and travelled extensively through key Latin American countries as president of a major multinational oil company. All the material from named and unnamed Argentine, Peruvian and other Latin American sources in this book has been derived from his interviews and researches over an 18-month period. Key military and political figures, sometimes at considerable personal risk, allowed him access to confidential official papers including transcripts of important Presidential telephone conversations.

Information about British diplomatic, political and military activity during and since the war has come primarily from Arthur Gavshon. His contacts with senior ministers, politicians, diplomats and servicemen have been developed during a career spanning more than 30 years of coverage as an Associated Press correspondent in London, Washington and other world capitals.

The writers' thanks go to those whose interviews, conversations, advice, speeches, letters or articles have been enlightening. In alphabetical order they include: Roberto Alemann, former Argentine Minister of Economy; Alvaro Alsogaray, former Minister of Economy, Labour and Industry; Dr Javier Arias Stella, Peruvian Foreign Minister during the 1982 war and now Ambassador to the UN; Peter J. Beck, principal lecturer in International History at Kingston Polytechnic; Hector Elías Bonzo, who commanded the *Belgrano*; Nicanor Costa Méndez, who was Argentine Foreign Minister during the conflict; Tam Dalyell, a Labour member of Parliament; José García Enciso, Aide to the Secretary-General to the Presidency under General Galtieri; Thomas D. Enders, who was Assistant Secretary of State for Inter-American Affairs before becoming US Ambassador to Spain; Capitán Jorge Luis Estévez of the Argentine Navy; Paul Foot, *Daily Mirror* columnist; Rogelio Frigerio, Vice President of the MID party; ex-President Arturo Frondizi of Argentina; former US Secretary of State Alexander M. Haig; Sir Nicholas Henderson, who was British Ambassador in Washington during the war; Dr Clifford Kirakofe, legislative assistant to US Senator Jesse Helms; Guillermo Makin, graduate research student and writer, Girton College, Cambridge; José Martínez de Hoz, former Argentine Minister of Economy; Paratroop General Rodolfo C. Mujica; Federico Ortiz; Social Democratic Party leader and former Labour Foreign Secretary David Owen; Emilio van Peborgh, a former Argentine Defence Minister; Capitán Miguel Pita, who headed Argentine military intelligence; Capitán Carlos Hugo Robacio, who commanded Argentina's 5th Marine Battalion in the Falklands fighting; Dr Paul Rogers, lecturer in Peace Studies at Bradford University; Alberto Silva, an Argentine newspaper and television commentator; BBC presenter Peter Snow; Esteben Takacs, former Argentine Ambassador to the US; William Wallace, Director of Studies at the Royal Institute of International Affairs; Andrew Wilson of the *Observer*; Philip Windsor, reader in International Relations at the London

School of Economics; Rear-Admiral Horacio Zaratiegui, who commanded the Southern Naval Region of the Argentine fleet during the war.

The writers, in the interests of balance, requested either formal or informal interviews with Britain's former Foreign Secretary Francis Pym, Commander Christopher Wreford-Brown of the nuclear submarine HMS *Conqueror* and Ambassador Jeane Kirkpatrick, who represents the US at the United Nations. Mr Pym, after examining a series of questions submitted at the suggestion of his office, decided against replying. The application to see Commander Wreford-Brown submitted to the Ministry of Defence in June was still being 'officially considered' in December. Written and verbal approaches for a meeting with Mrs Kirkpatrick finally drew the response that the Ambassador, a member of President Reagan's cabinet, was 'under instructions not to discuss matters relating to the Falklands' with journalists or writers.

Publication of this book in March 1984, and a subsequent BBC Panorama investigation brought to light important new evidence relating to the sinking of the *Belgrano*. This not only stirred controversy inside and outside Parliament but also caused serving and former members of the government and their officials yet again to amend their much-revised portrayal of what had happened. The Prime Minister confirmed the accuracy of our information which was that the Argentine cruiser was first detected two days, and not just a few hours, before being sunk. Alexander Haig and Francis Pym, then incumbent US and British foreign ministers, offered diametrically opposite versions of the conclusions they had reached in their Washington meetings. Cecil Parkinson revealed that he and fellow-members of the War Cabinet knew a Peruvian peace initiative was under way before they decided to attack the *Belgrano*. Admiral Lord Lewin, then Chief of the Defence Staff, appeared to contradict Mrs Thatcher when he emphasized that the *Belgrano* was 'not an absolutely immediate threat' to the British task force. Defenders of the government's position, nevertheless, seized upon Panorama's presentation of the view expressed by Argentina's Rear-Admiral Juan Jose Lombardo who had been asked if he would have sunk 'a British *Belgrano*' if he had come across her. 'Yes,' Lombardo replied. 'If I were the commanding officer of the submarine I would try to sink enemy surface ships or submarines.' The question, of course, was loaded. It would have been fairer and a better analogy if Lombardo had been asked: 'Would you have sunk "a British *Belgrano*" if you had come across her knowing promising peace talks were under way?'

We are indebted especially to Peter Grose of Secker and Warburg for his enthusiasm, encouragement and wise counsel; and we appreciate deeply the patience, perceptiveness and tenacity of Steve Cox's excellent editing.

Arthur Gavshon
Desmond Rice

London, June 1984

PROLOGUE

At 17.44 Lima time (19.44 Argentine time) on 2 May 1982, after a press conference announcement by President Belaúnde Terry of Peru of a new development in the confrontation between Argentina and Great Britain in the South Atlantic, the Associated Press agency man in Lima filed the following message to his New York headquarters:

> PRESIDENT FERNANDO BELAUNDE TERRY SAID TODAY THAT GREAT BRITAIN AND ARGENTINA WOULD TONIGHT ANNOUNCE THE END OF ALL HOSTILITIES IN THEIR DISPUTE OVER THE FALKLANDS.
>
> THE BASIC DOCUMENT WAS DRAWN UP BY US SECRETARY OF STATE ALEXANDER HAIG AND TRANSMITTED TO THE ARGENTINE GOVERNMENT BY THE PERUVIAN PRESIDENT.
>
> HE SAID THAT LONG AND CONTINUOUS CONTACTS BETWEEN THE TWO SIDES BEGAN YESTERDAY, CONTINUED LAST NIGHT AND EARLY THIS MORNING AND WILL BE PUBLISHED TONIGHT.
>
> BELAUNDE SAID THAT HE WAS UNABLE TO MAKE KNOWN THE TERMS OF THE AGREEMENT IN ADVANCE EXCEPT FOR THE FIRST, ABOUT WHICH THERE IS NO DISCUSSION: IMMEDIATE CEASEFIRE.[1]

Unknown to President Belaúnde, the crucial act of the war had already been committed when he went to meet the press that afternoon. At 16.01 Argentime time (14.01 Lima time) the British nuclear submarine HMS *Conqueror* had attacked the 44-year-old Argentine cruiser *General Belgrano*, with a crew of 1,138 men, at a position later given to the House of Commons as 55 degrees 27 minutes south, 61 degrees 25 minutes west.[2] At 17.01 the captain and surviving crew of the *Belgrano* had watched their ship go down into the waters of the South Atlantic.

Within two days of that attack, an air-launched Exocet missile fatally damaged the British destroyer HMS *Sheffield*, with further loss of lives. The final death-rolls for the two ships numbered 368 men killed on the *Belgrano*, 21 men killed on the *Sheffield*. Negotiations continued, but neither government could seem to overlook those casualties without endangering its own survival. The Belaúnde proposals had offered a sane conclusion to the war which began with the Argentine invasion of the Falkland Islands on 2 April 1982. Unhappily the real conclusion was not reached until six weeks and more than a thousand deaths later, with the surrender of Argentina's occupying forces on 14 June 1982.

British official accounts of the Peruvian peace proposals have uniformly disparaged them, presenting them as a totally separate (and minor) issue from that of the sinking of the *Belgrano*. Government versions of the sinking itself have been inconsistent both in the factual details and in the military and political reasoning put forward. An artificial fog surrounds the pivotal weekend of 1–2 May when the *Belgrano* was torpedoed and President Belaúnde's initiative foundered. This book sets out to penetrate the smokescreen.

PART I

I

International Bandits?

A century and a half ago, in January 1833, Great Britain expelled the Argentine garrison of the Falkland Islands. No one seriously doubts that within another century and a half the Falklands will become Argentine territory again.[1] Fortress Falklands is too far away, and too expensive, for Britain to be willing or able to maintain it indefinitely. Until 1982, the sovereignty, and even the whereabouts, of the islands had been matters of near-total indifference to the British people. To Argentines, though, they were a close and burning issue whose settlement had been much too long postponed, and the strength of this 'Malvinas factor' is a vital dimension of the events we cover here.

The difference in the Argentine perspective is first a question of distance. Argentina is a country four times the length of Great Britain. The Falkland Islands, some four hundred miles away, are as close in these terms as the Shetlands are to the British mainland. Mere propinquity gives no claim to ownership in international law – otherwise Gibraltar would be Spanish and the Channel Islands French – but what appears to the British as a dot in the South Atlantic, 8,000 miles away, appears to Argentines as the only sizeable body of land lying off their coastline, whose ownership would be an immediate strategic consideration even if Argentina had no legal claim upon them.

As for the legal claim, it is impossible after 150 years of British occupation to be so clear-cut as was one famous defender of British rights and sovereignty at the time. In July 1829 the Duke of Wellington, then the British prime minister, wrote: 'I have perused the papers respecting the Falkland Islands. It is not at all clear to me that we have ever possessed the sovereignty of these islands.'[2] The British claim to prior discovery of the islands in the 1590s was by its nature difficult to prove, and subject to counter-claims of earlier sightings, for instance by Amerigo Vespucci in 1504. A British garrison had occupied the Falklands for a few years in the eighteenth century, and been permitted to remain by the Spanish government, which then occupied most of the South American mainland with a legal title recognized by European nations if not by local inhabitants. When the garrison left the islands in 1774, it had left behind a plaque insisting upon British rights there, as you might leave your coat on your seat while lunching on a train.

The young Argentine republic which had inherited Spanish claims in 1816 was in no position to oppose the overwhelming power of the British navy, and Great Britain has remained on the Falklands since Captain Onslow sailed in on HMS *Clio* early in 1833. In the nineteenth century their ownership had several very practical advantages. 'The rationale was that possession of the Falklands would strengthen British sea power and provide a base for whaling and the suppression of piracy. In addition, the growing trade with Australia via the Straits of Magellan would make such a colony advantageous. Britain's interest grew at a time when it was seeking to dominate the seas and world trade.'[3] Argentina never stopped asserting its claims; Great Britain stayed put, while generations of British Falklanders were born; history applied its customary patina of immemorial practice.

On 25 May 1910, Argentina celebrated the centenary of the revolution which deposed the Spanish viceroy, and took the opportunity to reiterate its Falklands claims. Gerald Spicer, head of the British Foreign Office's American department, asked the FO's assistant librarian, Gaston de Bernhardt, for a detailed historical study of the dispute, and on 7 December he received a 49-page analysis of all official files and other relevant sources. What he read must have made him feel retrospectively relieved that Great Britain had refused even to answer the one proposal ever made by either country to submit the Falklands question to international arbitration, 26 years previously.[4] De Bernhardt's memo so undermined the British claim that a shaken Spicer minuted on 12 December 1910: 'From a perusal of this memo it is difficult to avoid the conclusion that the Argentine Government's attitude is not altogether unjustified, and that our action has been somewhat high-handed.'[5] A successor of Spicer's as head of the American department, John Troutbeck, noted in 1936 that 'the difficulty of our position is that our seizure of the Falkland Islands in 1833 was so arbitrary a procedure' that it would not be 'easy to explain our position without showing ourselves up as international bandits'.[6]

The British answer was to shift the basis of the argument for sovereignty away from prior discovery and legal title and towards a justification resting on the grounds of 'prescription', defined in the Oxford English Dictionary as a 'claim founded upon long use'. Much of the available information on the official British view of the legality of their Falklands claim comes from the researches of Dr Peter Beck, Principal Lecturer in International History at Kingston Polytechnic, who had been investigating the question before the outbreak of the Falklands war in 1982. The Foreign Office promptly withdrew from scrutiny many of the key records which he and other academics wanted to consult in the Public Records Office in London. Beck summarizes the British shift: 'Thus, as Anthony Eden observed in 1936, the British case had been argued hitherto upon the wrong grounds. This rendered it necessary to adopt an alternative perspective, which replaced the traditional emphasis upon *pre*-1833 criteria with one based on *post*-1833 criteria.'[7] Instead of arguing that they had found the seat and then left their coat on it, in effect the British were now saying that whoever the seat might have belonged to in 1833, they had now been sitting in it for so long that a century's practice made it theirs. No matter how valid this principle of prescription may be in the international law which Great Britain has never put to the test, it does not require much imagination to work out the likely Argentine response to the new British rationale. If Britain had stolen their Malvinas in the first place – and no one can say with confidence whether it had or had not – it was now adding insult to injury. From 'It's ours, so we took it', the British had transposed to 'We took it, so it's ours.'

Beck's researches led him to share the conclusion reached as far back as 1927 by Julius Goebel, the American author of a standard work, *The Struggle for the Falkland Islands*, which Yale University Press reprinted in 1982. Goebel wrote: 'There is a certain futility in interposing the lean and ascetic visage of the law in a situation

which, first and last, is merely a question of power.'[8] As Beck
saw it, the events both of 1833 and of 1982 'appear to confirm
that, in the last resort, power and will are the decisive factors.
Thus, the Buenos Aires government complained in 1833 that the
British occupation represented "the exercise of the Rights of the
Strongest to humiliate a powerless infant people". Again in 1982
Britain possessed both the will and the power . . . to regain
control over the Falklands.'[9]

So here is the second crucial difference of perspective between
Great Britain, peering out at the distant Falklands, and Argentina, which by the early 1980s was providing the Falklands' only
regular air service (Mondays, from Comodoro Rivadavia), looking after those hospital cases too serious for the facilities of
Stanley, and supplying all the islands' oil needs through the
Argentine state company YPF. It is hardly an exaggeration to say
that the British people noticed the Falklands in three disparate
contexts only: at school, learning about the naval battle fought
there in 1914; or looking at the shrunken list of British colonies
and their dependencies; or when some new Argentine initiative
caused its fleeting stir in Parliament and the media, before
oblivion fell again.

For the Argentine people it was a different matter. The Malvinas were an ancient grievance and a present objective. Every
schoolchild knew where they were and to whom they rightfully
belonged. In South America in general, let alone Argentina, they
were seen as a political anachronism, the last vestige of an
otherwise bygone colonialism. In the words of Sir Derick Ashe,
British Ambassador in Buenos Aires in the mid-1970s: 'No one
in London could ever understand the degree of almost religious
fervour that the Argentines had for the islands. It was more like
the Holy Grail for them, the one cause that could unite all the
Argentines.'[10] Yet the Argentines also felt that they had shown
exemplary patience. Beck has pointed out that as well as the
British government's 'proposed offer . . . to reunite Falkland
Islands with Argentina' (in a file not accessible until the year
1991), 'there is evidence . . . that in 1940 a leasing scheme was
considered but not pursued. But, in general, Argentina did not
take undue advantage of Britain's wartime preoccupations to
press its claims to the Falklands'.[11] In 1948, the Argentines made
another offer to put the question to adjudication; nothing came of
it.

By the 1950s, the Falklands' population was in decline from the maximum of 2,392 it had reached in 1931: in 1953 the figure was 2,230, and by 1980 it would have fallen to 1,813. With the opening of the Panama Canal between the wars, most shipping bound for the Pacific had cheerfully abandoned the route around Cape Horn, and the islands found themselves relegated to being a mercantile and geopolitical backwater. Sheep had long ago replaced whaling and fishery as the principal source of income, but the wool industry too had begun to decline, and was made more insecure by the large and unpredictable price fluctuations of the 1960s and 70s.

The British media, during their brief involvement with the new-found Falklands in 1982, tended to present the population as rugged individualists tilling the recalcitrant soil, shearing their own sheep on their own farms, quietly dedicating themselves to their own stubborn destinies. This had been very much the orthodox version well before the invasion. One standard guide-book to South America stated in 1977 that the inhabitants were 'almost exclusively of pure British descent, and descendants of the early pioneers own the greater part of the land. They are hard-working and thrifty.'[12] The reality was that absentee land-lords possessed most of the land and controlled practically the entire economy. One group, the Falkland Islands Company (FIC), set up in 1851, owned 42 per cent of the land area of 4,700 square miles, and controlled 66 per cent of the wool clip through a system of interlocking directorships with other independent but smaller companies. The FIC ran the single shipping link with Britain which carried the annual wool output, running at about £2 million. It also provided the islands' internal trade. A postwar study by the Latin American Bureau claimed that: 'The absentee landlords who control the islands measure success solely in terms of the levels of profit which they are able to extract.'[13] The survey commissioned by the British government from Lord Shackleton in 1975, and published in May 1976 as the Shackleton Report, said: 'If there is one cause of the decline in population and in the Falkland Island economy, it is the drain of resources from the Falklands to the UK. Given the choice between local reinvestment of after-tax profits and investment in the UK, the companies have chosen the latter option.'[14] To illustrate the rapid rate of decapitalization, Lord Shackleton cited figures showing that over four years the absentee landlords had ploughed back into the islands just one-sixtieth of their profits. Thus by the 1980s the Falklands could boast no more than 24 miles of roads, 11 miles paved, the rest gravel.

The effect of all this for the average islander was to make him an FIC servant, earning perhaps £60 weekly – three-fifths the wage of a British farmworker. He lived in a company house on company land and bought his needs at a company store. The first ruling power in his life was the Falkland Islands Company, now the property of Coalite Limited. The second ruling power was the British Foreign and Commonwealth Office, represented by its South America Department and by a governor appointed in London and assisted by an executive council. This same governor and council were also responsible for the Falkland Islands Dependencies, which 'are not part of the colony of the Falkland Islands, but constitute a separate colony'.[15] The Dependencies are the island groups of South Georgia, lying some 800 miles ESE of the Falklands (about $54\frac{1}{2}°$S, $36°$W), and South Sandwich, another 400 miles to the southeast ($58°$S, $26\frac{1}{2}°$W). Only South Georgia is inhabited, by scientists of the British Antarctic Survey. One of the South Sandwich Islands is Southern Thule, where a helicopter from HMS *Endurance* discovered 'an Argentine military presence' on 20 December 1976 which was still there when the Falklands were invaded.[16]

No gunboat showed up to evict these Argentines for the rest of the 1970s. That fact was only one item in what appeared to the British as a series of disconnected events; however Argentine officials were able to interpret them as sentences in one and the same encoded statement from a colonial power which had already unloaded most of its old possessions. This misunderstanding (if misunderstanding it was) is matched on the British side by an habitual underestimate of the Argentine longing to regain the Malvinas. Where Argentina inflated Britain's apathy, Britain discounted Argentina's ambition. The British continued to do so even after the Falklands war, when the committee headed by Lord Franks was asked to report only on 'the period leading up to the Argentine invasion'. Ignoring the long history of the Argentine claim, the Franks Report refers to its reiteration in 1963 and 1964 merely as 'a resurgence of Argentine interest', and chooses to examine the history of the dispute only from 1965, 'since it was then that the issue was first brought formally to international attention'.[17]

On 16 December 1965, UN General Assembly Resolution No. 2065 (Appendix 1) invited the British and Argentines to negotiate a peaceful settlement of their Falklands dispute, and implicitly recognized the strength of the Argentine case by placing the issue in the context of ending 'colonialism in all its forms'. The resolution asked both governments to bear in mind 'the interests of the population'. In an age of decolonization there were signs at some levels of the British government of a readiness to contemplate an orderly disengagement from what was felt to be a burdensome commitment in a far-off place. The Franks Report provides a lucid account of the main events following the UN resolution. In 1968 a 'Memorandum of Understanding' between the two governments mentioned Great Britain recognizing 'Argentina's sovereignty from a date to be agreed', subject to whether 'the interest of the Islanders would be secured'.[18] The initiative foundered, and in 1973 a second UN resolution called for a speedy solution, as did yet another resolution in 1976.

On 26 April 1977, after a Foreign and Commonwealth Office minister, Ted Rowlands, had held meetings and talks both in the Falklands Islands and in Buenos Aires, the new Foreign Secretary, Dr David Owen, announced that negotiations to be held from June or July 1977 would concern 'future political relations, including sovereignty, with regard to the Falkland Islands, South Georgia and South Sandwich Islands'. During these talks with Argentina, the British government would 'consult' the people of the Falklands.[19] This is how the Franks Report sums up the view of the British Defence Committee in July 1977:

> The aim should be to keep the negotiations with the Argentine Government going so as to allow time for the education of public opinion at home and in the Islands to be carried forward. Broadly speaking, the Government's strategy was to retain sovereignty as long as possible, if necessary making concessions in respect of the Dependencies . . . while recognising that ultimately only some form of leaseback arrangement was likely to satisfy Argentina.[20]

It was Owen who, during a critical period of bellicose Argentine naval activity in 1977, arranged for a nuclear-powered submarine and two frigates to be deployed in the area. The purpose was to reinforce Britain's negotiating position at a time when further Argentine military action was thought possible. Owen has emphasized that this was a secret deployment, not for the purpose of provoking Argentina, but as a defensive precaution. On the other hand James Callaghan, then prime minister, has said that he ensured that the unit's presence was made known through undisclosed channels to the Junta of the day. According to Martin Walker, writing in the *Guardian* in 1982, 'the Argentines were informed of its presence by the Americans, at Britain's request'.[21]

This episode is particularly worth noting because of the high level of confusion it has generated. It affects the British government's message not only to the Argentines but also to itself. Dr Owen has subsequently claimed that the rules of engagement drawn up for the expedition allowed the force dispatched to sink Argentine ships. Admiral Lord Lewin has flatly denied that claim. Much more damaging, because it points to a lost opportunity to stop the Falklands war before it started, is the assertion about the force made in the Franks Report: 'We have found no evidence that the Argentine Government ever came to know of its existence.'[22] Certainly the news was never made public in Argentina. Perhaps Mr Callaghan's message was never delivered. At any rate on 5 March 1982, when the diplomatic temperature was rising, but before the South Georgia incident on 19 March, Lord Carrington was informed that 'at an earlier period of heightened tension in the dispute, the previous Government had covertly sent a small naval task force to the area. Lord Carrington asked whether the Argentines had known about it and, *when told that they had not, he did not pursue the matter*' (emphasis added).[23] Whether or not the Argentines had been warned in 1977, in 1982 Lord Carrington knew of no useful precedent for using a naval presence for purposes of deterrence.

Carrington had been warning the British Cabinet for some time that if Argentina saw no prospect of progress (he himself favoured some sort of leaseback solution) then the dam was likely to burst. His memorandum to the Defence Committee on 12 October 1979 said in part that 'the "Fortress Falklands" option and the option of continuing talks but without making any concessions on sovereignty both carried a serious threat of invasion'.[24] This was the first of many examples cited in the Franks Report to show that Britain's diplomats, service chiefs and intelligence units had accurately assessed the perils in the deteriorating situation during the months and years before the invasion. It was followed in November 1979 by a report of the Joint Intelligence Committee – Britain's top group of diplomatic, political and military analysts – which said that: 'If negotiations broke down or if for some other reason the Argentine Government calculated that the British Government were not prepared to negotiate seriously on sovereignty, there would be a high risk of their resorting quickly to more forceful measures'.[25]

Mrs Thatcher's reaction was to postpone any formal discussion of the Falklands until a Rhodesian (Zimbabwean) settlement had been reached in the negotiations then in progress. It took more than three months, and further pressure from Carrington, before the Defence Committee looked at the submissions from the Foreign Secretary and JIC; and even then the warning of invasion seems not to have been taken seriously, because ministers hardened the government's stance on sovereignty. Carrington persisted in looking for a more reasonable solution, however, and late in November 1980 he sent Nicholas Ridley, the Minister of State at the Foreign and Commonwealth Office, to 'put forward several possible policies, including leaseback', to the Falkland Islanders. Ridley reported on his Falklands visit to the House of Commons on 2 December, and suffered an all-party mangling as MPs queued up to assert the 'paramount importance' of the wishes of the Falklanders. Sir Nicholas Henderson, British ambassador to the United States during the Falklands crisis, subsequently commented: 'Governments often take fright when there are strong upsurges of backbench opinion – instead of providing leadership, information and education on subjects or policies which could involve the nation in huge expenditure and commitments.'[26]

To the outside world, British policy appeared to be in a state of agonized suspension: the British had rolled up their trousers, but did not dare to dip their toes in the water. They were ready to talk, but not about substantive changes. The wishes of the Falklanders were paramount, and yet Britain was ready to leave essential services – energy, transport, health – in Argentine hands. In June 1981 the British government announced that the ice-patrol ship *Endurance*, lone warship guarding the islands, was to be withdrawn in order to save its £3 million annual maintenance costs. In October of the same year the British Nationality

Bill proposed to deprive one-third of the Falklanders of the benefits of full British citizenship.

In mid-September 1981, military and political planners began submitting to the Cabinet's Defence Committee their assessments, proposals and estimates for meeting various possible contingencies. One scenario which Mrs Thatcher, to judge by her lack of reaction, found merely academic was submitted by the Chiefs of Staff. Merely to deter an Argentine attempt to invade, they said, would require the presence of a naval task force complete with an aircraft carrier and a brigade of troops. But if deterrence failed, or was not provided, and Argentina occupied the islands, then a far bigger and more formidable force would be essential to repossess them.[27] Foreign Office specialists at the time focused on less extreme possibilities, hoping – and wishing – that total confrontation might still be avoided. They submitted that the Argentines might first cut off their air and sea links and other services. These would be difficult and costly to replace. The annual cost of substitute air and sea links alone would run to around £20 million, quite apart from such indispensable facilities as emergency medical services, schooling, fuel, freight and other supplies.[28]

These assessments were made in response to a note from the Argentine Foreign Minister, Dr Oscar Camilion, expressing his country's growing impatience with the pace of negotiations. It was accompanied, on 27 July 1981, by a communiqué which stated that a Malvinas settlement 'had become an unpostponable priority for its foreign policy'. Intransigence was to become one of the key words in the Falklands dispute. Lord Carrington had inherited 150 years of it, and was having to deal with its new embodiments in the form of 'domestic political constraints' and the opposition of the Falklands establishment. On 14 September 1981 he told Mrs Thatcher and the Defence Committee that although he still advocated a leaseback solution, 'given the Islanders' views, there was little prospect of doing more than keeping some sort of negotiation with Argentina going'. His exasperation survives even the Delphic prose of the Franks Report: 'Lord Carrington proposed to tell Dr Camilion that the British Government wanted to end the dispute, but that they could act only in accordance with the wishes of the Islanders, and to invite the Argentine Government to put forward constructive proposals of their own.'[29]

Now the tempo accelerated. Before the invasion, and particularly following the failure of talks held in New York on 26–27 February 1982, nearly a score of precise appraisals had reached the Prime Ministerial desk warning that confrontation, almost certainly military, appeared unavoidable during 1982. Mrs Thatcher and her inner circle of ministers were reminded regularly, and with growing urgency, that time was running out and that the options for a political compromise settlement were narrowing. None of this seems to have rung any bells in the Cabinet room, where it was not judged important enough to rate a formal discussion. The Franks Report records, with a deafening lack of comment, that: 'Government policy towards Argentina and the Falkland Islands was never formally discussed outside the Foreign and Commonwealth Office after January 1981.' Until, that is, about a week after Argentine scrap merchants had landed on South Georgia and a week before Argentine marines, troops and airmen descended on the islands. 'The time was never judged to be ripe,' the Franks Report laconically observed.[30]

The days of lofty indifference were long gone. The British government might continue to assert, as Ridley had done for form's sake in 1980, that it was in 'no doubt about our sovereignty over the islands', but even an economic blockade by Argentina would make the Falklands hard and expensive to hold, while any sizeable military commitment would entail an enormous drain on the Exchequer and would practically hamstring the British commitment to NATO. The British government was caught in two minds (at least) about what to do with the Falklands, and how seriously to take the Argentine claim which was as old as Argentina. Its response was to freeze: having no comfortable alternatives on offer, it just stood still. In mid-1983 William Wallace, Director of Studies at the Royal Institute of International Affairs, commented on the Franks Report: 'It is difficult to read it without some sympathy for, and understanding of, Argentine impatience [and] deep sympathy for the frustrations of a [British] Diplomatic Service which had done its best over the years to present the choices to the ministers and had seen those choices repeatedly avoided.'[31]

Battle Lines

The same period which had seen Great Britain shed all of its major imperial possessions, and much of its influence as an industrial and trading nation, also had witnessed a dramatic decline in the prosperity, and therefore the stability, of Argentina. In 1928 Argentina had the fifth largest gold holdings in the world, after the US, France, Britain and Germany.[1] In 1945, according to Alvaro Alsogaray, ex-Minister of Economy, Labour and Industry, it was still 'the seventh country in the world: now we're between the fortieth and fiftieth'.[2]

By 1982, Argentina was in severe economic difficulties. This was due partly to an unfavourable shift in the terms of trade during the 1970s,[3] but the root causes of the problem go much further back. Argentina's rulers had debauched the economy consistently for nearly 40 years, ever since Juan Domingo Perón came on to the political scene in 1943, as Secretary of War and Secretary of Labour and Social Services. In 1945 army and navy leaders imprisoned him on Martín García island, after forcing his resignation as War Minister and Vice-President. But Perón had forged close contacts with organized labour, and on 16 and 17 October hundreds of thousands of his *descamisados* ('those without shirts') brought Buenos Aires to a standstill to call for his release and won.

Perón, with his passion for the grandiose and spendthrift, began as President in 1946 with a Five Year Plan to spend US$1.9 billion to industrialize the country and to nationalize the US-owned Telephone Union and the British- and French-owned railways. The British had built their railways in the nineteenth century to link the great interior meat-producing areas to the coast, but by 1946 the country's whole productive pattern had changed, making the railways a white elephant whose British shareholders were delighted to get rid of them at the generous price paid by Perón. He financed his plans by nationalizing the country's Central Bank to control credit, then forming the IAPI, Instituto Argentino de Promoción del Intercambio, to control all imports and exports. What Alsogaray called Perón's 'statist and interventionist doctrines' have ruled the country ever since, whoever theoretically was in power. By the end of 1948 Perón had run the country's reserves down by 77 per cent.

Ever since the late 1940s, economic protectionism has become deeply entrenched in Argentina. Sub-standard companies were 'import-substitutive' or 'hard-currency-saving'; the least fit were positively rewarded. A huge and inefficient public sector has sprung up which consumes more than it produces, creating vast deficits which the state meets by printing money. The resulting inflation is recycled by wage increases indexed to it, giving rise to hyperinflation, devaluations, stagflation. In a state with two or more parties, strains like these bring in the opposition, but Argentina has never really had more than one major political party at a time during the twentieth century, and the force which periodically fills the gap is always the military. Yet it is a giant of a country, more than a million square miles in area, second in size and third in population among the countries of South America, and with the highest adult literacy rate. It is not an easy place for soldiers and sailors to govern.

In 1976 Isabel Perón was deposed from the Presidency (the seventh out of eleven presidents to have suffered that fate since 1955). She was succeeded by a Junta led by General Jorge Rafael Videla, who brought in José Martínez de Hoz as Minister of Economy. The new Minister set two objectives: to cut the public sector out of all day-to-day business, and to eliminate all import, export and price controls – a policy of proto-Thatcherism. In five years he cut the budget deficit from 13.5 to 4 per cent of GNP, annual inflation rates from 920 to 26 per cent. He closed 10,000 km of uneconomic line – one quarter of the State Railways' network – and improved foreign reserves from US$0.6 to 7.7 billion. He made every state enterprise apply modern accounting methods (YPF's first inventory showed that it had 500 years' supply of one spare part). He cut Perón's iniquitous IAPI 'retentions' on cereals and grains – 50 per cent of their export value – and the 100 per cent tax on imports for farmers, who at once doubled areas under fertilizers. Compared to the previous five years, grain production and export volumes boomed, the annual value of all agricultural exports rising to US$6 billion, or by 140 per cent.[4] But the mystique of Perón's public sector resisted him. He could not cut it far. At the end of his term, as Galtieri's Economy Minister, Roberto Alemann, noted, the public sector that contributed 37 per cent of the GDP was absorbing 45 to 50 per cent of current and capital expenditure.

Videla left another legacy when he quit office in March 1981. Before his Junta took power, Argentina had given birth to two radical political movements, the Trotskyist ERP (Ejército Revolucionario del Pueblo) and the Peronist Montoneros. An official publication, *Terrorismo en la Argentina*, estimated that in the nine years ending 1978 the guerrilleros killed 688 men, women and children. In the six years preceding Perón's death in 1974 they occupied 52 towns, robbed 166 banks and took US$76 million in ransoms for the kidnapping of 185 people.[5] The Junta's answer was the 'dirty war' of 1976–9, when murder squads of police or army agents in plain clothes picked up anyone whom they suspected of answering to Videla's definition: 'A terrorist is not just someone with a gun or a bomb, but also someone who spreads ideas that are contrary to Western and Christian civilization.' A UN investigating body, the Working Group on Enforced or Involuntary Disappearances, estimated that as many as 9,000 Argentines simply 'disappeared', never to be seen again. Other human rights organizations set the figure at up to three times that number.

Videla was still in power when Cecil Parkinson, then Minister for Trade, and later to be a member of the British war cabinet, paid his official visit to Buenos Aires in August 1980 and told his hosts: 'The British admire the efforts made by Argentina to reduce inflation and their achievements so far.'[6] Only *after* the invasion did the Thatcher administration begin to complain in public that human rights had for years been trampled upon by Argentina's security forces. It was the first time that Britain's Conservative government had ever expressed so much as distaste for the repressive actions of any right-wing government anywhere in Central or South America. The message of British silence had not been lost on the Junta at the time. Mrs Thatcher's government also had been a dutiful defender of the United States in its backing for regimes in Central America which had for years been emulating the use of death and torture squads as instruments of state policy. The point is made by Sir Nicholas Henderson:

> The government in Buenos Aires had been giving America support for its covert operations in Central America and its anti-communist causes throughout Latin America, a stance . . . that might well, in the eyes of the Argentine Junta, have secured American acquiescence in a forward Argentine policy over the Falklands.[7]

What Henderson leaves diplomatically unexamined is that his account of Argentina's role puts it into an unsavoury alignment with Great Britain's. It was true that Mrs Thatcher had expressed a great deal of belligerence since taking office, but all of it had been directed against communist countries: there were no British enemies on the right. Furthermore, from 1979 on, Britain sold more than £200 million worth of naval, aerial and electronic equipment, missiles and other weaponry to Argentina, even though the JIC had been warning of a possible military threat since November of that year. If that was not acquiescence, it certainly was not deterrence.

A similar British – US – Argentine alignment was implicit in a project long desired by the United States and revived by their ambassador-at-large, General Vernon Walters, during a number of visits to Buenos Aires and other key Latin American capitals between June 1981 and February 1982. Walters, once a Marine Commando and Deputy Director of the Central Intelligence Agency, hoped to rally support for a security system in the South Atlantic with the aim of blocking Soviet penetration of the area. The project for a South Atlantic Treaty Organization (SATO) supplementing NATO was designed to accommodate South Africa, Uruguay and Argentina among other regional states. Within such a system the facilities of the Falkland Islands would be vital, commanding as they do perhaps the most important of all US naval routes (given that the Panama Canal would not be hard to interdict), linking the Atlantic with the Pacific through the Magellan Straits and Cape Horn. Walters discussed this

SATO project with the then President, General Roberto Eduardo Viola, during a visit to Buenos Aires in November 1981, but he spent his most intensive time with the three commanders-in-chief, of whom the most important was General Leopoldo Galtieri, army C-in-C. No such project could work without some sort of Falklands deal between Britain and Argentina: practicalities, not abstractions, were Walters' business.[8]

Viola was put in office in place of Videla in March 1981, partly to insulate and cover up the military from the consequences of their role in the 'dirty war'. His administration and his successor's were to cover up the traces of the *desaparecidos* and immunize the murder squads against investigation and trial by any civilian administration. But Viola was too weak a pawn, and proved incapable of taking decisive action in any sphere. The effect on the economy was that by December 1981 inflation had shot back up to an annual rate of 100 per cent, and the peso, worth 2,000 to the US dollar a year before, now stood at around 10,000 – a loss of 80 per cent of its value in dollar terms.

Galtieri was propelled into the Presidency in December 1981 just when the Junta's 'Process of National Reconstruction and Reorganization' had reached the point of breakdown. The foreign debt was approaching £27,000 million, and whereas in the rest of Latin America the real wage of industrial workers had risen by 15 per cent in the period 1979–82, in Argentina it had fallen by 26 per cent.[9] Disenchantment with the performance and promises of the Junta was spreading even among its supporters. Among the political parties there was a recognition that the worsening situation held possibilities for achieving an end of military rule. Early in 1982, Galtieri and his colleagues were bracing themselves to meet the challenge they expected by the end of summer. They could choose between two foreign diversions: either a confrontation with Chile after the unfavourable outcome of Vatican mediation in their dispute over three islands in the mouth of the Beagle Channel south of Tierra del Fuego,[10] or pumping up the pressure on the Falklands. The decision to *consider* exercising the military option for recovering the Islands was energetically canvassed in the national media from January 1982 onwards.[11]

The British government knew already, as stated earlier, that Argentine impatience with the British attitude on the Falklands was coming to a head, and was likely to find some military expression some time during 1982. 'Self-determination' and the Falklanders' own 'paramount wishes' were a criterion for sovereignty which would keep the islands British indefinitely, no matter how dubious the original claim, and no matter how chary international law might become of the doctrine of prescription – ownership by long possession, the legalization of the right of the stronger. Now it seemed that the 1,800 Falklanders were to have the right to dictate the islands' future to both governments, simply because the British had put them there in the first place.

From late January for two months the Junta used formal as well as informal channels to convey to British diplomats in Buenos Aires that the invasion option was a reality, not only under consideration but also under preparation. Short of throwing a brick through the Embassy window with maps of the landing plans attached, the warning could not have been plainer. This was not done out of any sporting instinct. It was done, according to some well-placed Argentines who have talked with the writers, in the hope that the British would react by visibly, even ostentatiously, strengthening their military presence in the South Atlantic. In this way, the regime's strategists reasoned, the Junta would be presented with an external threat on which to focus its call for Argentine unity. The Franks Report made it clear that these Argentine signals were either misinterpreted in London or just ignored. Lord Franks and his colleagues were disposed to accept as reasonable the mistaken analysis of the Foreign Office, which was that the Argentine resort to force was indeed a serious possibility, but that the crisis was likely to develop only gradually, later in the year.

The prestigious International Institute for Strategic Studies, in its *Strategic Survey* for 1982–3, lends weight to reports that British diplomats in Buenos Aires had been made aware of invasion preparations. This took place between February and April 1982, the survey says, 'in the expectation that a frigate or two, or a submarine perhaps, would be despatched to prevent any actual landing. . . . British obstruction would then serve to reinforce a sense of national legitimacy and a temporary form of unity would once again be created in a country which notoriously lacks a viable political culture. But what took the Junta completely by surprise on this occasion was the total lack of British response.'

Dr David Owen, leader of the Social Democratic Party, who

was Foreign Secretary in the Labour government of 1974–9, noted that this development was not mentioned in such precise terms by the Franks Committee, but 'would not exclude it as a possibility'. He said in an interview that there were 'pro-British elements at various levels in the Argentine Foreign Ministry at the time'. Owen said that if London had picked up any such message an overt or covert display of force could have been arranged, and even a process of bluff. 'We could have told the Argentines through the Americans not only about our ability to deploy force, but also about the fact of our deployment.' (As James Callaghan claims to have done in the crisis of 1977, though the claim is not confirmed by Franks, and Lord Carrington had never heard of it before the invasion.)[12]

The British government did not respond because the Foreign Office analysis was mistaken. It left out of account the seismic force of immediate domestic pressures that triggered cumulative grievances. It ignored – as the Franks Report ignores – the possible validity of the Argentine case over the Falklands, and the power of a national sense of injustice to fuel dangerous behaviour and obscure its self-destructiveness. It did not consider what Sir Nicholas Henderson was later to call 'the irrationality and chaotic nature of the Argentine leadership',[13] as Cecil Parkinson had not considered it when expressing his 'admiration' some eighteen months before. The Franks Report doubted 'whether the Joint Intelligence Organisation attached sufficient weight to the possible effects on Argentine thinking of the various actions of the British Government'.[14] This is a momentous accusation, considering that it is one of the primary tasks of diplomacy, and an elementary duty of any government, to examine what the effects of its actions may be *before* the event, let alone after it. The Franks Committee's doubts are founded upon Britain's action and inaction on and around the Falklands, its tantalizing diplomacy of continually opening and then shutting the door, its absence of firm response to a history of feints and threats. Franks might have added, but does not mention, Britain's apparent approval, expressed in diplomatic as well as economic and even military terms, for the Argentine regime. Nor does it fall within the remit of the Report to examine whether Mrs Thatcher, who had become known as the 'Iron Maiden' for her assiduous rhetorical defiance of the communist East, was capable of imagining that the threat might come from the reactionary South.

The Junta too miscalculated. It assumed that President Reagan's administration was too anxious about events in Central America to want to alienate a valued ally, and would therefore remain at least neutral in any showdown. It did misread the British signals, and from them it drew the conclusion that also suited the Junta's own wishes: namely that the British would huff and puff diplomatically but not react with force in the event of a takeover. Costa Méndez had asked Argentine diplomatic missions in New York and London for their assessments of British reactions to an invasion of the Falklands. In each case the answer pointed to a diplomatic rupture, temporary economic and financial sanctions, but no counter-force.

Just as British analysts overlooked the pressure of events in Argentina, so their opposite numbers misread the British scene. Throughout 1981, Mrs Thatcher's fortunes had been flagging. The country was preoccupied with the realities of well over two million unemployed; a series of strikes and disputes among health, transport and other public sector workers; and company bankruptcies exceeding 200 weekly. Other grim developments faced the embattled Prime Minister. Irish Republican Army prisoners in Northern Ireland were staging hunger-strikes, heightening tensions in the province, where more than 2,000 people had died by violence since the British army had gone in, 13 years before. Investment funds were flooding overseas in search of havens more lucrative than those offered by the country's stagnating industries. The Gross National Product was only four times greater than that of little Switzerland. Race riots swept the towns and cities of England in mid-1981, though it might have taught the Argentines something useful about the British leader to witness her unblinking assurance in asserting that the causes had nothing to do with either unemployment or deprivation.[15] On the political scene, the newly formed Social Democratic Party was on the march in alliance with the Liberals, threatening – at least in public opinion surveys – to break the monopoly on power shared for most of this century between the Labour and Conservative parties.

It seemed to the Argentines – as it had seemed to most Britons for 25 years – that Suez had been the last hurrah of the British empire. Great Britain was a northern hemisphere power, committed to the European Common Market, to NATO, and to its 'special relationship' with an American President who had revived his country's anti-communist crusade for the first time since Vietnam. Would Britain not be secretly relieved to be rid of this 'pimple on the ass of progress', 'that little ice-cold bunch of land down there', as General Haig and President Reagan described the disputed islands?

The trigger of the pent-up forces at work in both countries was straight commercial greed and a touch of jingoism. In 1979 an Argentine scrap-merchant, Constantino Davidoff, had made a contract with the Scottish firm of Salvesen to pull down and carry away all he could of the defunct whaling station at Leith in South Georgia. The scrap metal price fell sharply, but the deal was still attractive when Davidoff's 41 workers arrived at Leith as commercial passengers on the Argentine fleet auxiliary *Bahía Buen Suceso* on 19 March 1982. One of them hoisted an Argentine flag on an old tower. A small working group from the British Antarctic Survey at Grytviken, 20 miles east, came upon Davidoff's party and their flag. They were appalled. Didn't the scrapmen know that they must have British permission from Grytviken to land?

The scrapmen did not know. Davidoff had been on South Georgia twice, in December 1981 and early March 1982, with no problems. On 9 March he had, so he thought, cleared this third visit with the British Embassy in Buenos Aires. He had met the ambassador, and later sent him a letter detailing his plans. The British group were perturbed. They radioed their base about the incursion, Grytviken then radioed Port Stanley who radioed London, each relay adding a degree of drama.

On 20 March Falklands Governor Rex Hunt signalled his orders to tell the Argentines that if they would not go to Grytviken and get their passports properly stamped, they must leave Leith at once. The scrapmen refused, but pulled down their flag. On the same day HMS *Endurance*, now in her last year on station, equipped with two rocket-carrying Wasp helicopters and two 20 mm cannon, sailed from Stanley to South Georgia with 22 Royal Marines on board. According to the Franks Report, 'there was no evidence at the time, and none has come to light since, suggesting that the whole operation was planned either by the Argentine Goverment or by the Navy'.[16] Nevertheless the subsequent course of events appears to be far from random. The British ambassador in Buenos Aires was instructed to inform the Argentines to remove the *Bahía Buen Suceso*, or the

British would take steps to deal with what they saw as a serious incident. On 22 March that ship was reported to have sailed, but leaving some men and equipment behind.

It was on 22 March that two senior men in the Argentine Marines, Rear-Admiral Carlos Busser and Captain Miguel Pita, his second-in-command, began speeding preparations to invade the Falkland Islands, because they alone knew that on 29 March the Argentine fleet would probably sail for a real objective, instead of taking part in its usual harmless annual manoeuvres with Uruguay.[17] According to the Argentine Foreign Minister, Nicanor Costa Méndez, the decision was taken in response to 'the severity of Britain's reaction' to the Davidoff affair, which compelled his government to meet 'a display of force with other force'.[18] General Galtieri made the same claim in an interview of 11 August 1982,[19] although that was in the context of *advancing* the invasion date originally set as 'about July' by a Junta decision which he said was taken in early January 1982. (Argentine politicians have told the authors that Admiral Jorge Isaac Anaya, C-in-C of the navy, made it a condition of his backing Galtieri for the leadership of the Junta in December 1981 that the new President would act to break the deadlock over the Malvinas.) This clashes with Costa Méndez' claim to the authors, when he admitted that Argentina had contingency plans for a Malvinas invasion – 'just as all NATO allies have their own contingency plans' – but insisted: 'We were going to implement them only in the very last resort, if Britain simply would not move constructively to fulfil Resolution 2065 of the UN General Assembly of December 1965.'

Implementing the plans would be fairly straightforward, because the Argentines were old hands at invading the Falklands on paper. The exercise was a hardy annual in all Military College training exercises. This particular model belonged to Admiral Emilio Massera. He had tried it on Isabelita Perón in 1975, but even she had rejected it flatly. He had revived it when he was the navy's man on the Videla Junta, again without success. When Massera retired, Admiral Anaya inherited it enthusiastically (it was the navy that was most vulnerable to a Malvinas in foreign hands), and Anaya sold it quite easily to Galtieri after helping him to take over the Presidency on 22 December 1981. The third member of the Junta, the air force's Brigadier-General Basilio Lami Dozo, was much the least enthralled. Nevertheless an order

dated 19 January 1982 went to a very senior officer in each of the
three arms requiring them to work out the plan together urgently
and in detail.[20]

The Franks Report concurs with Costa Méndez in asserting
that 'the decision to invade was taken by the Junta at a very late
date'.[21] If that is true, and the South Georgia incident was simply
a convenient pretext, then the next development in the story is
sheer coincidence. On 25 March another Argentine fleet auxiliary, the Bahía Paraíso, arrived in Leith. Observers reported that
she was working cargo and flying the pennant of the Argentine
Navy's Senior Officer, Antarctic Squadron. Captain N. J.
Barker, of the Endurance, stated that 'in his view the operation
must have been planned for some time as the Bahía Paraíso had
arrived from Antarctica, not from Argentina'.[22] What the ship
had brought from Antarctica was not only three landing craft and
a helicopter, but also Captain Alfredo Astiz, former head of the
GT33/2 kidnap squad which had tortured or murdered some
hundreds of people during the 'dirty war'. With Astiz came more
than a hundred Argentine marines. Astiz was a navy hatchet
man. If the Bahía Paraíso had been sailing Antarctic waters on a
routine patrol, it is difficult to see why it should have needed him
and his well-armed unit, equipped for a landing. Perhaps
Admiral Anaya, the hardliner, had a plan of his own to precipi-
tate confrontation and so forestall a diplomatic compromise.[23]

Another curious incident recorded by the Franks Committee
came following reports on 25 March that Argentine warships
had been sent to prevent Endurance from evicting Davidoff's
scrapmen and intercept her if she did so. Later that day, Britain's
ambassador in Buenos Aires was asked 'to sound out Dr Costa
Méndez on whether a personal message from the Prime Minister
to President Galtieri or the visit of a special representative of Lord
Carrington would help'.[24] The Franks Report does not revert to
these soundings, nor did Mrs Thatcher ever send a message, let
alone pick up the telephone and talk to Galtieri. Having conceded
the initiative in South Georgia, it is as if the British were now
asking the Argentines what to do next. What the Argentines
themselves did next, as British sources reported, was to send to
sea all the submarines at their naval base of Mar del Plata,
followed by a destroyer and a corvette. Two days later, on 28
March, Costa Méndez sent the British Ambassador in Buenos

Aires a note clarifying the linkage between the South Georgia events and the broader Malvinas issue. One sentence ran:

> I feel I must point out to Your Excellency that the present situation is the direct result of the persistent lack of recognition by the United Kingdom of the titles to sovereignty which my country has over the Malvinas, South Georgia and the South Sandwich Islands.[25]

In Gibraltar that day – a Sunday – the officers of the Royal Fleet Auxiliary replenishment ship *Fort Austin* went into sudden unexpected conclave. Extraordinarily big military supplies came on board, and were loaded at speed. The ship's crew had been nearly six months on station in the Gulf. Their spokesman, Michael Flockhart, asked Chief Officer David Heslop whether or not the *Fort Austin* was bound for home, as the men had been given to understand. Yes, said Heslop, and the spokesman passed the message on. Then he went ashore and into a bar. 'The barmaid could tell me what was going on and where we would be heading,' Flockhart later reported to the National Union of Seamen. 'That, most certainly, was not home.'

Before the *Fort Austin* weighed anchor at noon next day, units of the Special Air Service (SAS) and the Special Boat Squadron (SBS) came on board with all their battle equipment. About 15.30 hours on Monday 29 March, after passing through the Straits of Gibraltar, skipper Commodore Dunlop announced over the ship's Tannoy that there had been a change of orders and the ship would be sailing toward the Falklands. The barmaid had been well informed. The first elements of Britain's embryo Task Force had set sail southward even before Argentina occupied the islands, and before the British Cabinet resolved formally to meet the challenge.[26]

Also on 29 March, as they flew to Brussels for a summit meeting of the European Community countries, Mrs Thatcher and Lord Carrington decided to dispatch a nuclear-powered hunter-killer submarine to the South Atlantic, and HMS *Spartan* set out from Gibraltar only hours later. The tempo was kept up by Argentina, which sent five more Argentine warships to sea (including the aircraft carrier *Veinticinco de Mayo*), supposedly 'towards South Georgia'. Together with the ships already at sea, that made quite a legion of sledgehammers to crack so small a nut as the *Endurance*. Hindsight alone reveals that South Georgia was now only a cover story, but cover story or not, massive Argentine overkill or not, the British Prime Minister still made no attempt to deal directly with General Galtieri.

Instead, the British government pinned its hopes on the USA. Lord Carrington asked the American Secretary of State, Alexander Haig, to mediate with Argentina on 28 March. The following day Walter Stoessel, Haig's deputy, communicated the US disposition to assume an even-handed approach in the dispute and Sir Nicholas Henderson made a tart complaint – 'the Americans could surely not be neutral in a case of illegal occupation of sovereign British territory'? Lord Carrington expressed his own displeasure to the US chargé d'affaires in London on 30 March, only to be informed by Haig on 1 April that US chances of influencing Argentina would be greater if they appeared to favour neither side.[27]

By then, the last steps had been taken. Argentina's invasion fleet was at sea. On 31 March their Fleet Air Arm, Aeronaval, gave the order to start adapting each of its five Dassault-Breguet Super Etendard fighter-bombers with AM 39 Exocet air-to-surface missiles. It was on the evening of the same day that the British Defence Minister, John Nott, informed Mrs Thatcher that the latest intelligence showed that the Argentines had set the early morning of 2 April as their precise invasion target. In the wording of the Franks Report: 'It was considered that, taken with earlier intelligence reports, this provided a positive indication of an Argentine intention to invade the Falkland Islands.'[28] Mrs Thatcher now sent a message to President Reagan asking him to talk urgently to General Galtieri. Reagan made the call a day later, asking the Argentine President to call off his forces. When he put the phone down, he said: 'I guess I spelled it out, but it didn't sound as if the message got through.'

Both inside and outside the House of Commons, Mrs Thatcher has maintained that Argentina's action took her completely by surprise. A *Daily Express* columnist, George Gale, asked her directly if the Falklands crisis had come to her 'more or less out of the blue'. 'Out of the blue,' she echoed. 'It was Wednesday evening [31 March] when there was a message saying that their fleet had broken off some exercises. It looked as if their fleet was going to Port Stanley. It looked as if they had armed equipment on board. All of a sudden I said: "This is the worst week I am ever going to live through." '[29]

Three months later, with time to reflect and perhaps refresh her memory, she was asked in the Commons by Labour MP Tam Dalyell: 'In saying that the Falklands crisis came out of the blue does the Prime Minister mean that she had no warning of the invasion before Wednesday, March 31?' Mrs Thatcher replied: 'I have already made it clear in my speeches during the debate on the Falklands campaign that that was so, so far as the Falkland Islands were concerned.'[30]

She was hardly doing herself or her government justice. The incumbent Defence Minister, John Nott, told the House of Commons on 3 April: 'If we were unprepared, how is it that from next Monday [5 April], at only a few days' notice, the Royal Navy will put to sea in wartime order and with wartime stocks and weapons?' Then Nott added, in a little-noticed aside that seems totally to contradict the Prime Minister's professed astonishment on 31 March: '*The preparations have been in progress for several weeks. We were not unprepared.*'[31]

The 79 British Royal Marines who garrisoned the Falklands were prepared but relatively helpless. They thought that the Argentines would land at Purple Beach, four miles east-north-east of Port Stanley, where landing craft could get in close, while a second wave would go in by helicopter to take the airstrip half a mile south of the beach. The Royal Marines took up positions above the north-facing Purple Beach, by the airstrip, and at intervals along the road to Stanley, as well as at several other observation points, and by Government House.

In fact, at 22.30 on 1 April, less than two hours after President Reagan's call to General Galtieri, the destroyer *Santísima Trinidad* put 77 Amphibious Commandos into small rubber boats off Mullett Creek, some four miles south-west of Stanley. At 02.00 on 2 April the submarine *Santa Fe* delivered 15 Buzos Tácticos, Tactical Divers, to clear any obstacles from the chosen landing beach. This took them an hour.[32] Captain Bardi, who led the Amphibious Commandos, talked about the attack in an interview at the Marine base at Baterías, near Puerto Belgrano, on 14 April 1983. He said that he and his men were ashore just after midnight, and heading north-east, to slip past the Royal Marine outposts. Subsequent Argentine reports stressed the deliberately kid-glove approach of the occupation, but at 06.10 Bardi's men cleaned out the Moody Brook Barracks, west of Stanley, with automatic fire and grenades. Fortunately they were shooting up an empty building. By 06.30 Bardi had surrounded Government House and most of the Royal Marines.

Meanwhile the main assault force was coming. At 05.15 the *Santísima Trinidad* and the frigate *Granville* took up landing support positions, and the destroyer *Hércules* and frigate *Drummond* escorted into the bay above Port Stanley the Tank Landing Craft *Cabo San Antonio*, under the command of Rear-Admiral Busser, with 800 men of the Marine Corps and a sliver of the Argentine army in support. The Royal Marines above Purple Beach were spectators as the *San Antonio* sailed past them to the unguarded Orange Beach, further into the bay, to the west. At 06.30 she disgorged her tracked and armoured amphibious personnel carriers, each weighing 22 tons, carrying 20 armed men and fitted with a 30 mm cannon.

Captain Pita,[33] Busser's 2 i/c, led 21 of these mastodons to take the airstrip, which was unguarded, because Royal Marine commander Major Mike Norman had pulled his few men back to defend Government House. Pita headed in that direction, and the Royal Marines did stop one armoured personnel carrier with an anti-tank gun and rockets, but the odds were too unequal, and at 09.25 on 2 April 1982 Governor Rex Hunt ordered Norman to surrender.

As it turned out, the invasion produced no British casualties, military or civilian. The Argentines admitted a Marine captain killed and a lieutenant and a corporal wounded – no high cost for fulfilling a 149-year-old dream. Argentina had poured a great deal into the operation, including most of her fighting ships – six of her eight destroyers, two of her three frigates, one of her four diesel submarines, her lone aircraft carrier, and her lone Tank Landing Ship. She had committed two helicopter squadrons and a strong army tactical reserve in the icebreaker *Almirante Irizar*, in addition to the forces already mentioned. From 08.30 on 2 April they were joined by more and more army reinforcements flown into Stanley airstrip by Hercules transports, until in the end the islands held some 12,000 troops.

Operation Rosario, the taking of the Malvinas, had been achieved by surprise and with vastly superior numbers. If there was a plan for the occupation its name has not emerged, because the Junta seems not to have planned for the long term at all. The

Islands' very temporary governor, General Mario Benjamín Menéndez, recalled in September 1983 that his briefing by Galtieri just before the landings had mentioned a force of 500 men to police the islands. Costa Méndez would argue later that no one could have forecast the violence of the British reaction, and influential Argentines who hardly admired either him or his ministry have confirmed the prevalence of this view. Dr J. C. Murguizur, lecturer in military history at the Argentine army staff college, recalled in 1983:

> When this author first learnt of the invasion plan in December 1981, he asked the obvious question: 'And what if the British come and kick us out again?' but received in reply any number of reassurances – everything was arranged, there would be no problems, and any reaction would be merely verbal invective.[34]

Dr Murguizur's version of events – reflecting a view still widely held in Argentina – is that:

> A trivial incident in South Georgia convinced the ministry of finance to urge the military junta to invade the islands immediately in an effort to save face. Operation Rosario was therefore launched several months earlier than originally intended.[35]

He claims that the massive army presence was injected 'for prestige reasons' and was intended to be temporary. There are factors which bear out the suggestion that serious fighting had not been foreseen. About half of the troops put into the Islands in April were conscripts of 18 or 19, called up for their year's military service at dates from 1 March 1982 onwards. Some had less than two weeks' training. Why put up so virginal a defence against the first-class professionals of the British army?

Part of the answer was given by retired Paratroop General Rodolfo C. Mujica,[36] a week after he had written two articles for *La Prensa* of 8 and 9 July 1982, lambasting the Argentine army's performance in the Falklands. It was not true that his country lacked trained fighting men, he said. He knew the quality of the men he used to command, and Argentina had had paratroops sitting up in the Andes, on the Chilean border, who were specialized in mountain warfare. Bitter conditions of climate and terrain were nothing new to them. That the High Command had not committed them was due to its traditional obsession that Chile was the greater threat.

General Menéndez had never directly commanded fighting units. One of his regiments, the 5th Infantry, was normally stationed in the subtropical province of Corrientes, and recruited most of its intake from the north: their health and morale were crippled.[37] Argentina had in stock mobile metallic runways. Had they installed them at various island sites and brought in some or most of their fighter-bombers, instead of leaving them to operate from the mainland at the extreme of their range, the centre of gravity of the war would have been shifted. As it was, they did not even move in the materials and equipment to lengthen the airstrip at Port Stanley. None of this would matter if the occupying forces were never going to have to fight.

From the point of view of a full-scale war, Costa Méndez has always insisted that he did not expect one, and that the eleventh-hour invasion decision of late March 1982 did not envisage one. If Argentina had wanted a war, he argues,[38] it would have waited a year or two. By then, with no Falklands war to revive the British navy's fortunes, the British would have sold the aircraft carrier *Invincible* to Australia, retired the *Hermes*, and run down the rest of their surface fleet. This issue had dominated the controversy about Great Britain's future defence policy for a year before the Falklands events. It was no secret that the costly Trident missile programme had forced the government to effect swingeing economies, and the Royal Navy was the prime target for cuts. Furthermore, in two years or so more, Argentina would have more than doubled its submarine strength with six new diesel-electric submarines to be built in conjunction with Thyssen Nordseewerke in West Germany and Buenos Aires, and also doubled its destroyer and frigate fleet by adding ten new missile-carrying craft due from Thyssen Rheinstahl and Blohm und Voss in Western Germany and Buenos Aires. Then again, at the start of the Malvinas war, Argentina had only five Super Etendards and six missiles for them. Over the next few months the rest of the order would have been filled – nine more Super Etendards and dozens more Exocets. (They had all arrived by the end of 1982.)

Much of this argument about the changing military balance

would seem to have constituted a case against *any* invasion in 1982, let alone in April. But it was Costa Méndez' own ministry which helped to swing the Junta towards an invasion by predicting that the United States would remain neutral, and by misjudging the nature of the British in their response to a humiliating setback in the Falklands. Even so, the expectation that the military would have nothing to do after the invasion but drive up and down the streets of Port Stanley for the benefit of the media could not and did not justify the absence of contingency planning for the worst case. It does not even seem to have crossed any Argentine mind that the British might use Ascension Island as a staging post.

Yet for a military regime above all, the decision, once taken, was not going to be easy to revoke. At home, the people were now feeling their economic plight in their flesh and bones, daily. Some were hungry. A doctor or engineer in Buenos Aires earned £110 a month. A chambermaid in a four-star hotel earned £16 a month, one quarter of it swallowed by her bus fares. A thing never seen before, people could now be approached by a respectably dressed man or woman in the best streets of the city and be asked for the price of a meal. The mothers haunting the Plaza de Mayo still pleaded for news of the *desaparecidos*. As a working force Argentines were generally docile and long-suffering, but if pushed too hard too long, they could go to blood. When the Junta channelled all these resentments into the ancient resentment of the Malvinas, it was making its last throw of the dice.

Ever since 1833, some sort of confrontation had been inevitable between the British and the Argentines. They had been like two locomotives trundling towards each other down the same length of track, each in full view of the other. In the words of one Argentine:

> The dispute has assumed the proportions of a national feeling going back to the childhood of every native of Argentina (without any political or class distinction) and uniting the national conscience in the knowledge of having been robbed and subjected to insult without apology.[39]

For the British, with hardly any national feeling invested until the Falklands war left graveyards both on land and sea, it was still a simple matter. The islands were a British possession – nine points of the law – and their people were of British blood and wanted no truck with Argentina. If these two national attitudes could not be reconciled, then the engines must collide. The Argentine invasion brought the collision much too close, but it would still take a great deal of malice and incompetence to make it inevitable.

PART II

3

Southward Ho!

Britain's effective decision to force Argentina from the Falklands was taken by Mrs Thatcher's Cabinet immediately after confirmation of the invasion reached 10 Downing Street on 2 April 1982. In emergency session next day, Saturday, the House of Commons endorsed that commitment in a mood of fervent indignation. The Prime Minister looked visibly shaken as she faced a packed and seething Commons, during a debate limited by prior inter-party arrangement to three hours' duration. She borrowed time for herself with the announcement that the vanguard of a strong naval task force was assembling and would sail south on 5 April if, in the meantime, diplomacy could not achieve an Argentine withdrawal.

Out of a Chamber of 630 members, 20 were selected to speak during the ensuing debate. The outrage of the government's own supporters was matched by that of the Labour and SDP leaders, all of them calling for the sternest military response to what Lord Carrington called a 'national humiliation'. The government had botched its Falklands policy. Great Britain had been first gulled then bested by Argentina. The moment that crystallized the mood of the House of Commons, and possibly sealed the fate of the *Belgrano*, came with the icy intervention of Enoch Powell, once a Conservative minister, since 1974 an influential Ulster Unionist, but still able on occasion to speak in the sterling accent of High Tory authority. He rose to remind the Prime Minister that she had earned from the USSR the tag of 'Iron Lady' for her proclaimed resolve to countenance no Soviet aggression. 'There was no reason to suppose that the Right Honourable Lady did not welcome and, indeed, take great pride in that description,' Powell went on, addressing both the House and a massive live radio audience. 'In the next week or two this House, the nation and the Right Honourable Lady herself will learn of what metal she is made.' A true 'Iron Lady' or a tinpot premier, he was saying, and no one could mistake the message – least of all Mrs Thatcher.

The Prime Minister authorized her Defence Minister, John Nott, to placate the government's critics with a firm promise which also contained a self-fulfilling prediction: 'We intend to solve the problem and we shall try to solve it continuingly by diplomatic means, but if that fails, *and it will probably do so*, we shall have no choice but to press forward with our plans, retaining secrecy where necessary and flexibility to act as circumstances demand.'[1]

Nott had already begun to jettison the prospects for a diplomatic settlement. Yet his statement denoted a volte-face in British policy. The Thatcher government, like its predecessors, had constantly stressed the virtues of negotiation, just as it had consistently dismissed suggestions that Argentina was beginning to pose a credible military threat. Mrs Thatcher had treated the Argentines, or at any rate their successive Juntas, as friends, but it was a phantom friendship which had cost her a severe decline in her standing. Now that Argentina was behaving like the military dictatorship which it had always been throughout her premiership, it had to be made to pay for its trespasses. The irony of the situation is that the posture of granite rigour which could never be a practical option with the Soviet Union – to sink a Russian *Belgrano* in the same circumstances would be unthinkably rash – suddenly seemed feasible with a third-rate military power that had not fought outside its own frontiers for more than a century.

Powell's message to Mrs Thatcher had contained both a threat and a promise. The threat was that for her to send the biggest task force since the Second World War to retrieve a situation halfway around the world was too great an expense of national power and treasure to end in anything but a total Argentine surrender. For that force to trail back home without securing a military victory would not have ensured the Prime Minister's survival. The promise was equally clear to a 'conviction politician' with the acute political instincts of Mrs Thatcher. She knew, because she felt them in herself, the strength of such immeasurable factors as wounded national pride, frustrated patriotism, and Britain's nostalgia for bygone imperial grandeur, 'Victorian' values. Sooner than her colleagues she recognized that the crisis in the South Atlantic offered opportunities for a spectacular display of tough resolution, the clinching proof that Britain still counted in a changing world.

Britain might have lost the initiative, but Mrs Thatcher could yet regain it, and not only abroad but at home. The Opposition parties were bound to support her, as became clear in the Commons, where only one Conservative and one Labour MP were given the chance to express any doubts about the government's chosen course. By resorting to force in the furtherance of an international dispute, Argentina had put herself in breach of the rule of law. The UN Security Council confirmed as much on the day of the debate, when by a majority of 10 votes to 1 it passed Resolution 502, which said:

> The Security Council, recalling the statement made by the President of the Security Council on 2 April 1982 calling on the Governments of Argentina and the United Kingdom to refrain from the use of threat or force in the region of the Falkland Islands (Islas Malvinas),
>
> Deeply disturbed at reports of an invasion on 2 April 1982 by armed forces of Argentina,
>
> Determining that there exists a breach of peace in the region of the Falkland Islands (Islas Malvinas),
>
> 1. Demands an immediate cessation of hostilities;
>
> 2. Demands an immediate withdrawal of all Argentine forces from the Falkland Islands (Islas Malvinas);
>
> 3. Calls on the Government of Argentina and the United Kingdom to seek a diplomatic solution to their differences and to respect fully the purposes and principles of the Charter of the United Nations.

The British government now had carte blanche to deal with Argentina, in the same way as a police force has carte blanche to deal with an armed man holding hostages in a stolen car. Now it was up to the marksmen and the talkers.

The marksmen had already begun to prepare. The quiet process of diverting ships at sea, and signalling new orders to naval units engaged on other missions, had begun as soon as the certainty of trouble was recognized by the Chiefs of Staff. They had offered their assessment of the kind of strength required to recapture an occupied Falklands in mid-September 1981 (see p. 12). In the absence of any subsequent directive, they had taken it upon themselves systematically to elaborate plans for assembling, arming, equipping and stocking a huge task force in case they were called upon to organize one at short notice. By the beginning of April, when Operation Rosario was launched, Britain's three forces, and picked elements of the Merchant Navy, were already in action. To many it seemed later that the swift assembly of the Task Force for Operation Corporate had been made easier by the return of a large part of the British Fleet to home ports for Easter, traditionally a rest period. That was partly true. But on the evidence of senior military men, speaking in confidence, it was hardly fortuitous that many more naval units than usual had been called home. 'You can put it down to the prescience of an alert High Command,' one senior naval authority remarked. 'It was clear from the turn of the year that, sooner or later, the balloon was bound to go up as the Foreign Office kept reminding us, and so you can say there was a judicious exercise of military initiative in the absence of clearcut orders from our political masters.'[2]

Had they needed a reminder, it was provided by Mrs Thatcher herself. On 3 March 1982 she saw a telegram from the British Ambassador in Buenos Aires reporting press hints of a direct seizure of the Malvinas. 'We must make contingency plans,' she noted, and on 8 March she asked Mr Nott how long it would take to get Royal Navy ships to the Falkland Islands. The Ministry of Defence replied on 12 March, pointing out that 'passage time for a frigate deployed to the Falklands, which would require Royal Fleet Auxiliary support, would be in the order of 20 days.'[3] The eventuality of a Falklands problem, which took the Prime Minister by surprise on the 31st, appears paradoxically to have been expunged from her mind by the intervening events on South Georgia.

Falklands, South Georgia – it was all one to the Royal Navy, whose role had always extended far beyond Europe and the northern hemisphere. It had been fighting a political battle of its own, to defend itself against the plan identified in Whitehall by the designation of the White Paper which proposed it: Cmnd. 8288. In the interests of the national economy, and in order to pay for Trident, the surface combat fleet was to be cut by one third, concentrating the Royal Navy on its NATO role of waging anti-submarine warfare in the North Atlantic. The First Sea Lord, Sir Henry Leach, was eager to save his ships from the Treasury axe by demonstrating their effectiveness, and the organization, assembly and dispatch of the Task Force proved, by any standards, a brilliant high-speed operation. It startled not only Argentina but also Britain's allies, who had been as dubious as the Americans about the feasibility, let alone the wisdom, of the undertaking.

While the Chiefs of Staff were planning for the assembly of the Task Force, urgent operations were going on elsewhere. A swift and secret intelligence survey was undertaken in the capitals of the NATO allies to obtain a picture of Argentina's most recent weapon acquisitions. The United States provided a detailed confidential assessment of Argentine capabilities at sea, in the air and on land. Chile, which had its own long-standing territorial dispute with its neighbour across the Andes, was assiduously courted for information about any military movements it could observe without being seen to violate its nominal neutrality. (The British government had removed its blinkers to perceive that Argentina's was 'a repressive régime' with an 'appalling human rights record'.[4] For Chile, it left the blinkers on.) And various other Latin American governments were sounded – although without success – about their making air and sea staging facilities available. All these behind-the-scenes activities proved invaluable in enabling the British planners to select the kind of equipment and weapons the Task Force should carry and the kind of modifications they would need to arrange for the ships and planes assigned to the zone of conflict.

As well as Montevideo and Punta Arenas, Lagos and Freetown had to be ruled out as possible staging facilities. A suggested request to South Africa for a temporary return to Simonstown, once a British naval base, was quickly discarded for its explosive national and international political implications and because the Apartheid government's relations with Buenos Aires had for some time been steadily improving. In the event Ascension Island, a speck in the Atlantic about 4,225 miles from Britain, part of the British Dependency of St Helena, was chosen as the halfway house for the sea and air supply line. Its only airfield, the Wideawake base, had been built by and leased to the United States back in 1942, and was operated by Pan American Airways for the US government. Under a 1962 agreement Britain was required to give the Americans 24 hours' notice of the arrival of British aircraft. In one of their many acts of cooperative support, the Americans waived the requirement.[5]

Within 24 hours of the 31 March alert, RAF Hercules transports headed towards Ascension, laden with supplies and men, in what became virtually a logistic cascade. In the space of two weeks Ascension's population of just over 1,000 was outnumbered by British services personnel, more than 1,000 of whom were encamped in tents. For a while Wideawake became one of the world's busiest airfields, outperforming even Chicago Airport at its peak period by handling up to 400 aircraft movements a day. Throughout the campaign and its aftermath most military personnel and freight destined for the Falklands were routed to Ascension, and thence by ship. The intensity of this activity called for the island's civilian and military infrastructure to be generally extended in terms of radio and cable communications, roadworks, garrison accommodation, runway reinforcement, defensive installations against the possibility of Argentine attack. There was common agreement among British political and military authorities alike that Ascension was vital in the Falklands war: without access to it the campaign would hardly have been possible.

On paper, Britain's air, land and sea forces easily outclassed Argentina's. The British defence budget for 1981–2, for instance, exceeded £12,000 million – roughly six times more than Argentina spent. That kind of difference in expenditure translated into superior fire-power, technology and training. A battle-hardened nation of the industrialized north, backed by strong and wealthy friends, was pitted against a Third World state which had never fought a major war, whose economy was in tatters, and whose people were subjected to an unelected and crumbling military leadership whose principal competence and practice lay in the coercion of its own civilians.

In manpower too, Britain was much the stronger nation, though obviously none of these ascendancies would matter if they could not be brought to bear. According to the Stockholm

International Peace Research Institute, the comparative military strengths were as follows:[6]

	United Kingdom	Argentina
Total active manpower	327,600	180,500
Army	163,100	125,000
Navy	73,000	36,000
Air Force	91,500	19,500

The UK's military establishment was not only much bigger in number: its manpower was also entirely volunteer and professional, and in general was far better trained and had a far greater morale and esprit de corps than most of the Argentines it faced. The bulk of these were conscripts on national service turning over fairly rapidly. Conscripts of 18 and 19 made up just under half of the Argentine navy's manpower, just over half of the air force's, and almost three-quarters of the army's.[7] Forces actually involved in the Falklands conflict were 28,000 British, of whom about 10,000 were to be put ashore, against some 12,000 Argentine defenders.

Regarding weapons, both sides had Blowpipe missiles, Oerlikon anti-aircraft guns, general-purpose machine guns, automatic rifles and artillery. The Argentines' postwar analysis showed that the British forces had far better communications equipment, that their computer-based weapons-locating radars worked to deadly effect against opposing artillery, and that the British mortars had the edge because of the infra-red homing ammunition they used.[8] Sometimes though, as with night-glasses, it was the Argentine infantry who were better equipped. It was in training, discipline, organization and above all initiative that the Argentines were generally outclassed.

It was basically a question of mental attitude. General Mujica has already been quoted on the quality of the troops which the Junta committed to the Falklands. He had equally stringent criticisms to make of their commanders, whose conduct of the war he regarded as dogmatic, rigid and superficial. Here the supreme instance is Menéndez' obsession that the British would attack only one way, and that was right up against the front door of Port Stanley. Thus the Argentine troops could not be dispatched in force to liquidate the San Carlos beachhead as soon as the British appeared there. There were no roads on which they could be transported with heavy weapons, and no one had thought to provide enough helicopters. That meant they could only slog there on foot over four or five days under British air attack and the accurate British naval bombardments (which, Mujica pointed out, put down no fewer than 450 shells of 115 and 125 mm on Port Stanley on the night of 7/8 June alone). The British would fling assault troops, mortars, cannons, even radars around battlefields by helicopter, even at night. The Argentines just sat still in their sopping wet trenches passively taking everything that was thrown at them. The command was not even consistent. If it was set on defending Port Stanley at all costs, then why did it not have enough heavy artillery and missiles there to do the job? No one had thought that through either.

These are the main armaments directly involved in the Falklands conflict:[9]

Type	United Kingdom	Argentina
Surface warships	62	11
Submarines	6	3
Aircraft	42	102
Helicopters	200	32

Only in aircraft does Britain look weaker than Argentina, and in fact both RAF and Army Chiefs of Staff took the view that the Task Force was being sent into battle dangerously short of air cover for the fleet and troops and with a glaring need for more ground attack planes. The overall British aircraft commitment to support and combat operations in the Falklands totalled 28 Sea Harriers, 14 RAF Harrier GR3s, at least four Nimrod maritime patrol craft, 16 Victor bombers, elements from three Vulcan squadrons and an undisclosed number of Hercules transports. Argentine aircraft involved directly in the fighting included Skyhawks, Mirages, Daggers, Canberras, Super Etendards and Pucarás. At the outbreak of war their total air strength was thought to comprise 68 McDonnell Douglas A4P and A4Q Skyhawks,[10] 58 Mirage IIIs and their Israeli-built equivalents, the Dagger,[11] 9 Canberras, 5 Super Etendards and an unknown number of the Argentines' own light twin-turboprop Pucará fighter planes. Seven Hercules C-130 transports ferried men and equipment to the Falklands through most of the campaign and 5

P-2H Neptunes and 10 S-2A/S-2E Tracker aircraft,[12] designed for anti-submarine warfare, were used both for that purpose and as spotters.

But the quality of these aircraft was variable. Many of the Skyhawks, if not all, were early 1960 vintage, sold off by the US air force. Some were not operational. For years the US had refused to sell Argentina spare parts for them due to her human rights record and the controversy created by the 'dirty war'. They were much slower at low altitude than Britain's Sea Harriers and RAF Harrier GR3s and not nearly so manoeuvrable. The Mirages and Daggers were more modern aircraft, delta-winged and capable of Mach 2.2 at height, but they were not much faster than the Harriers at sea-level, and clumsy by comparison. Brigadier-General Lami Dozo said that when the war started he had only 82 Skyhawks, Mirages and Daggers available for action,[13] a figure consistent with SIPRI's above. They were armed with the original unsophisticated American Sidewinder air-to-air missile, effective only from the rear, because it needs the heat of a jet exhaust to lock on to. (Research by the *Sunday Times*'s Insight Team has revealed that the British Harriers, equipped with the Sidewinder's most recent version, the AIM 9L, borrowed them from NATO stocks for which the US supplied 100 replacements. The AIM 9L's guidance system allows it to be launched from any aspect.)[14]

The failure of the Argentine planners to provide runways on the Malvinas meant that instead of operating from the security of a nearby land base, the Argentine bombers had to operate from the mainland, in particular from Comodoro Rivadavia and Río Grande, respectively in Chubut and Tierra del Fuego provinces. That meant having to fly four or five hundred miles before reaching their target area, with only a few minutes in which to act before turning for home. Again the Harriers would be better placed. The British could keep their aircraft carriers east of the Falklands, clear of the Skyhawks' and the Mirage/Daggers' range. Dr Murguizur states that: 'At night, the ships came in closer to bring down harassing fire on the garrison troops and provide gun fire support for their commandos, withdrawing again before dawn. As the avionics of our aircraft did not permit night attacks or bad-weather operations, the sea was usually empty when they arrived.'[15] Finally, the Mirage/Dagger and Skyhawk pilots knew, because their instructors had made no

bones about telling them, that the probability of being shot down
if they openly attacked warships as sophisticated as the British,
armed with Sea Cat, Sea Dart and Sea Wolf missiles and with
long-range cannon automatically focused by radar and throwing
up a wall of shrapnel, was not less than 90 per cent.[16]

Yet the Fuerza Aerea Argentina, the Argentine air force, was a
formidable opponent, with a very high level of training and
dedication. Perón made it a separate arm in 1946, the year Lami
Dozo joined it, and its first instructors were ex-Luftwaffe pilots.
The most dominant of these was Hans-Ulrich Rudel, who had
flown 2,530 missions in Stuka dive-bombers during the Second
World War, helping to level Warsaw, and eliminating – so it was
claimed – 519 tanks, one battleship, one cruiser, one destroyer
and 70 landing-craft. He was shot down 30 times, relearned to fly
after losing one leg, and became the war's most decorated
German officer.[17] Later the Argentine pilots were trained by
France and Israel. The French war ace Pierre Clostermann
thought highly of them, and they prided themselves on rivalling
the Israeli pilots whom they considered the best in the world.

Though Lami Dozo himself reputedly was a moderate man,
his air force's philosophy was Catholic, nationalistic and exalted.
It was *Dios y la Patria* – God and Country. Cadets entering the
College of Military Aviation in Córdoba had to swear to 'follow
the flag always, and defend it unto death'.[18] They kept that
promise. They were to lose 55 killed and have 72 aircraft shot
down, 71 per cent of all their aircraft involved, 52 by missiles or
gunfire from ships or ground troops, and 18 helicopters, against
British losses of 10 Harriers and 24 helicopters, of which 10 were
on the *Atlantic Conveyor* when it was sunk by Exocets on 25
May.[19]

Argentina's ground forces in the Malvinas may have lacked
direction and initiative, but its air force did not, and nor did
Aeronaval, the fleet air arm. Its main strike aircraft were its 14
Skyhawk A4Qs, based on the 39-year-old aircraft carrier *Veinticinco de Mayo*, and the five Super Etendards which it began to
adapt to carry Exocets on 31 March. The Aérospatiale AM 39
Exocet was the latest air-to-surface version of the original surface
missile. It had its own miniature computerized guidance system
by which it locked on to its target. A Super Etendard could fly in
under the enemy's radar screen, pop up into it from 10 to 40 miles
away, localize the target with its radar, transmit the direction to

the Exocet's computer, launch the missile then duck beneath the horizon again and turn for home. The Exocet would skim on a few metres above the sea at near-sonic speed, almost impossible to detect or stop as it carried its 360 lb of explosive to hit targets up to 40 miles away.

The French played a key role in arming these lethal aircraft. At the outbreak of hostilities a technical team from Dassault, the manufacturer, was helping the Argentines with the sensitive task of marrying Exocet accurately to the Super Etendards' wings. France vigorously supported Britain in the Falklands war, and applied military and economic sanctions against Argentina, but although she stopped an Aérospatiale team which had been due to fly out to fit the Exocet, she omitted to recall the Dassault experts. Asked if they went on preparing the planes and missiles for war after 2 April 1982 a senior Argentine officer at Aero-naval's Espora base, 7 miles from Bahía Blanca, would only say: 'Well, they certainly never went on strike.'[20]

Capitán de Fragata Jorge Luis Colombo, squadron-leader of the Super Etendards during the Falklands war, was given a deadline of 30 days to install the missile launchers on the planes which he had received late in 1981. Working round the clock, the Espora technicians did the job in 15. His pilots had had 45 hours basic training in France; by the time hostilities began, each had 100 hours experience. They practised the launching technique hundreds of times, making dummy runs near Puerto Belgrano, Argentina's major naval base by Bahía Blanca. Colombo always practised his aircraft in pairs, flying at 625 mph a few feet above the water and in total radio silence. His pilots practised particu-larly intensively against their own Type 42 destroyers, the *Santísima Trinidad* and the *Hércules*, one built in Britain, the other under licence in Argentina. The British *Sheffield* was the first Type 42 built. Colombo's non-flying pilots would watch from the Type 42s, to study on their radars how the attacking Super Etendards could best surprise them.

Colombo did experiment with operating from the Port Stanley airstrip, but found that it was unusable when wet. If the Super Etendards were to operate from the mainland, they would need aerial refuelling, and so the squadron rehearsed that too, with an air force Hercules KC 130. Finally they practised the complete operation: take off from the mainland, refuel 300 nautical miles out to sea, get the enemy's position from a spotter aircraft, attack at top speed and skimming the waves, launch missile and turn at once for home – fire and forget. In fact, the squadron's attack on the *Sheffield* involved one aerial refuelling 250 miles from the target, and that on the *Atlantic Conveyor* – approached from the north-east for surprise – took two.[21] Colombo's squadron worked hard and professionally for its results, leaving little to chance.

A similar professionalism on the Malvinas themselves would have made an opposed landing into the scene of carnage which military observers were warning of before the Argentines' passive tactical dispositions became known. Even so, after it dawned on the Argentine high command that the British were going to fight, there was still time to stiffen the resistance. Galtieri had been moved to tears as he stood on his Casa Rosada balcony on 2 April and opened his arms to the cheers of an exulting crowd of 100,000 or more. The cheers came even from some Montoneros guerrillas who were themselves risking death if taken. His euphoria did not last long.

One of his fellow-optimists had been the commanding admiral to whom Capitán de Fragata – a naval rank equivalent to lieutenant-colonel – Carlos Hugo Robacio reported in Río Grande, on the Patagonian coast.[22] On 4 April he said to his admiral: 'Wait and see. The British will come.' The admiral shook his head and laughed. Then the Task Force was reported to comprise 36 ships (7 April), with four nuclear submarines (8 April), and it was on 8 April that his admiral asked Robacio: 'How ready is your battalion?' Robacio left by air for the Malvinas within four hours, and the full 1,000 marines of his Fifth Battalion were there by 12 April. They were the Marine Corps' only representatives, for all the forces who had captured the islands had handed them over to the army and returned to the mainland, together with their armoured personnel carriers. (According to Dr Murguizur, this left the defenders with 'no armoured vehicles except for half a dozen tracked personnel carriers, and later four Panhard wheeled APCs'.[23] The Task Force brought light Scimitar and Scorpion tanks, movable by helicopter, and as mobile on the ground as could be expected, given that the waterlogged Falklands are just not tank country.)

Robacio was given a front to defend just south-west of Port Stanley, about eight miles broad and nine miles deep, facing roughly south-south-west. He saw the basic concept at once, and did not like it. It was to defend Port Stanley at all costs from a sea attack, by static defences all round it. Robacio told his senior officer of his misgivings. If he were the British, the very last thing he would do would be to try to take the islands' only town by mass frontal amphibious assault. That would cost heavy casualties and would probably fail. There were several better landing possibilities around the East Malvinas. They could not all be guarded, but the Argentines should keep most of their forces highly mobile, so that they could hit the British wherever they were landing, when they would be at their most vulnerable. The senior officer told Robacio to get on with the job.

Robacio was 49 years old, and had been a marine for 30 years. Three years previously he had been lent to Peru to help train their marines, and he had been promoted to command the Fifth Battalion early in 1982. It was a crack regiment with ancillary commandos, engineers, and an artillery group of six 105 mm howitzers. In addition it had six 106 mm, eight 81 mm and thirty light mortars, plus twelve 50-calibre and 30 light machineguns. Some 80 per cent of its men were conscripts, but experienced: most had had more than five months of intensive training. They were almost professionals, and were built around a permanent core of 30 regular officers and 130 NCOs. On top of that, they had been trained at Río Grande, facing the Antarctic, in conditions worse than those on the Malvinas themselves, in temperatures down to 30 to 40 degrees C below zero. Physical fitness was high, gruelling forced marches nothing new. Properly mobile, with helicopter support, the Fifth Battalion was potentially a dangerous strike force. With his tortoise tactics of clinging to Port Stanley to oppose an amphibious attack that never came, Menéndez threw away that card.

The Fifth Battalion might be unwillingly static, but it did not have to be a sitting duck. The marines dug in hard. Robacio built his command post between Sapper Hill and Mount Tumbledown, to house five men. He dug it deep between two rock walls running north to south, using corrugated iron frames for protection, with rails from a disused railway across the roof, then 200-litre oil drums filled with earth, the mass packed down with peat. (When the battle came, the Command Post took five direct hits, but its occupants emerged unscathed.) Robacio had a clear field of view, and twice as much liberated telephone-cable as regulations permitted gave him first-class communications with all his battalion's forward observation posts. With immediate reports available by phone from all parts of his front, he could call down fire not only from his own six howitzers and mortars but from 42 105 mm howitzers and two 155 mm heavy guns of the Argentine army's artillery.

For many young Britons preparing to face the distant Argentines, the mounting phase which began officially on 31 March was a thrilling experience, enacting something of the achievements of forty years before in the heat of the Second World War. 'That week remains in my mind one of the most exciting in my service,' Major-General Sir Jeremy Moore, Commander of the Falkland Islands Land Forces, recalled.[24] 'Everyone was full of enthusiasm – the marines and soldiers preparing stores, or embarking in ships, were full of vigour; ships' companies, whether professional troop movers or not, appeared to fall over backwards to be helpful.' Stores seemed to appear almost before they were ordered. Ammunition and equipment were loaded well ahead of deadlines. A well-planned operation was under way, each service knowing exactly where it was heading and what it was expected to do. The industrial base in the civilian sector had swung into supportive action with similar speed. Items which normally might take ten years to deliver would now take ten days. 'This was a magic week,' said Moore, who presided over the mounting of the 3rd Commando Brigade of the Royal Marines, reinforced with two infantry battalions and an air defence battery.

To reach a state of readiness within six days involved the refitting, supply and loading of the warships, some with military contingents; the modification of merchantmen to take on helicopters and other aircraft and to refuel at sea; the conversion of Vulcan bombers, Nimrod reconnaissance aircraft and Hercules transports for in-flight fuelling receiver roles plus the parallel conversion of Victors, Vulcans and Hercules to serve as flying tankers; and the simultaneous adaptation of certain contingency plans prepared to meet emergencies in Europe. Such a catalogue of hurried yet successful improvisations and improvements tells only part of the story. There were numerous other aspects.

Nimrods were modified to carry bombs, the Harpoon anti-ship missile, the Sidewinder AIM 9L. RAF Harrier GR3 combat support planes were equipped to take on American-equipped

Sidewinders and laser-guided bombs. The American Vulcan-Phalanx gun system was introduced into HMS *Illustrious* and *Invincible* for point defence. Ship-borne chaff and electronic counter-measures (ECM) were developed rapidly to deal with sea-skimming missiles like the Exocet and were also adapted for use by tactical aircraft and helicopters. Flight decks were designed and fitted in a matter of days in those merchantmen chosen to carry helicopters or Harriers. Trawlers were equipped to work as mine-sweepers. New radio receivers, electronic navigational aids and coding units were provided for ships chartered from the trade. Water production plants were installed into most civilian vessels. Civil air carriers were called in to augment the RAF transport facilities. The Defence establishment worked closely with civilian factories and firms to assess specific threats, to modify or develop new equipment. Portable radio-jammers were invented, produced, tested and delivered within ten days of being ordered.[25]

The requirement which the Chiefs of Staff constantly emphasized was that the Task Force they were forming of 113 vessels – including nearly half of the Royal Navy's surface fighting ships – had to reach an operational area halfway around the world, and then to sustain itself in terms of fuel, food, arms, water, ammunition and every other conceivable necessity for at least three months. That this was done, and capped with a land campaign of the fiercest drive and energy, has been recognized as an extraordinary logistic achievement, fit for the courage it accompanied.

The major concern of the Task Force's organizers naturally focused on ways of ensuring the safety of their 44 fighting ships, 24 auxiliaries and 45 merchantmen, which included the liners *Canberra*, *Queen Elizabeth* and *Uganda*. Although the Argentine navy was unlikely to offer any great threat, the 100-plus combat aircraft of the enemy's navy and fleet air arm made manifest the need both for inventiveness and flexibility if command of the skies were to be denied to Argentina. As a consequence the concept of air-to-air refuelling had to be urgently broadened in order to make the most of the scanty air cover which the Force could take with it. We have mentioned the conversion of Victors, Vulcans and Hercules to tanker roles, Vulcans, Nimrods and Hercules to receivers. Short-range Harriers were also adapted as receivers, and some of the RAF's were enabled to fly thousands of miles nonstop to the battle zone from Ascension within hours. The Hercules transports were kept aloft for 24-hour periods for their supply mission. A Vulcan from Ascension bombed Argentine positions on the Falklands with the help of 17 refills from the fleet of 16 relatively small Victors based at Wideawake (at 07.23 GMT on 1 May). This was the equivalent of an 8,000-mile flight over to the Pacific and back, and went down as the longest operational combat mission ever recorded. Nimrods from Ascension were able to patrol Soviet and Argentine ships trailing the Task Force in a radius of action exceeding 3,000 miles and encompassing Cuba to the west and Guinea and Angola to the north-east and south-east. In addition the Nimrods, with their AD 470 Marconi transceivers, were equipped to intercept and decode operational messages to and from the Argentine fleet and air force – a crucial advantage. If the Argentines had been able to match, or even to approach, the flexible efficiency of the RAF in midair refuelling, their limited-range attackers might well have posed an almost unanswerable threat to Britain's carriers and troopships. It worked for the Super Etendards, with their handful of Exocets, and it was tried with the Skyhawks, though not always successfully. RAF monitors once intercepted the curses of a returning Argentine pilot after he had missed linking with his tanker control and had to ditch in the sea. Against that, RAF pilots had to divert for emergency landings only six times in more than 600 midair fuel transfers, according to the Defence Ministry. On 3 June, one of these diversions was to take a Vulcan bomber to Brazil, where it was disarmed.

The 8,000-mile sea bridge, measuring 21 days in sailing time, saw 28,000 men pass over it, plus 400,000 tons of fuel, 100,000 tons of freight in merchantmen alone during the seven weeks until the landings.[26] No one knew how much resistance the Argentines were willing or able to put up, operating just outside their own back door. The Falklands were right at the end of Britain's reach: sinews must be strained in order to get there, and kept at full stretch in order to stay there. And the whole Task Force was reliant on its two light aircraft carriers, Hermes and Invincible. The loss of either would jeopardize both Operation Corporate and the government which ordered it. Normally three carriers are considered essential in order to keep just one on station, but the Royal Navy had its orders, and it too was eager to demonstrate of what metal it was made. In any case the Thatcher government had resolved on an extraordinary step to deal with the extreme emergency which would arise if either or both the carriers were to be lost. 'We would have had to ask the Americans to make one available to us,' Sir Nicholas Henderson recalled.[27] Whether or not President Reagan would have authorized the sale or lend-lease of a carrier was not ascertainable when fighting ended. The Prime Minister was gambling so much already that she may have gambled that the sight of his most loyal supporter about to fall would force Mr Reagan to reach out and catch her.

For the whole Task Force mission was a gamble. It divided the Chiefs of Staff, defied American advice and entreaties, and dismayed even some of those senior ministers who knew that certain British submarines were still carrying nuclear weapons which they had not had time to unload. Britain's then ambassador in Washington, Sir Nicholas Henderson, a diplomat with forty years' experience reaching back to the Second World War, still sounded dismayed when he wrote about the situation more than 18 months later:

> . . . if an account is to be given of how things really were at the time, it must not be forgotten that when the British task force was despatched to the South Atlantic few of those responsible for the decision had any idea how the Argentines were going to be ejected by force from the islands.

Henderson quotes a remark made by Admiral Fieldhouse on a visit to Ascension Island in April – 'I hope that people realize that this is the most difficult thing that we have attempted since the Second World War' – before recalling:

> A great deal was at stake, the risks were very great and I know how much ministers realized this . . . It was impossible to know what our casualties were likely to be, or how much British public opinion would tolerate in the way of losses.[28]

If the Task Force was as vulnerable as that, then the commanders on the spot were going to shoot first and ask questions afterwards in the event of anything that looked like an immediate threat. With something less immediate, they might ask their Chiefs of Staff, 8,000 miles away, and *their* instinct must be to shorten the odds. If their political bosses were gambling for high stakes too, then that alone was likely to predispose them towards the sure solution.

In Britain, there were not many voices raised in caution. Lord Carrington resigned as Foreign Minister on 5 April, along with two of his ministers, Humphrey Atkins and Richard Luce. It was Carrington who had prevailed upon Mrs Thatcher to subdue her natural instincts, and the infuriated right wing of her own party, and back majority rule in Zimbabwe – not welcome, but work-able. The debate of 3 April 1982 had shown that not even the prospect of an unpredictable war was going to shift the Com-mons out of the mood of all-party outrage which had savaged Nicholas Ridley in December 1980. Seeing that there was no role left for him to play, and that the British government's loss of face demanded a scapegoat, Carrington was not unhappy to with-draw. He was succeeded by Francis Pym, whose influence on his leader remained imperceptible.

Any reservations there might have been were drowned in any case under the cheers of the crowds, the farewell hoots of ship's sirens and the martial brass of military bands as the vanguard of the Task Force set out from Portsmouth, bound for the South Atlantic. The moving spectacle of wives and mothers, sweet-hearts and sisters bidding farewell to their menfolk as troopships lined with waving servicemen moved slowly out into the Eng-lish Channel brought back memories of other separations in bigger wars. Generations which had grown up in an age of decolonization found that they could still respond to the fervour of 'Rule Britannia' and 'Land of Hope and Glory', and the feeling that the eyes of the world were fixed on Great Britain again. Two powerful streams of British feeling converged and surfaced – nostalgia for the exciting days of imperialism, the Victorian and Edwardian splendours recalled by so many books and TV pro-grammes in the last twenty years, and a sense of heroism and sacrifice last felt in the Second World War. Somehow it did not matter that that war had been fought against a stronger enemy, a murderer of races and nations: the rhetoric prevented the contrast from being drawn. Argentina was outnumbered and outgunned, and more by luck than judgement it had managed not to kill anybody in its seizure of the Falklands and South Georgia. Yet Mrs Thatcher was able in all sincerity to strike the Churchillian attitude, as she did in 1983 when she quoted Churchill on the humiliations which are forced upon those who feel unable to defend their rights against aggression. She then went on to say:

> True in the face of the Nazi menace in the 1930s, true in the face of the threats to our way of life today. True, too, in the South Atlantic last year, when . . . Britain again had to demonstrate that aggression must not be allowed to succeed and that international law and the right of people freely to choose their own way of life must be upheld.[29]

Neither then nor since could the British Prime Minister perceive the epic disproportion between the two cases, and she was not helped to do so by a campaign by four of Britain's mass circulation tabloid newspapers – the *Sun*, *Star*, *Express* and *Mail* – in which opponents of the war were damned as appeasers, fainthearts, traitors. Jingoism, hysteria and racism were blended, patriotism exploited. Vindictiveness was turned into an ethic. Two days after the Task Force set out, a *Financial Times* editorial protested that the Falklands issue involved 'no vital national interest in any material or strategic sense'. The very presence of the Task Force in the Falklands would change that assessment, but the vital national interest committed by the government right from the start was Britain's pride.

Argentina had its own genius for creating myths. Having seen one of them exploded – the myth that Britain would not react strongly to an invasion, nor promptly send a powerful battle fleet – they shifted to another. Now it was that something would just stop the fleet and turn it round. It might be dreadful weather, or grave logistical difficulties, a fierce resolution from the Organization of American States, a sudden peace agreement, or the discovery that the Falklands under hostile occupation had become too difficult to repossess by assault. This delusion flourished at august levels. Admiral Anaya held it and argued it forcefully right through April. President Belaúnde of Peru was horrified by the *triunfalismo* – the blind optimism and euphoric self-deception – of some of the senior Argentine military officers who visited him in Lima during the Falklands war. The British Task Force couldn't take the place now, they said authoritatively. '*Es un baluarte*' – It's a bulwark.[30]

Their President's own view was equally far removed from the facts. In an interview of 29 July 1982 he looked back on the war

like some helpless spectator. Asked why the Junta had used so
many green recruits, Galtieri replied airily that he had had no idea
of the state of preparation of the soldiers who went to the front;
that was the responsibility of his subordinate officers. (He had
remained C-in-C of the army all through his presidency.) Asked
if the communiqués of the Joint General Staff had not been too
triunfalista, he cheerfully acknowledged: 'That's true, I agree. My
wife pointed it out to me. I myself was surprised when I got the
news of the fall of Puerto Argentino [Port Stanley]. I thought that
they could go on fighting longer.'[31]

Below this cloud of Anglo-Argentine myth and rhetoric, the
military realities took shape. Before the Task Force's emotional
send-off, Britain's five nuclear-powered hunter-killer submarines (SSNs) were already on their way.[32] Their role was
crucial because of their speed, firepower and operational independence. Argentina had nothing to match them. They were
responsible not to the Task Force commander but directly to the
operational headquarters of the Chiefs of Staff at Northwood,
Middlesex, on the outskirts of London. Of course reports of their
movements, sightings, activities and problems were relayed to
Rear-Admiral John 'Sandy' Woodward on board his flagship
Hermes.

The precise mission assigned to HMS *Conqueror* and her four
identical sister submarines was to police the area around the
Falklands and to help secure the Total Exclusion Zone imposed
by the British when it came into force on 30 April. Powered by
Rolls-Royce nuclear reactors, the SSNs were able to remain
submerged for months, move underwater at 30 knots, and spot
an enemy 40 miles away. Thousands of sonar 'ears' fitted to their
hulls were able to pick up the sounds of a distant target, eliminate
superfluous noise and transmit details of their find to a battery of
screens in the sonar room. Navy specialists, working round-the-
clock shifts, then interpreted the computerized messages which
told the commander what he needed to know about the target –
the type of vessel, its course and speed, and even its support.

Depending on the nature of their orders, the SSN commanders
could decide whether to attack the target, shadow it or seek new
instructions from their superiors in London. Their highly sophisticated radio communications systems enabled them – if fully
operational – to make contact with Northwood or with Defence
headquarters almost instantaneously, given the right conditions.

Armaments included the Mark 24 Tigerfish torpedoes which can be set to detonate either near the target or upon impact. The Tigerfish is almost a craft in its own right, weighing nearly two tons, with a speed of more than 45 mph and a range of roughly 40 miles. These torpedoes were not popular with the commanders or their crews: they had a record of running amok, with the risk of rebounding on the craft that launched them. However the SSNs also carried Mark 8 torpedoes of the type used during the Second World War, a reliable killing machine. Their 810 lbs of Torpex high explosive would blow a wide enough hole in any ship the Argentines might put to sea.

4

Tilting for Britain

The role of the United States in the Falklands confrontation was bound to be decisive. American opposition would probably have stopped the Task Force before it started. A benevolent American neutrality directed towards Argentina instead of towards Britain would have made it so difficult for the Force to operate that the British government would have been forced to negotiate on sovereignty rather than take the spectacular risk of intruding on the hemisphere without a friend. One of Mrs Thatcher's first moves on the evening of 31 March 1982 when John Nott received the 'positive indication' that the Argentines would invade was to send a message to President Reagan to ask him to intervene. In order to 'ensure a rapid reaction from the White House'[1] she also instructed the British Ambassador, Sir Nicholas Henderson, to speak to the US Secretary of State, Alexander Haig, once military adviser to Henry Kissinger, White House Chief of Staff to President Richard Nixon, and Supreme Allied Commander Europe.

'You know the American scene,' Henderson later observed.[2] 'There isn't always a unified view on a major matter of policy. You have the lobbies, the White House, Congress, the State Department, CIA. You have Haig on the one side, [UN Ambassador Jeane] Kirkpatrick and Thomas Enders [then Assistant Secretary of State for Latin America] on the other, and they favoured a Latin American orientation. But Haig leapt into action after my meeting with him on 31 March.'

Thomas Enders, who had visited Buenos Aires earlier that

month, was also present at Henderson's meeting with Haig. While Haig's reaction to the British intelligence assessments of an imminent invasion was 'electric', as Henderson described it, Enders remained sceptical. 'Evidently an assurance had just been received from Costa Méndez that in Buenos Aires no invasion was being contemplated and Enders said that the information had been confirmed elsewhere.' Asked in 1983 whether the reputed hardliner in the Junta, Admiral Jorge Anaya, might have acted independently in staging the invasion, Henderson's response was sharp: 'Definitely not. Costa Méndez and the others were in it up to their necks as much as Anaya.' So Costa Méndez had misled Washington? 'Not for the first time,' said Henderson.

There was a great deal of criticism at that time in Britain, and some in the United States, of the apparently neutral American stance. Henderson recalled how useful it had been: 'If Haig had not acted as he did, if there had been no mediation – however much it was resented by some people in London – we would never have had US support. And that support, across the board, may very well have been a decisive factor in the outcome. It was very important to us.'

2–4 April 1982. HMS Conqueror *lay at her base at Faslane, on the Gare Loch, which opens on to the Firth of Clyde, taking on stores, and 14 men of the Special Boat Service, for the voyage to the South Atlantic. She sailed at 21.15 on Sunday, 4 April.*
6 April 1982. News arrived that the Marines on South Georgia had shot down a helicopter, damaged a corvette and killed three Argentines before surrendering. The ship's new captain, Commander Christopher Wreford-Brown, addressed the ship's company. It was his first voyage in command, and he sounded grim and serious.

Haig threw himself into the role of mediator between Britain and Argentina with frenetic energy. On 6 April he talked separately to the British and Argentine ambassadors in Washington, Henderson and Esteban A. Takacs, and with the Argentine Foreign Minister, Costa Méndez.[3] He told them that if confirmed as the United States' mediator in the conflict he would be attempting to negotiate some sort of mixed administration to run the Falklands. Henderson stressed that the British government was not going to negotiate under duress: the Argentines must first withdraw their forces. General Galtieri would need something in return, Haig answered, or he could not survive as President. Too bad for Galtieri, Henderson shrugged. 'It was he who had brought about the present occupation in order to distract public opinion from economic and political difficulties.'[4] The British policy throughout the crisis was to ignore the long-standing Argentine claim to sovereignty and present the invasion as a piece of opportunism by a militarist regime characterized as intransigent and irrational.

Haig told Henderson that he accepted that the Argentines must withdraw before Britain could negotiate:

> But, thinking aloud, he wondered whether it would be possible for him to appoint a commission comprising, say, some distinguished but impartial American figure, a Canadian, some Latin Americans and one or two others, who might act as intermediaries and serve as some kind of interim administration.[5]

Although some Americans considered that Vice-President George Bush would be a better choice, because less inclined towards Europe, and therefore towards the United Kingdom, on 7 April the National Security Council accepted Haig's mediation proposal. That same day, Britain announced the imposition of a 200-mile maritime exclusion zone around the Falklands, to come into effect on 12 April.

7 April 1982. The Conqueror *was making a fast passage, with one periscope-depth (PD) run every 30 hours. The evening film was* One Flew Over the Cuckoo's Nest.
8 April 1982. The Conqueror *passed Madeira.*

Haig flew to London on 8 April, taking with him a powerful team which included General Vernon Walters. One stumbling-block in the negotiations proved to be Mrs Thatcher's insistence on the paramountcy of the *wishes* of the Falkland islanders – in effect, a right of veto. This went against the determining UN Resolution 2065 (see Appendix 1), which spoke only of taking due account of their *interests*. Britain's position was that the right of self-determination ('to be British') was absolute – a matter of principle.

From London, General Walters flew on to Paris to see his old friend, the Argentine Ambassador to France, Gerardo Schamis. Schamis at once sent a coded telegram to Buenos Aires to inform his government of the three key points which Walters had made about that first Haig – Thatcher meeting. They were that:

1 Mrs Thatcher had adopted a rigidly non-negotiating stance.
2 She was deliberately staking her entire political career and future on maintaining the belligerent line she had taken.
3 Reagan would support her in the long run and the last extremity, *and she knew that.*

The Thatcher government had taken the initiative in Europe in backing the US policy of introducing cruise missiles to counter the Russian SS20s. Mrs Thatcher had also backed Ronald Reagan in his Central American policy and his overall strategy of militant anti-communism. Despite Reagan's Caribbean and Central American worries, the US grip on South America was secure, and none of the American-backed governments there could afford to take too strong a line against their mentor. In Europe, a hostile or disenchanted Britain would be an unpredictable and dangerous factor. Writing in 1983, Sir Nicholas Henderson stressed the genuinely friendly feeling towards Britain which he found at high levels at the time of the Falklands crisis. He also recalled:

> Haig emphasized to me in the early days that the United States was not at heart impartial, that HMG had always supported the Reagan administration in foreign policy, and that America could not privately be even-handed in anything involving its closest ally . . . Haig frequently assured me at the time that, notwithstanding the public stance, the president was our staunch supporter.[6]

So the Argentine government knew from early in the crisis that Haig was combining the roles of mediator and of surrogate negotiator on Britain's behalf. By the same token, Mrs Thatcher knew that if and when the talking turned to fighting, the US could afford to drop Argentina, but not to drop Britain.

9 April 1982. The Conqueror *passed the Canary Islands.*
10 April 1982. The Conqueror *passed the Cape Verde Islands. The ship's crew learned that a 200-mile exclusion area was in force around the Falklands, and that their sister-ships* Spartan *and* Splendid *might*

*attack Argentine shipping inside it. They themselves were to make for
South Georgia.*

On Friday, 9 April, Haig and his team flew from London to
Buenos Aires. He found that Argentina would not budge on its
old and fundamental claim of absolute sovereignty over the
Malvinas, but was ready to discuss a stopgap neutral administration. The American Secretary of State stressed repeatedly that if
it came to a shooting war, Britain was much the stronger
country, and was bound to win. He was already arguing strongly
on Mrs Thatcher's behalf, or so the Argentines thought. From
the beginning, he made it clear that in the event of war, Washington would have to side with the British, the most stable of its
European allies. The US could not permit the precedent of a
small nation imposing its will on a friendly world power.

The transcript of the second mediation talks held on that first
Haig visit, at 21.30 on 10 April, shows how vigorously Haig
presented the British case. The talks were attended by Galtieri,
Costa Méndez and the deputy foreign minister, Enrique Ros;
Haig was assisted by Tom Enders.

Haig was proposing a period of 'transition' during which the
Falklands would retain their established machinery of govern-
ment: an Executive Council (the islands' Cabinet) and a Legisla-
tive Council. A Consortium of four countries – Canada or the
US, the UK, and two Latin-American countries would vet the
Councils' decisions. There would be no Governor.

Haig: The final authority would be the Executive Committee
and its decisions would have to be approved by the Consortium. (. . .) There would be a representative of the Argentine
Government with direct access to the Consortium to confirm
that the viewpoint of that Government was being protected.

Galtieri wanted an Argentine Governor in day-to-day control,
possibly under the Consortium. He would not recall his
Governor, or lower the Argentine flag.

Haig: I think that we can have flag representation during the
transition period which would involve five authorities. I believe too that the Argentine Governor can remain, but the idea
of him as the ultimate authority would be thrown out in

London. If it were accepted Mrs Thatcher would fall. Let's tread softly around this lady who outfaces statues. A solution like the one I've proposed will permit her to assure her parliament that the authorities have been re-established.

Haig went on to envisage 'a secret protocol in which Mrs Thatcher with President Reagan's guarantee would commit herself to finishing the process before the end of the year. President Reagan would transmit these agreements to the Argentine President.' Costa Méndez jibbed: 'After 17 years we don't believe anything any more. Every year we talk the same. Fourteen years ago I was Foreign Minister and I spoke understandingly to the British, but we always ended up with nothing.'

Galtieri: They took away our flag for 150 years. Now that we've reinstalled it we can't ask the Argentine people to accept our taking it away again.
Haig: This would mean political suicide for Mrs Thatcher. I don't think she can accept it.

Haig stuck to the Executive Committee: 'Maintaining the make-up of this group is the only thing that Mrs Thatcher still has. If she loses sovereignty, she loses immediate control.'

Costa Méndez: Since the signature of the 1971 agreement [a communications accord under which Argentina supplied the Islands with air and sea transport, oil, and mainland secondary school scholarships] we Argentines have been refused access to the Islands.
Galtieri: They can't ask us to turn everything back. What's proposed will be accepted by Mrs Thatcher, but not by the Government of General Galtieri.

The discussion drifted on, with mention of a smaller consortium – Haig called it a 'transitional triumvirate' – of Argentina, the UK and the US, the right for Argentine citizens to reside on the islands (hitherto denied by the British, for fear of an Argentine influx creating a new set of 'wishes' and a different goal for 'self-determination'), the removal of Parliament's veto on the sale of shares in the Falkland Islands Company, and so on. Things had become inconclusive, and Galtieri withdrew.

General Walters was not idle during Haig's two mediation visits to Buenos Aires. On the first, 9–11 April, he spent much time with senior Argentine army corps commanders. There he learned that only two of the country's twelve divisional generals had known about the invasion before it happened. Again Walters stressed the British demands: unconditional withdrawal; a mainly British and American interim administration with a few Argentine representatives; the wishes of the islanders to come first. During the team's second visit ending 19 April Walters arranged a private talk with Argentina's ex-President Arturo Frondizi. Five days later Frondizi's MID political party published the first of its articles criticizing the Junta for getting into the Falklands war.

General Walters' final appearance in Buenos Aires was conclusive for Galtieri. On 10 June, with a British victory now a foregone conclusion, he spent his time with those generals most critical of the President, recommending that they should throw him out. Walters had helped to make Galtieri. In the end he helped to break him.

11 April 1982. Conqueror*'s reactor 'scrammed', and she started sinking, at 01.45. She pumped out some thousands of gallons of water and regained buoyancy. They passed the latitude of Trinidad later that morning.*
12 April 1982. Conqueror *crossed the Equator at 10.09.*
13–14 April 1982. A fast passage past the 10th and 15th parallels.

A British fleet of 107 surface ships was on its way, 62 of them Royal Navy, 45 merchantmen,[7] led by the *Hermes*, 24,000 tons, launched in 1953, and the *Invincible*, 17,000 tons, launched in 1977, her sale to Australia for 1983 postponed. The Argentine carrier, the *Veinticinco de Mayo*, 16,000 tons, launched in 1943, led a smaller fleet. The one cruiser, the *General Belgrano*, commissioned in 1939, was due to be taken out of service as a floating museum in 1982, as her sister ship, the *Nueve de Julio*, had been in 1979. Of the four destroyers committed to the Falklands war, two of them were Second World War vintage – the *Hipólito Bouchard* and the *Piedra Buena* – and the other two were the Type 42 *Hércules* and *Santísima Trinidad*. Argentina put three diesel submarines to sea for the campaign: the *Santa Fe* was a Guppy class SSK submarine, also 38 years old; the *Salta* and the *San Luis* were modern German-built Type S209s. Of the Task Force's surface warships, 15 were fitted with surface-to-surface Exocets with 20-mile ranges, compared to seven so armed on the Argentine side. These were the four destroyers already mentioned, and all three of Argentina's French-built Type A 69 corvettes, the *Granville*, *Guerrico* and *Drummond*.

Argentina put its fighting navy to sea between 15 and 17 April, progressively, from the major naval base of Puerto Belgrano, by Bahía Blanca.[8] It constituted Task Force 79, of three groups. The northern group was the *Veinticinco de Mayo*, with her complement of 18 A4Q Skyhawks and Tracker S2E reconnaissance aircraft,[9] with four Sea King and Alouette helicopters, and the two Type 42 destroyers. The central group consisted of the three French-built corvettes. These two groups were far too small successfully to take on the formidable British force now ploughing towards them on the surface, let alone the six submarines, five of them nuclear, which were also in the offing.

The southern group was composed of the 10,800-ton *Belgrano* and the two venerable destroyers – though armed with Exocets – the *Piedra Buena* and *Hipólito Bouchard*, with a total of 119 years' service between them.[10] The *Belgrano* carried no Exocets, as the British Navy knew: her only missiles were surface-to-air Sea Cats, with a range of 2½ miles. Her main armament was her 15 six-inch guns, with a range of 13 miles. An Exocet-fitted frigate could sit seven miles further than that and blow her out of the water. The *Belgrano* had been in dock for regular maintenance on 2 April, and had taken no part in the invasion of the Falklands. She and her escorts were to act as a barrier against any British ship trying to attack the Argentine Patagonian ports and Ushuaia from the north-east, or from round the Horn,[11] and against any Chilean ship that might venture into the fight.

Haig had been pursuing the best traditions of shuttle diplomacy, the necessary rituals of long plane journeys and too little sleep. He and his team returned to London on 11 April, but the British stood pat on the issue of sovereignty, would not agree to lift restrictions on Argentine citizens settling in the Falklands, and refused more than a token Argentine presence in any interim administration. There was nothing to be gained by further discussion. Haig flew back to Washington, and then on to Buenos Aires.

This was a crucial visit, because here the two later versions of the Haig diplomacy diverge. According to the orthodox account Haig, blocked by Argentina's refusal – 'intransigent refusal', rather – to contribute any positive peace proposal whatsoever, left Buenos Aires empty-handed on 19 April and headed despondently back to Washington. (London had cabled to say discreetly that it saw no point in another session.)

Sir Nicholas Henderson gives a rather different account:

> After prolonged discussion with Haig . . . the Argentines put forward a proposal that Haig said, in transmitting it to Pym, was not something that he could urge the British government to accept.[12]

According to Henderson, 'their idea for troop withdrawals would heavily favour Argentina' – they would be 400 miles away, the Task Force 8,000. The Argentines also wanted a 'disproportionate representation' on the interim island councils, and they wanted a provision which would enable them to flood the Falklands with their own immigrant nationals. Lastly, 'the text would exclude a return to the status quo ante and did not preserve the principle that the islanders should choose their own future'.[13] It may be remarked about these latter criticisms that the Falklands had been desperately looking for immigrants to bolster a shrinking population, and that the Argentines had plans to develop the islands which were much more practicable if run from the South American mainland than from the islands, which are thinly populated, under-capitalized, and not self-sufficient. The wishes of the islanders were a sticking point, but it was not the Argentines alone who rejected them as a 'principle' in any settlement: UN Resolution 2065 had stipulated no such principle.

In the orthodox account of the Haig negotiations, the Argentines are utterly intransigent. In Henderson's modified version, they put forward 'a proposal' but it is obviously not acceptable. Henderson goes on to explain that they were probably playing for time, waiting for the world to get used to their occupation as a fait accompli, and for the coming winter to make a British military presence in the South Atlantic untenable.

However, according to a source in the Presidency in Buenos Aires,[14] before Haig left on 19 April the Argentines had put to him no less than five separate peace proposals copies of which were made available in Buenos Aires to Dr Clifford Kiracofe, Legislative Assistant to the ultra right-wing Chairman of the US Senate Foreign Relations Subcommittee on the Western Hemisphere, Senator Jesse Helms.[15] The final Argentine proposal of 19 April (see Appendix 2) incorporated several concessions to the British; however it also set a 31 December 1982 deadline for its implementation, failing which Argentina would insist on appointing its own chief administrator.

15–16 April 1982. The Conqueror's *southward passage took her past the 35th parallel. The SBS contingent practised its landing methods, to be used on South Georgia. The submarine's workshop was producing a gun mounting for the bridge.*
17–18 April 1982. Conqueror *entered the Northern Iceberg Limits. She was almost on station. (The Task Force was now at Ascension Island.)*

On 20 April, back in Washington, Haig began to formulate a Memorandum of Agreement – proposals to be sent to London and Buenos Aires. The following day he talked to the British Ambassador:

> He described the irrationality and chaotic nature of the Argentine leadership. He said there seemed to be 50 people involved in decisions. If he reached some sort of agreement on one of the points at issue with a member of the junta, this was invariably countermanded by a corps commander entering the room an hour or so later.[16]

The picture was one of growing impatience with the dilatory Argentines.

Galtieri flew out to the Islands on the 22nd, and he and Menéndez went on a three-hour tour of inspection by helicopter. He noticed that Menéndez did not really know the terrain: clearly he had not been moving around his command enough.[17] Galtieri was in two minds about sacking him, but the Task Force was approaching.

On 23 April, Senator Helms learned that officials of the State Department had begun drafting a motion for passage through the Senate and House of Representatives recommending that the US should end mediation and give Britain all-out support short of military intervention. Helms had always argued that by forcing Argentina out of the Falklands in 1833 Britain had violated the Monroe Doctrine, which had been designed by the US in order to keep Europe's empire-builders out of the Western Hemisphere. He felt that the US ought to stick by its partners in the Río Treaty of Reciprocal Assistance, signed by 21 American countries, including the US and Argentina, in 1947.

Then Helms received a report that the Democratic senators Joseph R. Biden and Paul E. Tsongas had promised to initiate a pro-British resolution, after being visited by British Foreign Secretary Francis Pym (in Washington since 22 April), a British Defence Minister, Peter Blaker, and US Secretary for Defence Caspar Weinberger. Helms was furious. He knew of no precedent for a mediator 'tilting' halfway through like this. It would simply make Haig appear pro-British.

19 April 1982. Conqueror *approached South Georgia at 6 knots, and was 20 miles offshore by early morning. She closed in to within three miles of the coast for a closer look, then moved back to begin an anti-shipping patrol.*
20 April 1982. Patrolling an area 100 miles north of South Georgia, the Conqueror *was followed by flocks of seals playing in her wake. The crew were now sensing that action was a strong probability.*
21 April 1982. Routine patrolling. A possible submarine contact turned out to be biological. Conqueror *spent much of the night surfaced, while a repair crew worked on a damaged wireless-telegraph (WT) mast. The crew felt envious of Spartan, whose job was blockading Port Stanley.*
22 April 1982. In a gale of Force 8-plus, with 20-foot waves, Conqueror *took a pounding during her runs at periscope depth, west of South Georgia. Intelligence had reported a merchant vessel in the vicinity.*
23 April 1982. Splendid *was taken off her surveillance on the* Veinticinco de Mayo *and her group.* Conqueror *headed towards the Falklands to join the British Battle Group.*

According to Sir Nicholas Henderson, on 23 April the British government announced to the world and the Argentine government 'its preparedness to attack any Argentine ship or aircraft wherever it was if it posed a threat to British forces in the South Atlantic . . . From that time any Argentine warship, submarine or military aircraft . . . could expect to be attacked on or over the high seas.'[18] Henderson is interpreting the mere existence of an Argentine ship in the South Atlantic as a threat. His version of the statement is slightly at odds with the account given in the British government's retrospective analysis *The Falklands Campaign: The Lessons*, which reads:

23 April The Government warns Argentina that any *approach by Argentine warships or military aircraft which could amount to a threat to the task force* would be dealt with appropriately. (Emphasis added.)

Henderson's version might be translated as an unambiguous statement: 'We will sink or shoot down any Argentine warship or aircraft that ventures beyond your territorial limits.' No such unvarnished warning was issued by the British government until 7 May. *Splendid* did not attempt to torpedo the Argentine carrier now on the high seas.

24 April 1982. Conqueror *was ordered back to South Georgia to find and sink an Argentine submarine reported in the area by British intelligence. This was the* Santa Fe.
25 April 1982. Conqueror *received news of the failed SAS landing on South Georgia on 22–23 April, when two Wessex 5 helicopters ditched in atrocious weather. Another signal stressed that military action was now practically a certainty in the Falklands. Later in the day came the news that one of HMS* Antrim's *Wessex 3 helicopters had found the* Santa Fe *on the surface and crippled her with missiles. Following a bombardment from HMS* Antrim *and* Plymouth *and a landing by the SAS and SBS, at 17.15 local time the Argentine forces at Grytviken surrendered. All* Conqueror *could do was to pass round the port in celebration.*

On the morning of 27 April Costa Méndez received Haig's Memorandum of Agreement from the US Embassy in Buenos Aires, together with Haig's request for a reply by midnight that day. It was a brusque message, and Costa Méndez wondered if the time scale implied some secret deadline that had to be met. These were the terms put forward in the Memorandum (Appendix 3A):

Immediate ceasefire.

No entry or deployment of fresh forces.

Elimination of Britain's Total Exclusion Zone (TEZ), and suspension of Argentina's operations within it.

Mutual withdrawal of existing forces under verification by the United States.

An immediate end to all economic and financial sanctions.

The establishment of a Special Interim Authority composed of British, Argentine and US delegates, to ratify all decisions, laws and regulations made by the local administration. This would function as before, but the six-man Executive Council would be enlarged by two Argentine appointees. It, and the nine-man Legislative Council, would also include representatives of Argentines living on the islands, in proportion to their number in the population, there being at least one such representative of the resident Argentine population (which was only 30) on each Council.

The flags of all three constituent members of the Authority would be flown. There would be equality of rights in travel, transport, residence, ownership, disposal of property, communications and trade between mainland and islands, preservation of earlier rights customs and lifestyles, and a definite solution by 31 December 1982, with due regard for the rights of the inhabitants and the principle of territorial integrity, in line with the aims and principles of the UN Charter and relevant Resolutions of the UN General Assembly.

The British – Argentine – US interim authority also would submit proposals to the London and Buenos Aires governments on ways of sounding islander opinion as to their 'wishes and interests' for the future; on the development of the Falklands' resources including the role of the Falkland Island Company; and on arrangements for compensating islanders who might choose to be resettled.

Mrs Thatcher's government found Haig's terms for a settlement to its liking, particularly the provision for a kind of opinion poll among islanders about their 'wishes and interests'. So the British lost no time in accepting the Secretary of State's memorandum as a basis for negotiation. Haig, when announcing the end of his mediating mission on 30 April, put it this way: 'We had reason to hope that the United Kingdom would consider a settlement along the lines of our proposal.' Then he added: 'But Argentina informed us yesterday that it could not accept it.' Reasons for the Junta's hesitation were easy to identify.

The Argentines had just been trounced on South Georgia, and with the British Armada fast approaching, Haig's deadline appeared ominous. Nevertheless, Costa Méndez spotted two political booby-traps in the Memorandum. The first was that it restricted Argentine representation on the island's Councils to levels below the British and below those previously implied by Haig as being acceptable. With no provision to increase the Argentine representation if the negotiating parties failed to reach a solution, Argentina could remain in a permanent minority on both councils. As Costa Méndez' reply would put it (see Appendix 3B), Argentina was 'faced with the real possibility of establishing a predominantly British administration indefinitely'.

The second and – for Costa Méndez – the more lethal trap was contained in paragraph 8.1 of the Haig Memorandum, which spoke of taking the '*wishes* and interests of the islanders' into account, as determined by some sort of opinion poll – 'a sounding of the opinion of the inhabitants'. This ran counter to UN Resolution 2065 and would be suicidal for Argentina, whose stock had fallen markedly in the islands even before the invasion, and was now at rock-bottom. The opinion poll was a new notion of Haig's, never raised before.

Haig had always told the British that both he and Ronald Reagan were fundamentally on their side once negotiations reached deadlock. Henderson characterized his activities as 'something to fill the diplomatic vacuum' in between the Task Force's departure and 'its readiness to repossess the islands'.[19] Interviewed on 22 November 1983, Henderson argued, however, that Haig's priorities 'did not stop him from trying to reconcile the two seemingly irreconcilable British and Argentine positions almost to the very end'.[20] Certainly he was not trying to reconcile those positions when he delivered a top-secret briefing to the Senate on the evening of Wednesday, 28 April, starting at 5.30 and finishing at 6.45 pm. It was held in Room S 407 on the fourth floor of the Capitol, known as the Star Chamber, unbuggable, electronically insulated and under 24-hour guard. Senators Biden and Moynihan were to put a pro-British motion to the Senate the following day, and what Haig told the 70-plus senators who attended the briefing would be vital.

He told them that Argentina was being intransigent. The word crops up repeatedly in the debate the following day. For instance Senator Dodd (Democrat, Connecticut) referred to 'Argentina's intransigence' and called that country 'an international outlaw'.[21] Two key points have emerged about Haig's briefing, and they help to explain why Dodd and his fellow-senators were so unanimous in their condemnation of Argentina. The first is that it was held *before* Haig had received the Argentine reply to his Memorandum delivered the previous day. The second is that apart from the two points already mentioned, virtually the whole Memorandum was an eclectic blend of the same five peace proposals which the Presidency had submitted. Dr Kiracofe's examination of these in Buenos Aires was to show that most of the other articles came from one or another of the five Argentine proposals, often verbatim. Yet Haig did not tell the assembled senators anything about the five proposals and he presented the Memorandum as his own work.

Like his diplomatic mentor, Henry Kissinger, Haig kept some things to himself, and that was his right, but this particular silence enabled him to show the Argentines in the most unfavourable light. Instead of their contributing positive proposals, they were shown as rejecting Haig's. Instead of negotiating, they were shown as intransigent. Given the minimum positions of both Britain and Argentina, Sir Nicholas Henderson could properly call them irreconcilable. The dilemma is put neatly and almost comically by the former Ambassador himself: 'A negotiated settlement was always the one most favoured, provided British interests and principles could be safeguarded'[22] – in other words, as long as Britain's sovereignty and its Falklands majority remained unchanged. Argentina was equally reasonable: any settlement would be welcome, as long as their sovereignty and their control were finally to be acknowledged in the Malvinas.

26 April 1982. Conqueror *patrolled the sea northward of South Georgia. There was more trouble with a WT mast in the evening, and she surfaced to repair it.*
27 April 1982. A helicopter picked up the SBS men and their equipment and transferred them to Antrim, *which was inshore together with* Brilliant, Endurance, Plymouth *and* Tidespring. Conqueror

spent all day attempting to fix her defective WT gear. In the evening she was dispatched to the Falklands.
28 April 1982. Conqueror set out for the Falklands in the early morning, with her communications equipment still not repaired.

The Argentine ambassador in Washington, Esteban Takacs, delivered his country's reply to the Haig Memorandum in person at 11 am on 29 April. He saw it as a vital step in a continuing negotiation – a view which he felt was confirmed by Argentina's subsequent readiness to negotiate with President Belaúnde of Peru, three days later. Yet when he delivered the reply Takacs had to sit and suffer 'a very tense conversation about it for some 20 minutes'. It was as if some unalterable judgement had been passed: Argentina was culpably intransigent, unwilling to accept a reasonable compromise, contributing nothing helpful to the search for a viable peace agreement. When Senator Helms rang Haig at noon, to ask what progress, the Secretary of State spoke of 'Argentine pride and reluctance to negotiate'.[24]

What Costa Méndez said in his reply was that 'significant differences have emerged, some of which give rise to difficulties that it is essential to overcome' (see Appendix 3B). Costa Méndez insisted that recognition of Argentina's sovereignty was an 'unrenounceable goal' and neither Haig nor Britain could have expected Argentina to give up what she had been seeking for 150 years. UN Resolution 2065 presupposed that this very question was negotiable and not immutable. The Foreign Minister linked sovereignty and the provisional administration of the islands: if sovereignty remained unsettled, then Argentina wanted broader powers of administration; 'if it were clear that Argentina's sovereignty would be recognized in the end, then we could be more flexible regarding the matter of temporary administration'. He might have been spelling out his country's acceptance of a leaseback solution.

If anything, the terms of the Argentine reply were ingratiatingly mild. Costa Méndez seemed at pains not to shut any doors decisively, or at any rate to be seen to be doing so. Referring to Haig's two 'British' conditions, he said only that he felt that 'other formulas must be found' – 'For this effort, we will always be at the disposal of the Secretary.' If the balance could be found between giving Argentina security about sovereignty in the long run or administrative power in the short, then 'agreement would be facilitated enormously and the final text of the document would not pose any insurmountable problems'.

Clearly this is not an outright rejection of the Haig Memorandum, but nor is it a diplomatic retreat. Haig would argue that the British had principles which they were bound to stand firm on. He found Mrs Thatcher 'very tough' in her attitude – 'I wish we had more like her.'[25] In Haig's version, the Argentines made excessive claims to sovereignty, prevaricated, and had trouble getting unified decisions out of their Junta. Costa Méndez' reply of 29 April was just such a prevarication, according to Haig's portrayal.

The Senate started debating the Biden – Moynihan Resolution 382 at 7.30 on the evening of 29 April. Senator Helms, with the help of Kiracofe and backed by the Republican senators John Warner and Paula Hawkins, bargained intensively to dilute the original motion. They succeeded in eliminating two references lauding the 'principle of self-determination' (a British veto, thereby breaching Resolution 2065), and they cut out a clause binding the US to prepare to 'further the efforts of the British Government to achieve in the Falkland Islands the full withdrawal of the Argentine forces . . .' This, Helms argued, would have the US almost in the front line alongside the British, pushing the Argentines out of the islands. All the same, the final version of Senate Resolution 382 still branded Argentina as the aggressor, resolved that the US could not stand neutral in implementing Security Council Resolution 502 (see p. 37), recognized the right of the UK and all other nations to self-defence and determined to advance the Resolution 502 requirement for all Argentina's forces to withdraw from the Falklands. A little after 9 pm the motion was carried by the crushing majority of 79 votes in favour to 1 (Helms) against.

The Senate resolution was not legally binding on President Reagan, but it had tremendous moral force. Haig had helped to create this force, and now he used it. By 10 pm he was on the phone to Ambassador Takacs, warning him to advise Buenos Aires that the US would tilt against Argentina next day and would impose tough economic and military sanctions against her. The same message went to Galtieri through the US Ambassador to Argentina, Harry Schlaudemann, at midnight Argentine time.

29 April 1982. Conqueror was still tussling with her communications problems, having to route her signals traffic through New Zealand as she headed for her new station between the Falkland Islands and Tierra del Fuego. Even inside the boat, the Antarctic cold was so intense that the crew had to wear their thickest pullovers.

At 11.30 am Washington time on Friday 30 April Haig went on television to announce the failure of his mediation mission. He explained in his speech (Appendix 4) that the US had been guided by the basic principle of the rule of law. He had presented a fair and sound settlement proposal which Britain could accept. But Argentina had advised the previous day that she could not. (Henderson puts the point more accurately: 'After the junta had referred the plan to corps commanders they replied in a manner that was construed by Haig as a rejection.')[26] Haig said that Argentina was insisting on prior assurance of eventual sovereignty or an immediate role in governing the islands which would lead to that. Britain continued to insist that the 'views' of the inhabitants (in fact their *wishes*) must be 'respected' (in fact *observed*). Consequently, he went on:

> In the light of Argentina's failure to accept a compromise, we must take concrete steps to underscore that the United States cannot and will not condone the use of unlawful force to solve disputes.

The US would apply military and economic sanctions against Argentina and offer material support to the British. Soon afterwards President Reagan endorsed Haig's statement, flatly condemning what he too called Argentina's intransigence.[27]

The then Peruvian Foreign Minister, Javier Arias Stella, saw the danger at once. 'The moment we learnt of Haig's speech,' he said, 'we knew that the risks of a British attack had increased immeasurably.' Two and a half hours after Haig's speech, Arias Stella phoned Frank Ortiz, US Ambassador to Peru, telling him of the Peruvian fears and suggesting urgent new peace talks.

Soviet diplomacy also made a move. After the Falklands landings Sergei Striganov, Soviet Ambassador to Argentina, had paid a visit to Enrique Ros, the deputy foreign minister, with an offer of arms. Hours after the US tilt was announced, Striganov called again, this time at the Presidential offices, the Càsa

Rosada, to see Galtieri himself. He repeated the Soviets' readiness to supply any arms that Argentina might want, to be delivered through third parties such as Libya, and he named his price:

a) Immediate withdrawal of all Argentine military advisers from Central America, and no others to be sent.

b) Argentina should abstain from now on in all votes against the Soviet Union in the United Nations on issues such as the occupation of Afghanistan.

c) The Soviets should be granted facilities to build fishery installations at Ushuaia – which presumably would involve rights to develop a communications system covering the South Atlantic.

d) Argentina should immediately cease its support for General Torelio's right-wing military government in Bolivia.

Galtieri and the Junta found this price too high, above all for a government so committed to combating communism. (It may also be doubted whether the Junta would have long survived the decision. The CIA might not be the force it had been – according to Sir Nicholas Henderson, 'after Kissinger the CIA was very nearly decimated'[28] – but Argentina did not need more than a firm push to destabilize her in May of 1982.) Nevertheless, had they been tempted to accept the offer it would have imposed an East – West geopolitical dimension on a hitherto limited local dispute. As it was, the American and Russian superpowers were hardly idle bystanders. Each monitored every development in the conflict by its satellite network. Both the British and the Argentines received useful military information about the other side's activities from the Americans and Russians respectively.

The world had been watching the British Task Force as it pressed southward towards the Falklands. With its arrival a new phase in the crisis must begin. The Haig and Reagan declarations publicly committed the United States: Britain was free to act. Haig had duly performed his role of filling the diplomatic vacuum, and in any case it was inconceivable that the Task Force just hang about and wait, dispelling its own momentum. Yet to have attacked a negotiating Argentina would have alarmed Britain's European allies, and alienated world opinion. An intransigent Argentina, on the other hand, might properly be given a sharp reminder that British patience was not inexhaustible. As Costa Méndez saw his last hope of US neutrality evaporate, he was left to complain bitterly that the American stand was 'unjustified and inopportune, and would appear to be scheduled to fit in with the operational plan of the British fleet'.

The position of Alexander Haig during the period of his own mediation in April, and then in early May, is difficult to fathom. There is no doubt that he was staking his reputation on a successful outcome. The question is what he thought that outcome should be. One strand in his thinking is clear: he knew that the British would make no concessions on the principles of sovereignty and self-determination. That meant that it was the Argentines who would have to make the concessions. To Haig that was a fact of life. He admired Mrs Thatcher. She was tough. She was militarily superior. She meant what she said. The United States needed her country more than they needed Galtieri's. She knew that. The Argentines were facing a choice between a crumb or two of petty comfort, and no crumbs at all, plus a bloody nose. If they could not see that, then they were simply too dumb to come in out of the rain. But if Mrs Thatcher meant to plunge in come what may, the United States could not afford too close an identification with an uncompromising ally. Their reputation for throwing their own weight around had been inhibiting their foreign policy ever since the wars in Indo-China. Before they could back the British preparations for a massive counterstrike, they needed some moral ground for action. Argentina's 'intransigence' provided it.

Hence the gratitude of Sir Nicholas Henderson for Haig's help. The former British Ambassador was at pains to acknowledge the significance of Haig's mediation process both during our interview of July 1983 and in his apologia printed in the *Economist* in November 1983. Without it, he argued, Britain would never have received the utterly crucial logistic and political support of the United States. Haig recognized very early that the British Prime Minister was determined to go through with the Falklands operation. He was convinced that the US must support Mrs Thatcher or jeopardize the policies in Europe which she had been foremost in supporting. Win or lose, a Conservative government snubbed by the US could be as much a thorn in their side as de Gaulle had been. And a defeat in the Falklands would almost certainly mean the return of a Labour government opposed both to the United States' Big Brother role in Central America and to their deployment of new nuclear weapons systems, and particularly the cruise missile, in Western Europe. In Henderson's words, Haig 'also saw how close a bearing the crisis had on the future of the Atlantic alliance'.[29] If the mediation came off, it would be a great triumph for Haig and the United States. If it did not, then although it might temporarily damage the Secretary of State it would preserve the alliance and its failure might be charged to Argentina's account. Not to have mediated at all would have bound the Americans either to accord immediate support to Britain (internationally difficult, and a kick in the teeth for South America) or to cause a breach that might also be further embittered in the event of a British failure in the South Atlantic. Haig backed Britain against the 'Latino lobby' – Kirkpatrick, Enders, Helms – who were Henderson's immediate opponents in Washington. He also helped Britain – possibly against the preference of a Prime Minister who would rather have had immediate US solidarity – to be seen as the reasonable injured party, instead of as the infuriated big power determined to get even at all costs with the insolent small one. Viewed in this light, Henderson's evident admiration for the man whom he described as the 'victim' of the Falklands episode conveys more than sheer gratitude. It is also compounded of fellow-feeling for a man who knew as well as Henderson himself how much harm Mrs Thatcher's own intransigence could do to both their countries' causes, if it could not be portrayed as resolution.

In his speech on 30 April, Haig was accepting the inevitable British resort to force, and putting the best possible face on it. The force came soon. At 24.00 GMT on the same day, less than eight hours after Haig's declaration, a British Vulcan bomber took off from Wideawake airfield on Ascension Island on its marathon 15-hour flight to the Falklands and back again. At 07.23 GMT it unloaded its twenty-one 1,000-lb bombs over Stanley airstrip. They made only one direct hit on the strip, which remained operational for Argentina's Hercules transports and Pucará light fighters throughout the campaign.

30 April 1982. Conqueror already knew that the Argentine ships in her patrol area were an elderly World War Two ex-US cruiser with no ASW capability and no sonar – a sitting duck – plus two old destroyers and an oiler. She reached the area, about 200 miles south-west of the Falklands and 120 miles east of Tierra del Fuego, in the afternoon of a clear sunny day, and with the sea calmer than at any time since her arrival in the South Atlantic. A signal received in the evening told Commander Wreford-Brown that the British government had decided to use 'more military force' and had ordered the 'destruction' of the Argentine carrier, the Veinticinco de Mayo. *She was not in Conqueror's area, and it looked as if* Splendid *would make the kill. In the afternoon some distant signatures were picked up on the tail.* Conqueror *went to periscope depth at 16.00.*

5

'Concentrating the Minds'

Saturday, 1 May 1982, saw a series of raids and clashes on and around the Falklands, starting with the Vulcan bombing raid at 04.23 local time. British and Argentine accounts of the day's events vary so much that it is impossible to correlate them. For instance, at 04.40 British Harriers began a series of attacks on Stanley and Darwin airstrips which went on all day. Twenty Harriers were involved. The Argentines claimed that they shot down two, but British accounts insisted that there were no Harrier losses (it was the day of 'I counted them all out and I counted them all back'). Both sides have stood firm on their own versions since this first day of serious fighting. It is difficult for the writers not to attach more credence to the official British accounts. Nevertheless, Argentina has consistently alleged that Britain concealed losses both of men and material for purposes of domestic propaganda.[1]

In addition to the aircraft attacks, the Task Force began intensive shelling in the afternoon from 11 units which approached within sight of Port Stanley. The record of the Argentine Joint Chiefs of Staff times various Harrier attacks at 04.40, 06.29, 07.50, 08.23 and 11.48, and times the fleet units' 'daring approach to Port Stanley' at 14.00. The same record reports that at 17.00: 'A Mirage hits an enemy destroyer near Puerto Enriqueta [in the region of Mullett Creek, south-west of Port Stanley]. The vessel sails east, giving off distress signals and asking for help.'

Dr J. C. Murguizur sums up other Argentine claims:

The British attempted three landings, two near Port Stanley and one near Port Darwin. All these attempts were repulsed, the first two on the beaches. During the third, which was the most dangerous, the Argentine anti-aircraft defences shot down the Sea King helicopters of an airborne force . . . The loss of these helicopters, plus the energetic Argentinian action in the air and the activities of the submarine *San Luis* prompted the enemy to retreat. Several British warships, including the aircraft carrier *Hermes*, were hit. A torpedo fired by the *San Luis* hit a frigate but did not explode and the submarine hunt begun as a result bore no fruit even after 20 hours.[2]

However Argentine casualties during the day were estimated at 56, and there was dismay in Buenos Aires at the ferocity of the British operations. 'Until 1 May,' said one informant, 'few members of the military hierarchy really believed that the British would mount a major assault.'

At 15.55 Vice-Admiral Juan José Lombardo, Argentine Naval Commander South Atlantic, ordered Rear-Admiral Walter Allara, the Fleet Commander, to use his Task Force 79 (including the *Belgrano* group, said Lombardo on Panorama on 16 April 1984) in a search and destroy mission against the British fleet, in response to its merciless aerial and naval pounding of the Malvinas. Also during the afternoon, between 15 and 20 divisional and brigade generals and field commanders met informally at the big Campo de Mayo military base outside Buenos Aires to discuss the worsening situation. General Llamil Reston, who was to become Minister of the Interior when General Reynaldo Bignone succeeded Galtieri, was in the chair. Their recommendation was that Argentina should negotiate and at all costs avoid all-out war. Some of the divisional generals from this meeting then went into Buenos Aires for a higher-level evening gathering at army HQ in the Edificio Libertador in Paseo Colón. Divisional General José Antonio Vaquero, Chief of the Army's General Staff, presided over this meeting attended by ten of the army's 12 divisional generals.

About 18.00 local time Francis Pym flew into Washington. At a brief press conference he announced that the day's military activity was intended to 'concentrate Argentine minds' on the need for a peaceful settlement. 'No further military action is envisaged for the moment other than making the Total Exclu-

sion Zone secure,' he promised. (The TEZ had come into force
the previous day.) A glimpse of developments in Buenos Aires
would have shown Pym that the generals were concentrating
hard.

1 May 1982. Yesterday's signatures proved to belong to the force which
Conqueror *had been sent to locate. In the late morning she closed in to a
range of about 4,000 yards: the* Belgrano *and her escorting destroyers
were in the middle of refuelling from an oiler – a tempting target, but they
were outside the TEZ. Intelligence forecast that the group meant to turn
north, and into the TEZ, but for the moment* Conqueror *sat on their
tails, about five or six miles back, while they continued westward
unawares.*

Rear-Admiral Woodward recalled in an address to the Royal
United Services Institute in London on 20 October 1982 that:

> My initial plan was to lay on a major demonstration of force
> well inside the exclusion zone to make the Argentines believe
> that landings were due to take place and thus provoke a
> reaction that would allow me to conduct a major attrition
> exercise before the amphibious force actually arrived to com-
> plicate my problem. And at the very least I might discover
> whether they had a coherent defensive plan. Port Stanley and
> Goose Green airfields were bombed, ships bombarded, mili-
> tary installations around Stanley and we carried out an offensive
> ASW [anti-submarine warfare] operation off a possible landing
> area where it seemed sensible for an SSK [submarine] to be on
> patrol. The reactions we got indicated that the plan succeeded,
> at least initially . . . .

Woodward went on to report that the demonstration was
accompanied by 'considerable air activity' that Saturday. By
about 19.00 the first phase of his 'demonstration' had ended, and
Woodward stated that Task Force units then headed eastwards
beyond the range of Argentine land-based fighter-bombers.

By nightfall, Rear-Admiral Allara had not located the British
fleet, and by then Vice-Admiral Lombardo knew from the
Malvinas garrison that the Harrier bombing had stopped and the
Task Force dispersed eastwards. With the backing of Admiral

Anaya himself, the arch-hardliner, Lombardo signalled Allara at 20.07 rescinding (*dejando sin efecto*) his prior order to attack, and telling him to bring Task Force 79, the *Belgrano* group included, back to port. On board his flagship the *Veinticinco de Mayo*, Allara was glad to obey. A Sea Harrier had just overflown him without attacking – probably at the limit of its range – and he could not get his own defending Skyhawks up as it was a still night and he needed a good headwind to launch them. So the Argentine fleet followed Allara's orders and began to withdraw after 20.07

Later, at 01.19 on 2 May, Lombardo signalled to Allara his confirmation of Allara's orders to individual fleet units, and to enlarge upon the earlier rather curt command. The recall message explained:

Your 012007 [yours of 1 May at 20.07 hours]: There have been no further air attacks on the Malvinas after 011900. I do not know the position of the enemy aircraft-carriers. The free-ranging enemy still constitutes a strong threat to Task Force 79.[3]

A Presidential source avers that Anaya approved the withdrawal order without consulting his Council of 8 Vice- and 15 Rear-Admirals. Two were outright hawks who would probably have tried to block it. These two suspected that Britain and the US were colluding to turn the Falklands into a massive Anglo–American military base. Grounds for their suspicions seem entirely circumstantial.[4]

About 20.30, General Vaquero called an even more high-level meeting at the nearby Joint General Staff building at Paseo Colón 200. Galtieri was there with Basilio Lami Dozo, C-in-C of the Argentine air force. Reports differ as to whether this meeting was also attended by the navy chief, Anaya. Vaquero summarized the recommendations of the two earlier meetings for Galtieri: '*No queremos guerra abierta*' – We don't want open war. Galtieri, himself stunned by the impact of the day's attacks, put up no argument. After all it was mainly these same generals, aided by Anaya, who had put him in power just four months before. The air force was as willing to negotiate as the generals, since Lami Dozo had never been enthusiastic about the seizure of the Malvinas.

These meetings of the generals were especially important in two ways. First, they were bound to reinforce Galtieri's growing disinclination to lock horns with the British. Second, it has been stated in the House of Commons by the Labour MP Tam Dalyell that by 1 May 1982 US Intelligence had penetrated the Argentine Military Command at all levels.[5] Everything that happened at the generals' meetings that day would have reached Washington in short order, and Washington was keeping British authorities informed. South America, then as now, was in the CIA's back yard. Unless they had totally lost their grip, then that night, or at the latest next morning, 2 May 1982, Mrs Thatcher's intelligence advisers should have known that there was a strong movement for a negotiated peace in the top echelons of the Argentine leadership.

After the generals had begun to 'concentrate', and with the Argentine fleet beginning to withdraw, the climate was propitious for a peace initiative. It came when Galtieri, still in his office in the Casa Rosada, took a telephone call at 01.30 Sunday 2 May from the Peruvian President, Architect Fernando Belaúnde Terry, in Lima. Belaúnde and his compatriots Manuel Ulloa and Javier Arias Stella, Peru's Prime Minister and Foreign Minister respectively, were friends to Argentina throughout the conflict. Peru quickly supplied ten Mirages when the Argentine air force started taking heavy losses in aircraft, and remained active on Argentina's behalf in the United Nations.[6]

Belaúnde gave the following account of the events leading up to his call to Galtieri:

From the moment the English fleet left port, I was deeply concerned, because I felt that the more time passed, the more certain it was that the forces would clash in the end. My position was to avoid that shock at all costs . . . I watched the days pass, the fleet get nearer, and saw nothing constructive emerge from General Haig's negotiation. Finally on Saturday night [1 May] I called our ambassador in Washington [Fernando Schwalb, the present Peruvian Prime Minister] and told him I was profoundly worried by the situation, and that if no solution emerged from the meeting between Haig and Pym [scheduled for the following morning, 2 May] a disaster could follow. Schwalb said: 'I'll talk to some friends,' and half an hour later Haig himself rang me. He told me: 'President Reagan's not in Washington right now. He's in Knoxville, opening an exhibition. But I know that you are very concerned, and so are we. What can we do? How can you help us?' I told him plainly that I was on very good terms with Argentina and that I understood that his negotiations with her had not succeeded. 'That's right,' Haig agreed, 'there was intransigence on both sides.' I said then that some acceptable formula had to be found. We talked by phone for three-quarters of an hour and I finally asked him please to dictate to me the essential points from Britain's viewpoint.

Haig read them over to me, and I for my part told him what word was unsatisfactory and what condition unacceptable for Argentina. We finally agreed on a plan which covered seven points, and I left it that I should call President Galtieri at once to put that formula to him.[7]

Belaúnde was in fact very well placed to negotiate successfully, if anyone could, in a dispute between these two countries, with the US inevitably playing a major role. Not only did he get on very well with both Galtieri and Haig, but he also had a special relationship with the British Ambassador in Lima, Charles William Wallace. Belaúnde talked of how during the two and a half months of the Falklands confrontation he had almost stopped governing Peru, instead worrying and constantly exchanging views with other Latin American Presidents such as Turbay Ayala of Colombia, searching for 'the best way of helping our Argentine friends. I stress to you that I was in a perfect position to do so, for I have a great friendship with the British Ambassador in Lima: his wife is a childhood friend of mine, and I have a great trust in him. So Peru could serve as excellent neutral ground for any negotiation between Argentina and Britain . . .'[8]

This special relationship also meant that the British Foreign Office, Chequers and 10 Downing Street could expect to be kept promptly informed about everything important that happened in Peru. That fact is worth noting because it is at this juncture in the Falklands crisis – this point when the military lesson had been delivered and when it might have been expected that some diplomatic initiative would yet rescue both countries from prolonged hostilities and further casualties – that official British accounts of events record a lengthy transatlantic silence. Yet Dr Arias Stella, for one, has since stressed that the Peruvians 'kept the British Ambassador in Lima very fully informed indeed' about everything to do with Belaúnde's pursuit of peace, and with what they were telling Haig about the responses of Galtieri and Costa Méndez.

Here in translation is the transcript of the complete telephone conversation which Belaúnde began with Galtieri at 23.30 on Saturday 1 May, Lima time, which was 01.30 on Sunday 2 May Buenos Aires time. It is quoted in full because it has been part of the official British case that they were not discussing anything so concrete as real 'proposals',[9] and because the air of urgency presents a striking contrast with the torpid aloofness of Britain's public response.[10]

Belaúnde: Here is the peace proposal in the South Atlantic:
1 Immediate ceasefire.
2 Simultaneous and mutual withdrawal of forces.
3 Third parties would govern the Islands, temporarily.
4 The two governments would recognize the existence of conflicting viewpoints about the Islands.
5 The two governments would recognize the need to take the viewpoints and interests of the Islanders into account in the final solution.
6 The contact group which would start negotiating at once to implement this agreement would be Brazil, Peru, West Germany and the US.
7 A final solution must be found by 30 April 1983 under the contact group's guarantee.

This is the text that emerged from a conversation in which the Secretary of State himself showed that he very much wanted to bring something concrete to his dialogue tomorrow with Mr Pym. Naturally we commented on all these points and tried to phrase them in a language that the British could accept. Naturally the document has no value unless your government accepts it, and it's in that sense that I put it to you. Now General Haig has suggested that the so-called contact group, or the friendly countries, should provisionally be these – no, I don't think that this is an indispensable condition, no, it's these provisionally . . .

Galtieri: That's to say Peru, Brazil . . .

Belaúnde: Hello, yes . . .

Galtieri: It would be Peru, Brazil, Federal Germany and the US? Doctor . . .

Belaúnde: We proposed Canada before these countries as a country friendly to Britain, to counterbalance our presence a little, which was required, but we were told that Argentina didn't share this viewpoint much so that it was automatically eliminated.

Galtieri: Yes, I agree, Doctor, it's been quite a while that we haven't shared . . .

Belaúnde: Then . . .

Galtieri: But still, well, I don't know, I have my doubts about the United States, Doctor . . .

Belaúnde: But look, there's us and Brazil and we're in very good . . .

Galtieri: That's fine, with you two I've no problem, but after the public attitude of the US towards the internal Argentine front it's going to be pretty difficult to accept a thing like that . . .

Belaúnde: The English will make the same objection about Peru, they'll make the same objection because they'll say that Peru's a country that's frankly on Argentina's side, won't they?

Galtieri: That's true too.

Belaúnde: So it's a matter of balance. And there's a text in English and if you like I'll read it to you quickly so that then you've got it recorded.

Galtieri: I'm already recording, though I shan't understand much, my English is very poor.

Belaúnde: But if you record me I'll read it fast.

Galtieri: Go ahead Doctor, I'm recording you.

(Text of the agreement in English, essentially as in the seven points above.)

Belaúnde: That's the end.

Galtieri: Very good, Doctor.

Belaúnde: Mr President, you'll understand with what emotion and fervour my colleagues and I have made this almost last-ditch effort to avoid what might be a bloodbath that would hurt us very much.

Galtieri: It already is, Doctor.

Belaúnde: Clearly the present circumstances are alarming, aren't they?

Galtieri: I mean, the bloodbath.

Belaúnde: So it is, so it is, but perhaps it can be controlled so that it doesn't get any bigger.

Galtieri: I agree.

Belaúnde: So what I'd like to insist, Mr President, is that you think deeply about these conditions [of the proposal] and if possible have ready by 10 am tomorrow – that's the time when the Secretary of State is meeting Pym – some agreement on these points of view, because if you could that would support the hope that we could achieve a solution.

Galtieri: Ten o'clock Washington?

Belaúnde: Ten o'clock Washington, you're two hours ahead.

Galtieri: What time is it in Lima?

Belaúnde: Now, for example, here where I'm waking you up, it's 11.30 at night.

Galtieri: No, I'm fully awake and working in my office, and it's 1.30 in the morning.

Belaúnde: I can understand your worries.

Galtieri: So we're two hours ahead of Lima?

Belaúnde: Yes, two hours, two hours. Tomorrow the Minister of Transport, Engineer Bernardo Chaves Belaúnde, is travelling to attend a road conference, and as well as being my minister is very close to me, and he'll be bringing a few lines from Prime Minister Ulloa to Minister Costa Méndez, because we didn't know if we were going to have the pleasure of talking to you tonight. I'd like to recommend very much that you analyse all these points – naturally they're not exhaustive, they're necessarily short and in some cases vague, but that's what makes them viable, isn't it? And if we had agreement tomorrow our delegates would travel to Washington that night to start the contact group's work there first thing on Monday, that's the plan as we've set it out.

Galtieri: Doctor Belaúnde, can you hear me?

Belaúnde: Yes, President, I'm hearing you very well.

Galtieri: Have you made these sorts of contacts with Brazil?

Belaúnde: No, the only contact that exists is with us. We're very close to Brazil now, we have got very close, because of the Washington meetings.

Galtieri: I know them.

Belaúnde: Good. I don't think there'll be any problems with them. Clearly, this is a point where one country can be substituted for another. For example, it's just struck me, didn't Germany have a naval battle in the Falklands?

Galtieri: Yes, sir.

Belaúnde: So that perhaps Great Britain won't accept them, or will suddenly have some reservation, it's just an idea that crossed my mind; I don't think it's fundamental which the countries are, but it seems to me as a first impression that the Secretary of State – if indeed it's he – has chosen them well, with the one comment that I've just made, if England doesn't make it then there's nothing to say, they're all friendly countries, aren't they?

Obviously Germany's not active in this matter, there's a fair degree of impartiality on the European side, and on the American side Brazil's friendly, not belligerent, while we Peruvians are very much inclined towards Argentina, and the US towards her traditional ally Great Britain. Anyway these ideas were dictated by the Secretary of State himself and we made him a series of objections, producing a text rather shorter, but we think much more viable. I'd like of course to be able to celebrate the end of this conflict, and to talk with you about more pleasant and less alarming things, but naturally we're just as absorbed in this affair as you are, and as concerned about the fate, in the end, of the soldiers and officers who are fighting so gallantly in this issue.

Galtieri: Thank you very much, Doctor Belaúnde Terry, really it's another gesture towards Argentina and towards America. I'll try – because here as I say it's 1.30 in the morning, in the early morning – to get something near to what you're asking tomorrow. I'll talk to you tomorrow, Doctor.

Belaúnde: Yes, then, it would be enough for you to say that the conditions expressed there are acceptable, no? We could start to work already on that basis, and our delegations could go off the next day. Of course we'd be very happy actively to take part and add our grain of sand.

Galtieri: I've heard your message with pleasure, Doctor Belaúnde Terry, and I thank you enormously in the name of the Argentine nation; you'll have my phone answer tomorrow. So I send you a firm embrace and the gratitude of the Argentine nation for this unbreakable friendship.

Belaúnde: It's my duty to tell you that I thought I felt in the Secretary of State a deep concern about a certain intransigence on the other side, no?

Galtieri: What's happening, Doctor, is that we're not going to change. You voted in TIAR,* we're not going to change sovereignty for anything, Doctor, eh . . .

Belaúnde: The victory won in the OAS, we judge that's an important precedent, no? No doubt it'll be a fundamental element of judgement, in the negotiations that will last a year, at the most.

Galtieri: Look, Doctor, for me, after a hundred and fifty years, a year or two doesn't bother Argentina. What worries me isn't one year more but fifty.

Belaúnde: Well, if we're here you can be sure, General, that we'll do all within our power to help fulfil the justified aims of your government.

Galtieri: Thank you, Doctor, I'll call you tomorrow.

Belaúnde: Well, I'll be here, I'm in the Palace, as you know, here. I don't know if you reside in –

Galtieri: I've been in this place permanently for the last four or five days without moving, Doctor.

Belaúnde: I beg of you to greet your colleagues. The Minister was going to call Costa Méndez, but he didn't find him. We were a bit hesitant about calling you at this hour, but with an affair so urgent we felt that we had to do so.

Galtieri: Please feel quite at ease. I'll contact Doctor Costa Méndez to get this matter analysed, and I repeat, Doctor . . . Ulloa, whom I thank for his intervention, and tomorrow we'll talk again, Doctor, though I don't know if at ten, eleven or twelve.

Belaúnde: Look now, this proposal is more recent than the one we've been working on during the day; the other was more elaborate, but we thought that unless we got to a really simple formula the Pym mission could fail, and for this reason this replaces the one we were working on till midday today – until this afternoon even we were talking to the US Embassy. Of

---

* TIAR, the *Tratado Interamericano de Ayuda Recíproca*, also called the Río Treaty, has as its key clause that: 'Any aggression against an American state shall be considered an aggression against all American states.' The British (and US) position was that the TIAR was not relevant to the Falklands dispute because, first, the above clause did not apply if an American state started the aggression, and second, TIAR was subservient to Security Council rulings, and 502 clearly found Argentina the aggressor in this case. The OAS had met on 28 April, backing the Argentine case strongly and announcing: 'The Argentine Republic has the unquestionable right of sovereignty over the Malvinas Islands.' Voting was 17 for, and 4 abstentions, which were the US, Chile, Colombia and Trinidad-Tobago.

course it doesn't annul what we'd done before, but it does simplify it into a quick substitute formula. The State Department will have the two texts, English and Spanish, they'll have them at the hour when you can give your reaction.

Galtieri: Well, we'll try and work in these hours that remain. It doesn't give me much time.

Belaúnde: I beg of you to keep in mind that we friendly nations are really as concerned as you are with this problem, and we're praying to God that He may enlighten us all, and especially you, to find a permanent solution.

Galtieri: Thank you very much, Doctor, you'll get my call tomorrow.

Belaúnde: My best wishes and my fervent hopes that there's no new destruction.

Galtieri: A thousand thanks and the gratitude of the Argentine nation to the Peruvian people and its Doctor President.

Belaúnde: A warm greeting, and I repeat the terms of my telex yesterday. Thank you, Mr President, till tomorrow.

Galtieri: Till tomorrow.

(Belaúnde's telex to Galtieri the previous day, 30 April, had been sent as an immediate reaction to Haig's tilt statement that morning. It promised Galtieri to 'lend all the support at our command in the defence of your legitimate national interests'.)[11]

The Belaúnde–Galtieri conversation is not mere talking about talking. Belaúnde wants something to show Pym by morning, and wants to have the contact group working by the following day. Galtieri's position does not allow him to express as much alarm as the President of Peru, but only a few hours before, his generals too had been pressing him for peace. Through his good friend and ally Belaúnde, he could now feel that there was yet some hope of a *salida elegante*, a stylish way out, by means of which both parties to the conflict could avoid further hostilities gracefully and honourably.

At 10.00 Argentine time (14.00 London time, BST) on the morning of Sunday, 2 May 1982, President Belaúnde phoned Galtieri again to learn that the Argentine President had passed the negotiation over to the Foreign Minister. Subsequently Costa Méndez made several more phone calls to Belaúnde to clarify or modify various points. Belaúnde had proposed that a mutually acceptable group of four countries should supervise the working of the peace agreement. He had also stipulated that the *viewpoints* and interests of the islanders should be taken into account in any final solution. The Argentines saw *viewpoints* as practically synonymous with *wishes*, and hence overriding the operant UN Resolution 2065. As Costa Méndez put it: 'We wanted to change two things. Instead of the US in the supervising group we wanted Canada. And we would not give paramountcy to the *wishes* of the islanders because we saw that as giving them an absolute veto over every single project we might want to carry out there. We *were* prepared to accept a formula which said that "the inhabitants' viewpoints regarding their interests must be taken into account".'[12]

That Sunday morning Costa Méndez discussed both points with Belaúnde, together with the question of an interim government for the Islands. Here is an excerpt from their transcribed telephone conversation:

Belaúnde: Good, very good. Look, then. About the text generally, no? Then the important part is 'the viewpoints regarding the interests'.

Costa Méndez: Correct.

Belaúnde: Then we'll be refusing what they're asking. That's the viewpoint . . .

Costa Méndez: Without doubt, Mr President, it's a subject we can't back away from.

Belaúnde: About the countries, it's simply the elimination of the US that's fundamental.

Costa Méndez: That's the fundamental thing.

Belaúnde: Yes.

Costa Méndez: Mr President, if you'll permit me, going back to the points of the plan that you made known last night to the President of Argentina, there's a third point that says: introduction of third parties to govern the Islands. I'd like to have it made very clear that the third parties would have to replace everything that was British administration.

Belaúnde: Well, of course, that's what's wanted. But you know, in this kind of urgent agreement, being too explicit can lead us to failure, no?

Costa Méndez: Yes, but still . . .

Belaúnde: I think that's clearly implied, isn't it?

Costa Méndez: Yes, but I'd prefer to leave that clearly formulated as an Argentine position, from which Argentina couldn't with-draw. And of course the US shouldn't be in the administrating group.

Belaúnde: Yes, surely. If they're eliminated, there's no problem.

Costa Méndez: Perfect.

In this conversation Belaúnde also got Costa Méndez' confirma-tion that there had been no further belligerent actions that Sunday morning. The lull struck him as an 'excellent sign'.

Belaúnde was hesitant about asking Haig to eliminate the US from the supervising group until Galtieri and Costa Méndez insisted. So, said Belaúnde: 'I called Haig, and he in turn told me that Britain was objecting to Peru's membership of the group. "Magnificent," I answered, "we're on equal footing. We can withdraw and look for two other countries." Haig replied: "What more could I ask than to have this problem lifted from my shoulders?" '[13]

Belaúnde and Costa Méndez solved their second point of divergence by devising the formula that 'the islanders' *aspirations* and interests must be taken into account in any final solution'. Although 'aspirations' were perilously close to 'wishes', the Argentines reasoned, they did have rather more of a connotation of lofty hopes, and less of mere whim: it was the fear of being dictated to by the caprice of the islanders – since islanders are traditionally conservative in any case, and these particular ones had been put there by Britain in the first place – that bothered the Argentines most. Thus, with these two points cleared up – and Costa Méndez recalled that Belaúnde now raised no objection – Galtieri advised Belaúnde that his peace proposal was acceptable in principle. In doing so, the Argentine leader effectively drop-ped his demand for replacing the British administration.

That, in Costa Méndez' words, just about completed the job. According to him, Belaúnde could 'take it as almost certain that our Military Committee [the Junta, sometimes with a few senior officers or advisers attending], which was to meet at 19.00, would announce formal acceptance of his proposal wihin the hour. We recorded all these phone conversations as vital. So did Peru and – we understand – Washington. The progress was so great that Associated Press and United Press International in Lima, after talking with Belaúnde, urgently reported to their New York offices that Argentina would accept the Peruvian peace proposal that night. [See the telex message quoted on p. xiv.] Throughout, Belaúnde had his direct phone contact with Haig.'

Costa Méndez insisted: 'I cannot believe that Haig, who had shuttled most of the previous month in search of just such an agreement, or Pym in his office with him that May 2, did not transmit the news of Belaúnde's success to Mrs Thatcher and her War Cabinet in London at once. In that case there could have been a good three and a half to four hours clear between London's receipt of the news and the torpedoing of the Belgrano.'

Costa Méndez' version of what happened on Sunday 2 May was corroborated independently and closely in a written account provided by a navy source close to the Junta:

On 2 May in the early morning the President of Peru spoke to the President of Argentina and offered him the peace proposal.

This proposal was analysed immediately by the Special Malvinas Team (chaired by Costa Méndez and made up of his deputy, Dr Enrique Ros, General Norberto Iglesias, Secretary-General of the Presidency, Rear-Admiral Benito Moya, Head of the Casa Militar, Brigadier-Major José Miret, Director of Planning, an ambassador and five Foreign Ministry officials). During the morning of 2 May more than six phone calls were made to Peru to expand or to discuss the proposal point by point. On our agreement that the proposal was acceptable save for one word of difference [presumably Costa Méndez' 'aspirations' in place of the proposal's 'wishes' or 'viewpoints'], we advised the Peruvian President that he could count on our reply being ratified at the level of the Military Committee at 20.00 hours Buenos Aires time.

Every conversation was recorded and exists in tangible form in three countries: Argentina, Peru and the US. The President of Peru continually advised what he had discussed with Argentina to Secretary Haig, and Haig in turn affirmed that he was keeping Foreign Secretary Pym informed as Pym was with him in the same office in Washington throughout the Argentine–Peruvian conversations on the morning of 2 May.

The conversations exist, in three American countries, in which Argentina specifically reiterates that her Military Committee will definitively confirm her acceptance at 20.00 hours on 2 May. That information was given in advance in the last

Argentine conversation with President Belaúnde on 2 May at midday when he transmitted it to Washington.[14]

Dr Javier Arias Stella was closely involved, as Peru's then Foreign Minister, with the course of the negotiations. He recalled Galtieri's words to Belaúnde when he accepted his proposal in principle: 'I've studied your plan. I think it feasible.'[15] Arias Stella stated that Belaúnde had constant and direct contact with Haig by phone and kept him fully informed. By that route, said Arias Stella, Peru had between 8 and about 12 noon Lima time on 2 May got across to Haig in Washington the whole of Galtieri's and Costa Méndez' reaction to the Peruvian peace proposal. The Peruvians knew that Francis Pym had been scheduled to arrive in Washington on the evening of Saturday 1 May and would be with Haig in his office the next morning: 'We understood that Pym and Haig's contact was so close that whatever Haig accepted was all right with Pym – that is, Pym passed it on at once to London, Pym spoke with London's voice.'

Haig knew that Galtieri had accepted the detailed peace proposal in principle, except for the outstanding disagreement between 'wishes' and 'aspirations'. Given that Haig himself had been involved in formulating the proposal, then it seemed to the Peruvians that with Haig conferring with Pym in his own office, and conveying no British objections, peace must be within sight. Arias Stella recalled that: 'President Belaúnde was so sure we had achieved peace that we arranged a ceremony for the British and Argentine ambassadors in Lima to sign the documents formally that evening. President Belaúnde also held a press conference in Lima that afternoon, about 16.30. It was televised. He announced that peace was imminent, and said that the agreement needed only to be ratified by the Military Committee in Buenos Aires that evening, as a formality.'

Asked if he was sure that the Peruvian initiative really was substantive and likely to lead to a ceasefire – since the official British view was and has remained that it was still vague, general and incomplete – Dr Arias Stella replied: 'I most thoroughly disagree that our seven-point peace proposal was at all vague or general or not ready to be put into effect at once. It was the result of very intensive negotiations, mainly with Haig, whom we always took to be speaking for Britain. We thought that we had worked out a completely practical proposal which had a fair and balanced text completely consistent with the rulings of Security Council Resolution 502.'[16]

Haig's own assessment of the practicability of the Belaúnde proposals, given in June 1983, was that although some difficult paragraphs remained, 'we did think that we had a formulation that provided hope that a settlement could be reached.'[17] Evidently 'Argentina's failure to accept a compromise', the ground for the US tilt only two days before, was no longer a hindrance. From the British point of view it might seem that the short sharp shock administered on 1 May had done the trick.

Yet another angle on the Peruvian initiative was provided by Prime Minister Manuel Ulloa. He rang Haig on Sunday morning, while Pym was with him, stressed how near the negotiations were to success, and begged him to obtain a 24-hour or even better 48-hour truce from the British. The Prime Minister observed that he found Haig very sympathetic.[18]

It had been Costa Méndez' assumption, when Belaúnde called on Sunday morning to say that Haig wanted the British 'wishes' restored, that the alteration had come from the British themselves – that Britain was participating in the latest moves. The Argentine Foreign Minister claimed that his talks with Belaúnde that morning ended thus:[19]

Belaúnde: With the sole exception of this word 'wishes', which the UK has just insisted on, the rest is acceptable?
Costa Méndez: Correct.

Costa Méndez painted a dramatic picture – grotesquely mistaken, according to the subsequent account given by Francis Pym – of a four-nation trans-oceanic telephone conference in which Galtieri confirmed the agreement his Foreign Minister had just made: 'At midday on 2 May, the Argentine President is in direct communication with the Peruvian President, who in turn has a telephone line open to the US Secretary of State. Mr Haig, for his part, has in his office British Minister Pym, linked in turn – it's impossible not to suppose so – with the British Prime Minister. The circle was complete.'

Three *Clarín* journalists[20] say categorically that Pym was in touch with Chequers during these negotiations, in which Belaúnde was permanently linked by phone with Haig, sitting in Washington with Pym, while Mrs Thatcher's War Cabinet debated in parallel. They note Belaúnde's haste to complete his deal: 'Belaúnde perceived the anxiety that Haig transmitted him by phone, Haig sensing in turn the nervous state of Pym, connected with Chequers, where the cruiser's lot in the South Atlantic would be cast.'

Costa Méndez could well assume that peace was won. Haig was London's emissary, as Belaúnde was Argentina's. They had agreed. When Costa Méndez left the Casa Rosada at 13.00 he told reporters:

'We're on the brink of an agreement. The difference is about a single word.'

Early that afternoon, when Galtieri confirmed to Belaúnde that Argentina accepted his proposal in principle, an exultant Costa Méndez cried out to his staff:

'We have an agreement! We can live with this!'

It is worth recounting the process which led up to Costa Méndez' jubilation. It began with Haig's departure from Buenos Aires on 19 April, taking with him the five Argentinian proposals for a settlement. These proposals, together with the British negotiating stance made known to Haig in the course of his various meetings with British officials and Margaret Thatcher, were combined to produce the Haig memorandum of 27 April. Haig said later that he 'had reason to hope' that the British would consider a settlement based on his proposal.

At this point, Argentina had two reservations: the Haig Memorandum did not give them the representation they wanted on the Executive Council and Legislative Council on the island during the period of interim administration; and it proposed that some undefined form of survey should be arranged to determine the opinion of the islanders as to their future 'wishes and interests'.

The next phase was sparked by the phone call from President Belaúnde to Alexander Haig in which he asked Haig to list the minimum terms required by Britain. After some discussion seven points emerged, which Belaúnde undertook to present to the Argentinian government. These were points which Belaúnde had every reason to believe were acceptable to Britain since the whole basis on which they were drawn up was Haig's perception of Britain's essential requirements. *These seven proposals were accepted by Argentina*, with two minor reservations. Argentina wanted the word 'aspirations' substituted for 'wishes', and wanted the United States eliminated from the international consortium to rule the islands. Britain wanted Peru removed, so there was a balance. Britain was kept fully informed of this development through Francis Pym, the Foreign Secretary, who was in the room with Haig during the final telephone conversations.

A central problem in the *Belgrano* controversy is the question of how much information reached London, either from American or from British sources across the Atlantic. Harry Schlaudemann, the US Ambassador to Argentina during the Falklands conflict, said in an interview with *Clarín* on 28 August 1983 that it was 'inconceivable' that Washington could have failed to achieve peace had the US really wanted it. Instead, his government had turned the situation in favour of the British by broadcasting 'several errors of information' about the peace negotiations.

Pym has insisted that he had nothing new to tell the British Prime Minister. Nevertheless there was another source available. Arias Stella insists that he was in constant telephone contact 'from about midday that Saturday' until well into Sunday 2 May 1982 both with the Argentine Ambassador in Lima and with the British Ambassador, Charles Wallace, whom he knew well. He spoke 'several times' from his office to their homes – 'since embassies don't usually work at weekends'. Wallace, a conscientious man, gave Arias Stella the clear impression that he was referring back to London all the time – 'that's what ambassadors have to do at such times, isn't it?'[21] Mr Charles Wallace, now British Ambassador to Uruguay, indicated to a visitor, Guillermo Makin, on 6 December 1983 that he had vital information about those two pivotal days, though he would not divulge it.

What strains belief is that the Foreign Office should have failed to keep itself fully informed about the progress of the Haig-Belaúnde peace initiative before London gave the order to sink the *Belgrano*.

That was the position at noon on 2 May, Washington time.

6

Dead Men Everywhere

The Argentine cruiser *General Belgrano* left her operational base of Ushuaia in Tierra del Fuego for the last time on 26 April 1982.[1] From there she sailed eastwards towards Staten Island, at the toe of Tierra del Fuego, and waited off the island for three days until a helicopter flew in with sealed orders. The instructions for her commander, Capitán de Navío Héctor Elias Bonzo, and his crew of 1,138 was to patrol a line of about 250 miles in the notorious seas eastward of Cape Horn, on a bearing of 110 degrees east-south-east, then back west-north-west on a bearing of 290 degrees. She and her two destroyer escorts were explicitly forbidden at any time to enter the 200-mile-radius Total Exclusion Zone which the British had drawn from the mid-point of the Falklands. Their task was to patrol the line described, to watch against any British approach either from the east or from round the Horn.

Captain Bonzo knew that his ship was growing too old for active service, and was destined for retirement, but he and his crew were proud of the old cruiser's past. As the USS light cruiser *Phoenix*, commissioned in October 1938, she had called at Argentina on her shakedown trip, before going on to her base at Pearl Harbor. There she fought the Japanese air assault of 7 December 1941, and emerged unscathed to help search for the raiders' carriers. She escorted troopships in Australian waters, and saw the evacuation of Java before the Japanese onslaught. In December 1943 she smashed enemy shore installations in New Britain and covered the US landings, and in 1944 she was active

around New Guinea, making night raids and supporting land-
ings. In May 1944, during MacArthur's amphibious assault on
Biak Island, when a shore battery hit two escorting destroyers,
Phoenix wiped it out with her 5-inch guns.

   Phoenix took part in the reconquest of the Philippines too, and
was part of the force that shelled Leyte beach before the October
landing. Sailing with Admiral Oldendorf's group that annihi-
lated the Japanese Southern Force in the battle for Leyte Gulf, she
hit the Japanese battleship *Fuso* with her fourth ranging salvo,
then used all her 6-inch guns to sink it in 27 minutes. In
November ten torpedo-bombers attacked *Phoenix* and her sister
vessels patrolling Leyte Gulf. A suicide plane crashed into a US
destroyer. *Phoenix*'s 5-inch guns brought down one attacker in
flames and her machineguns brought down a third as it made its
torpedo run. Hours later the enemy returned, and she shot down
another. She helped destroy two enemy aircraft in December,
then brought down a kamikaze with 40-mm fire only 100 yards
off, capping that later by downing another kamikaze at 8,500
yards. En route to Luzon, *Phoenix* dodged two torpedoes from a
midget submarine; an escorting destroyer sank it. She survived
Bataan and Corregidor, and supported the assault waves at
Balikpapan. Altogether she won nine battle stars in the Second
World War. Perón bought her in April 1951, and named her the
17 de Octubre after the day that brought him to power in 1945. In
1956, after the fall of Perón, the name was changed to *General
Belgrano*, after one of the leaders of the revolution of May 1810.

   Captain Bonzo described his ship's final departure from port.
At about 16.00 on 26 April they pulled out from the eastern side
of the great concrete jetty which juts out at right-angles from
Ushuaia's waterfront like a prolongation of the town streets
Veinticinco de Mayo and Laserre. Glacier-covered mountains
capped by huge motionless banks of cloud looked down over
Ushuaia's spacious, sheltered bay. The clouds were often heavy
and sullen here, thunderous and blue-black, matching the sheer
cliffs in the Magellan Strait. There were no townsfolk, dockers
or sailors to wave them out of harbour. Theirs had been an *entrada
operativa*, an operational entry into Ushuaia to refuel and to
replenish supplies. Security was tight – though not tight enough
to prevent *Conqueror* from being informed that the *Belgrano* was
at sea, with two destroyer escorts, by 30 April – and all the ship's
crew had been kept strictly on board. At the end of March,

Bonzo had watched the Argentine invasion fleet leaving Puerto Belgrano, equally matter-of-factly. Now his ship turned east towards the South Atlantic, past rocky islands festooned with seabirds and seals.

The crew were well trained and their morale was high. They and the *Belgrano* made a well-oiled fighting machine, slowing down a little, but still something to be reckoned with. During his four months in command, Bonzo had put her through her paces. In January he had pushed her hard for twenty-four days of intensive navigation along the Patagonian coast and then far out onto the high seas. The crew were mainly keen cadets from the naval college, and they and their captain had had an exhilarating time.

But every man on board the *Belgrano* knew the difference between those gymnastics and this voyage, where danger could strike from the air, the sea, or from under the sea. Bonzo knew that some of his crew had had the eerie experience of hearing foreign radio broadcasts reporting the *Belgrano* sunk, or at any rate seriously damaged. The rumour had even been reported in one of the bulletins that were circulated on board, credited to a news agency. So perhaps there had been a touch of anxiety in the air, in these turbulent latitudes, with an enemy whose hunter-killer submarines must certainly have reached the South Atlantic before now. Bonzo felt little change in the mood of his crew as the news spread that they were to return to base. There was no boisterous response, no change in discipline. They still slept fully clothed, their personal effects close to hand, just in case.

Conqueror had followed the *Belgrano* all of the night of 1/2 May along a line parallel to the Exclusion Zone. There had been no official indication of the whereabouts of the centre of the TEZ, but putting it about halfway along Falkland Sound, even the *Conqueror*'s circle still left the *Belgrano* around 20 miles outside the limit, ploughing along at between 10 and 13 knots. No evasive jinks, no sonar, now and then a leisurely radar sweep.

'What the hell were they doing there?' asked Admiral Sir Terence (now Lord) Lewin, then Chief of the Defence Staff.[2] He said that when he called at his Northwood HQ that Sunday morning, Wreford-Brown had just reported: 'I have the *Belgrano* in sight.' Lewin had had some time to consider his own question, because *Conqueror* had located the group some 40 hours before, and it was Northwood which had dispatched the submarine to meet it. And the Chief of Staff was confident of the answer to his question: 'It didn't matter what direction the *Belgrano* was going. She might just have been wasting time so as to be able to attack the Task Force at night. Critics who say she was steaming for home have no idea what they are talking about. I went straight to Chequers and called the war cabinet into a side room and told them the situation. I said we could not wait. Here was an opportunity to knock off a major unit of the Argentine fleet.'

Lewin seemed to suspect an elaborate Argentine bluff. He knew that the *Belgrano* group had not been used aggressively the previous night, after the Task Force had attacked the Falklands all day. But they might be attempting to lull the invisible observers whom they had made no attempt either to locate or to evade into a false sense of security. The man who was confident enough to talk about calling his country's leaders aside under their own roof was not going to be diffident about what he thought necessary, and that was to sink the *Belgrano* while he had the chance. If not now, she might be a threat in future. He represented Britain's military arm. It was his job, as he saw it, to destroy any enemy unit that the politicians would let him destroy.

And 'the cabinet said go ahead,' Lewin related. 'Once Mrs Thatcher trusts your judgement there is no problem. She was superb. But first she had to get over the ghastly shock of losses in war. [This must mean the thousand or so Argentines who might be killed if she sank the *Belgrano*. There had been no British losses so far.] It is terrible for anyone to have to face . . .'

Lewin says elsewhere that, trusting his judgement or not, there was then a lengthy debate.[3] This contrasts with two other accounts. Sir Nicholas Henderson refers to 'a decision reached by the war cabinet meeting at Chequers around midday' (which is around 08.00 Argentine time).[4] According to Task Force commander Rear-Admiral John Woodward too, approval to sink the cruiser was given 'in remarkably short order, reputedly in the entrance porch at Chequers'.[5] Woodward had urgently signalled Northwood pressing for revised rules, since the standing Rules of Engagement said that Britons were only to attack Argentines inside the TEZ, unless the Argentines seriously threatened the Britons. Woodward was aware that the main Argentine battle group had been somewhere north of the Falklands on the evening of 1 May, when one of his Harriers had spotted the *25 de Mayo*. A

British nuclear submarine – probably *Splendid* – had found and followed (Admiral Lewin denied this in recording for Panorama 16 April 1984) then lost her. Woodward did not want to lose the *Belgrano* too, and rather than apply a Nelsonian eye to the Rules, he decided to try to change them, with Lewin's full backing.

The Royal Navy was at risk in the Falklands, and it was also eager to retain its prestige. The war cabinet could take that into account, together with the expertise of the British military leadership, but the final decision to sink the *Belgrano* had to be a political one. The Prime Minister and her colleagues had to ask themselves if there was any alternative – to warn the Argentines that the entire South Atlantic beyond their coast was now a TEZ; to ask Pym, in Washington, whether there were any hopeful new developments; to seek some lesser but more lethal target, such as one of the escorting destroyers, with their Exocet missiles.

There is a further discrepancy. Lewin has stated, in a radio comment for 'The World This Weekend', that 'communications with nuclear submarines are not continuous and one hundred per cent, because this would restrict nuclear submarines' operations. But on this occasion the communications worked very quickly.'[6] *Conqueror* received the order to sink the *Belgrano* at 14.00, local time, which was 18.00 BST – in other words about 46 hours after the cruiser was first detected. Northwood already knew that for more than 25 hours the hunter-killer submarine had been trailing her target at periscope depth.

Mrs Thatcher said in her letter to Denzil Davies, MP, of 4 April 1984 that she and her War Cabinet decided at 13.00 BST to sink the *Belgrano*. The 5-hour gap between transmission and receipt of the attack order could, of course, be due to the fact that Northwood came on circuit to its nuclear submarines at pre-arranged times – when it was safe for them to raise their radio-masts above surface.

Conqueror continued to follow her quarry, then went to Action Stations around 15.00. No one on board had ever fired a torpedo in anger, and the realization of what they were about to do caused a growing sense of strain. Even through the insulation of the hull, they had been feeling the cold of the South Atlantic. That was where the crew of the *Belgrano* would float – those who would not die when the torpedoes hit.

Commander Wreford-Brown took the submarine deep and

went to about 4,000 yards from *Belgrano*'s port side, as she steered the same straight course between her escorting destroyers. At 15.57 by the *Conqueror*'s time, 16.00 by *Belgrano*'s, he fired three Mark 8 torpedoes. The men in the Control Room watched the seconds tick by in total silence. Forty-three seconds, then came the first explosion.

The *Belgrano* was sailing steadily west-north-west, Bonzo said, on a bearing of 290 degrees and at a speed of between 10 and 11 knots, pointing towards and some 90 miles away from her refuelling base of Staten Island. His estimate of her position was latitude 55° 24' south, longitude 61° 32' west, on the edge of the Antarctic. The sea was wicked, with choppy waves three to four metres high, and there was intermittent fog. Temperature was near freezing. The icy wind of 50 kilometres an hour intensified the hypothermic impact of the sea. A man might stay conscious in it for five minutes, then he would go gently to sleep and die. The ship was in the condition which the Argentine navy calls *crucero de guerra*, with a third of her crew at battle stations, a third working, and a third resting.

The first torpedo hit the *Belgrano* on the port side, amidships, at her operations centre. It blasted inwards and upwards, bursting up with incredible power through four thick steel decks to the main deck. That killed any hope of keeping the ship afloat: with four ruptured decks there were not enough watertight compartments. The second torpedo struck four seconds later, fifteen metres from the prow. Here the force of the explosion ripped the bows clean away from the hull.

Two hits. *Conqueror*'s Control Room was a mass of cheering men. Wreford-Brown at the attack periscope had to shout his orders – ten down, starboard 30, half ahead, 150 revs. For the two dozen or more men in the Control Room there was jubilation, back-slapping, roars of triumph.

Bonzo was coming out of his quarters on the main deck and donning his heavy overcoat when the first torpedo hit. The huge impact made curiously little noise. What there was sounded deep and muffled. Every light went out and there was a sudden penetrating acrid smell. The movement seemed gigantic. It was as if the ship had suddenly struck and climbed up a great underwater mountain of sand. Then utter silence. The ship lost way abruptly. There was the shock of the second torpedo.

He reckoned afterwards that of the 368 men whom he lost

from his crew of 1,138, probably 330 died in those two apocalyptic explosions, especially in that first appalling internal blast with its great waves of heat, smoke and steam. It cut off all the power and light. There was no energy to drive the pumps to bale the water. A switchboard explosion killed the emergency generators, which broke loose from their bases. The ship was dead.

Survivors said that they never even saw the submarine which hit them from the south. *Conqueror* was going deep. Corporal Miguel Angel Alvarez was woken by the explosion:

> I threw myself off my bunk as I was, wearing only a sweater and a wind-cheater. I tried to get out the usual way. I slept in the poop, a metre or so from where the torpedo hit. The lower decks, where we slept, were just above the fuel oil tanks . . .
>
> But ahead I saw the explosion, a giant powder-flash, and behind it a huge jet of fuel oil, so I turned back. There was an emergency escape manhole, you can just get your body through one, but when I tried there was fuel oil up to the ceiling. I had to plunge into the oil and climb a ladder with the bit of air I had left. I was almost drowning from the oil and the gases from the explosion . . . the fuel oil was only ten centimetres from the ceiling, and I had to let my mates in front of me get out first . . . And I got out on deck . . . [7]

> It was suddenly totally dark, and there was a crushing lack of oxygen. Tubes were burst everywhere and the smoke kept getting thicker, and the heat more intense. (Conscript Able Seaman José Gonzales) [8]

Bonzo ran up to the bridge and gave the orders to take up emergency stations. He had to use voice-tubes and word of mouth. The crew seemed remarkably calm but he was taking no chances. He went back to his cabin for his pistol and stuck it in his belt for the next 40 minutes. He would have to use it on any man who might start to panic.

> I was almost in the centre of the ship, on the lower deck . . . From the impact I thought it was a six-inch shell. The ship weaved about. There was a noise like a liquid gas cylinder exploding, a sharp crack . . . I went to get my lifejacket and an Antarctic windcheater. I was going up to the gun-battery

mounting; we all knew our combat stations . . . I wanted to knock down an Englishman . . .

I got up to the main deck and immediately saw a lad covered in fuel oil, all black. You could see that the attack caught them sleeping, because he only had a vest on. They told me afterwards that this kid was running around the deck because the fuel oil was burning him up inside . . . I gave my blanket to a burnt lad so he could cover himself. (Conscript Gun Mechanic Oscar Alfredo Pardo)[9]

Within five minutes of the explosions the *Belgrano* was listing 15 degrees to port. Bonzo still had some hope that he could somehow keep her afloat, and some of the crew were doggedly trying to repair her. Pardo recalled:

Then they called for volunteers to rescue men from inside the ship, which was sinking. The boilers had burst and there was no light . . . With several of the lads, I went down into the cruiser. She was split open from side to side. There was lots of smoke everywhere, a thick fog. We had to use a lantern, you could hardly see . . . There were dead men everywhere, bits of bloody bodies, an arm here, a leg there. We could only help the one who cried out or asked for help, because you could hardly see and the smoke was hurting us badly. I couldn't last five minutes, and even then I swallowed a lot of smoke. I nearly drowned, getting back up from the lowest down below to the main deck.[10]

The *Conqueror* had almost scored a second kill, when her third torpedo ran on past the *Belgrano*, hit the destroyer *Hipólito Bouchard*, but failed to explode. At 16.20 the *Bouchard* radioed urgently to the Theatre of Operations South Atlantic (TOSA) in Comodoro Rivadavia: 'Bouchard attacked. Torpedo struck but did not explode. Am beginning withdrawal.' So it must have been the *Bouchard*'s sister ship, the *Piedra Buena*, that dropped a depth charge so close to *Conqueror* that Commander Wreford-Brown took desperate evasive action. He took her down to 500 feet, and spent the next hour driving his ship at full speed while the crew froze into silence and could not tell which way to tense themselves for the next explosion.

The sea was flooding into the *Belgrano*. By 16.22 the Breakdown Control Centre was itself under water and the list had gone to 21 degrees. Bonzo gave the order to abandon ship.

She was equipped with 72 rubber rafts, each able to take 20 men. The crew managed to get 62 into the water, and then they abandoned ship in a good seamanlike manner. In one case nerves gave out, when a midshipman, on a raft already holding 20, shot two conscript sailors trying to clamber aboard.[11] Bonzo got 770 men out finally, a high figure under the circumstances. He still had to face 36 hours in that wild and icy sea, where 25 more died, most that Sunday evening, when rough weather sprang up and capsized a raft. No one emerged.

Bonzo was 50 years old, a career officer, but he felt as proud of his 300 conscripts as he did of the great bulk of his crew who were regulars like himself. The conscripts were civilians from all over Argentina, young men of 18 and 19, but they stayed disciplined. That is why the survival rate was comparatively high. Each man knew at least two ways of getting out of the ship from his post. Their team spirit and readiness to sacrifice themselves for their mates was high.

By 16.40, after inspecting the deck, he was as sure as he could reasonably be that no one was left on board alive who was able to save himself or to be saved. Bonzo was the last to leave, or almost. He was now on the main deck with the tilt at 45 degrees, cutting the last rafts free from the ship, worried that there would not be enough for the men in the water. He could walk down the deck straight into the sea, which was clogging with oil.

Bonzo discovered now that he still had company – a petty-officer who kept asking him to abandon ship, and refused to do so himself until Bonzo did. Meanwhile he helped the captain to cut loose the last rafts. When they had finished, Bonzo looked at the petty-officer and shrugged: the man was not going to budge.

The captain of the *General Belgrano* walked down to the edge of the sea. The pistol was still in his belt. He took it out and threw it away. In the water he glanced back and saw the petty-officer following at last. In the maelstrom of events that followed, he did not see the man again until two days later, aboard the *Gurruchaga*, an ocean-going tug dispatched by the Naval Commander, Southern Region, Admiral Horacio Zaratiegui, to search for survivors.

Bonzo swam some 15 metres, fully clothed, through the icy sea and oil, then hands pulled him on to a raft. His outer clothes were soaked but his inner still protected him. The men huddled together in the raft to keep themselves warm and alive. They were re-enacting the experience of the men of the Arctic convoys during the U-boat war of 40 years before.

The rafts worked well. Bonzo was surprised that so many were able to survive through those seas. Those with their full complement of 20 men or thereabouts were the most efficient at preserving life. It was in the rafts that carried only three or four survivors that most deaths occurred from cold or exposure, and these were also the most easily capsized by the huge waves. Apart from huddling close together, the men found other tricks to survive. Urine in a plastic bag, its temperature 36 degrees C in an ambient of two or three degrees, could keep a weakened man warm and alive.

At 17.01, just an hour after the torpedoes struck, the cruiser *Belgrano* rolled ponderously over and sank stern-first beneath the waves. When she rolled Bonzo saw a deep 20-metre scar on her hull amidships, running inboard from her port side. Because the torpedo appeared to have exploded underneath the ship's side armour, which was three metres broad and 15 centimetres thick, Bonzo was inclined at the time to suspect that the British had used one of their Tigerfish torpedoes. Nevertheless, the evidence is that the damage was in fact done by the old-fashioned Mark 8s.

The *Conqueror* had been running for an hour. Commander Wreford-Brown decided to take her back up to periscope depth, about 20 miles from the scene of the sinking – the datum, in ship's jargon. She slowed and was preparing to rise when another resounding bang forced her off again, wriggling away from the spot under total silent drill. The ship's company was mystified and frightened. There was no indication of sonar from the destroyers, so how had they been located? Could the Argentines be using Neptune spotters with Jezebel buoys? *Conqueror* twisted and fled for another hour, to a distance of some 30 miles from the 'datum'. This time she was able to go to periscope depth with no enemy response, and she transmitted the news that she had hit and probably sunk the *General Belgrano*. With the news that the *Veinticinco de Mayo* had escaped, the *Conqueror* gained the distinction of becoming the first British submarine since the Second World War to have attacked an enemy ship, and the first British nuclear submarine ever to do so. The Task Force Commander informed Wreford-Brown that Her Majesty's Government had

HMS CONQUEROR

c o BFPO Ships

ARGENTINIAN SHIP 'GENERAL BELGRANO'

Sunk by HMS CONQUEROR at 1558 (Local) (1858 GMT)
on the afternoon of Sunday 2 May 1982.

Position: 55°30' South   61°40' West
95 miles South West of Isla de los Estados
210 miles South of West Falkland Island

Three Mark 8 Torpedoes fired. Two hits. The
third weapon hit the escorting destroyer
HIPPOLITO BOUCHARD but failed to detonate.

Each weapon contained 810 lbs of Torpex high
explosive.

a.   The first Nuclear Submarine ever to carry out
      an attack.

b.   The first British submarine to carry out an
      attack since World War 2.

c.   Probably the most Southerly engagement in the
      history of the Royal Navy.

'authorized the destruction of all Argentinian warships'. It was very much in line with Admiral Lewin's view that enemy shipping should be targeted if it seemed to pose even the slightest threat to the Task Force.

By 18.30 it was dark over the South Atlantic. The wind was rising and the rafts drifted apart. At first the men roped them together, at 10-metre intervals, to prevent it happening, but after holding that pattern for two hours, they cut the ropes. They had been putting the rafts in danger; they were more sea-worthy floating free.

Just after dark the *Bouchard* radioed again:

18.36. To TOSA. Confirm appreciation. Torpedoed without damage. Explosion outside the hull. Three white Bengal lights fired from *Belgrano*. Communications with drifting cruiser interrupted. *Bouchard*.

After the action the *Bouchard* is reported to have spent several days in an isolated bay in Tierra del Fuego, probably undergoing repairs to damage caused by the *Conqueror*'s near-miss.

That firing of distress flares from the *Belgrano*'s life rafts had not been much more than whistling in the dark. No help came, and by 19.00 the wind had developed into a *temporal*, a 120-kilometre-per-hour blow that whipped up the waves to twice their earlier height. It lasted throughout the night, until 07.00 next morning.

To stop the rafts from overturning the men sat with their backs stressed against the walls of the canopies to withstand the huge weight of cascading water. So they passed that night, singing, telling stories, praying. Bonzo said that he did not have too bad a time. He and his men had done all they could, as naval discipline demanded.

From 07.00 the weather became calmer, after a sullen dawn, but Bonzo saw that the sky was still in turmoil. They could expect no aerial search as yet. He judged from the position of the cloud-masked sun that they were being carried south-east. That would do them no good at all. That way there was nothing but cold grey sea and Antarctic ice. The conscript next to him in the raft asked: '*Pero donde vamos navegando?*' – But where are we sailing to? Bonzo told him: 'It's OK, we're doing fine.'

About midday, perhaps nearer 12.30, came the first aircraft.

The men in Bonzo's raft were convinced that it had spotted them, but he was not so sure. By now all the rafts were completely scattered and they could see no other. The waves cut their field of vision to 60 metres.

The men in the other rafts were having an equally nerve-racking time. First Signals Corporal Alvarez, the man who had swum through fuel oil to get out, spent an agonized 26 hours on his raft before the tug *Gurruchaga* picked it up. For the first four hours he had no idea who his companions were, because he kept needing to clean fuel oil out from under his eyelids in order to see at all. Then someone gave him a pair of knitted underpants to wipe enough of the oil off his hair and face to make him feel human again.

At first they were hungry as well as cold. There were iron rations on the rafts, chocolate and fruit blocks and a kind of serum, but the rule was that they must not eat or drink in the first 24 hours, and then must eat only the minimum. The idea was to spin out the planned survival time for the 20 men on each raft as far as they could. All the time they had to keep baling out the sea blown in off the rearing wave tops by near gale-force winds. And they must move their hands and feet and slap and slap again at their legs to keep the circulation going, so as to avoid frostbite.

Petty Officer Bruno Inaudi had 40 hours adrift on his Raft No. 57 in the vicious icy seas. He had the regulation 19 men with him, two of them badly wounded. In spite of everything their shipmates could do, these two died within hours of abandoning ship. Inaudi was the senior man on board. He rationed out the food and chose the watch, and took charge of baling the raft. The first night came, and he did his best to keep morale up. Mostly they sang, the Navy March or popular songs. They prayed too, for their own lives and their mates'. That night the winds were almost hurricane force. The *temporal* was slowly rising, with waves ten metres high. Apart from the two dead men, the raft also had one badly wounded crewman with grave burns from the explosion on his face and hands. The cold was agonizing. Inaudi knew that in these conditions of being permanently up to their ankles or higher in cold sea water, the sailors were bound to suffer from trench foot. At last the *Gurruchaga* found them.[12]

The first rescue vessel reached the area about 16.00. It was a destroyer. The men on Captain Bonzo's raft had seen no more aircraft, because the weather had worsened again. At 17.00

another *temporal* started up, and it was still blowing hard when Bonzo's raft – the last to be rescued – was picked up on Tuesday, 4 May, at 04.00, with two dead men in it.

It was the *Gurruchaga* that took him and his men on board. Two other ships arrived later, a Chilean vessel and the *Bahía Paraiso*, last seen at South Georgia before the invasion. These two stayed behind for a while, to scour the zone for any last survivors.

Some *Belgrano* crew members still died up to 24 hours after their rescue. Several had been burnt, although Bonzo learned later that only a small proportion of his dead had been burnt by direct contact with flames.

The former captain of the *Belgrano* arrived at Ushuaia on Wednesday 5 May in a state of considerable strain, both physical and mental. He stayed in the zone till the last rescue ship was back, and at 19.00 he was flown to the main naval base of Puerto Belgrano. With him were 18 wounded, two dead and two doctors. On the flight to Puerto Belgrano one of the wounded, a burnt man, died.

Interviewed in his office in the Edificio Libertad, the Argentine navy HQ in Buenos Aires, Captain Bonzo confessed to feeling some resentment towards Rear-Admiral Woodward for blaming the Argentine navy for the loss of life involved in the sinking of the *Belgrano*. He was alluding to Woodward's assertion that the casualty toll might have been much less had rescue operations been swifter. That was nonsense, Bonzo said. It was the explosion of the two torpedoes in those first four seconds which had caused 330 or 340 of the *Belgrano*'s 368 deaths: his salvage operation in getting his men from that point to the rescue ships and Ushuaia had cost only 25 lives.

Bonzo had no more sympathy with the suggestion that his own escorting destroyers should have stopped to pick up survivors. 'They had their own job to do,' he said, and that was to search and destroy any attacker as top priority.

Part of the propaganda image generated by British officials during the Falklands campaign was that which portrayed the Argentines as being careless of their own men's lives. The charge that it was Argentine incompetence that killed some of the *Belgrano*'s crew may have salved some British consciences. Sir Nicholas Henderson has produced a more elaborate statement of Argentine fecklessness. Writing about the *Belgrano* sinking, he observes:

The Argentines have said subsequently that they were taken
unawares by the attack. One can only say that this is not
surprising given the endemic unawareness of the Junta and
their confidence that the British would never react militarily to
the invasion of the islands.[13]

This picture of the Junta dispatching valuable ships and men to be
picked off by the British like fish in a barrel seems to ignore the
fact that a day before the sinking the British had indeed 'reacted
militarily', causing 56 Argentine casualties. The Junta might be
careless with its men and property, but it must go without saying
that the men – well over a thousand of them – and their captain,
steering a dead straight course and making no evasive moves,
would have to have been suicidal to behave as *Conqueror* watched
them doing if they had not had the best of reasons for feeling safe.
However in this situation the issue is not 'the endemic unawareness of the Junta', but the nature of British intentions. The gen-
eralized warning to Argentine ships coupled with the creation
of a limited TEZ was at best loaded with ambiguity, at worst a
deliberate trap for the unwary.

Captain Bonzo has rejected the British claim that the attack
was legitimate because even though the cruiser was 36 miles
outside the TEZ (or 20, by *Conqueror*'s guess) she could have
imperilled the Task Force. Informed of the statement by John
Nott, then British Defence Secretary, that 'this heavily armed
surface attack group was close to the total exclusion zone and was
closing on elements of our task force which was only hours
away',[14] Bonzo claimed that this allegation was, literally, all
wrong. His group had not been particularly heavily armed by the
standards of the British fleet. The *Belgrano*'s main armament of
15 6-inch guns with a range of 13 miles could not match Britain's
surface-to-surface missiles, including Exocets with a range of 20
miles. Her two escorting destroyers carried Exocets but were
themselves vintage pieces, 38 years old.

So this was no attack group. When assaulted, it was *not* part of a
pincer movement with the *25 de Mayo*. Even if designed to be part,
as Lombardo claimed, it was ordered home before it ever turned
north. It would have been an odd pincer movement, Bonzo
said, with the prongs some 350 miles apart. The *Belgrano* had
specific orders to patrol a defensive line, and that is what she did.
Again, the *Belgrano* was well outside the TEZ when tor-

pedoed, pointing straight at the Argentine coast on a bearing which she had been following for hours. She was not 'closing on' the British Task Force but sailing just the other way. Bonzo was nettled when, in a telephone interview on 3 June 1983, he learned that in her election news conference the day before, Mrs Thatcher had said that when sunk the *Belgrano* was only about six hours sailing from the nearest British surface vessel. That was 'absolute nonsense', he retorted. The nearest British surface vessel must have been at least 250 nautical miles away, east of the Falklands. He would have needed 14 hours to cover that distance at the *Belgrano*'s top cruising speed of 18 knots, always provided the British ship had had the decency to stop dead in her tracks and wait for him.

Bonzo thought no better of Mr Nott's alternative explanation that 'because HMS *Conqueror* might lose the *General Belgrano* as she ran over the shallow water of the Burdwood Bank the task force commander sought and obtained a change in the Rules of Engagement to allow an attack outside the 200-mile exclusion zone'.[15] The implication was that whereas a surface ship like the *Belgrano* could float above these shoals, a bulky nuclear submarine could not. Bonzo sketched the Burdwood Bank's location, south-south-west of the Falklands, on the rim of the TEZ, and mostly inside it, about 200 miles east to west, and 50 north to south. Even if the *Belgrano* did turn suddenly and cross the Bank, he said, the *Conqueror* could have followed. It was nowhere shallower than 50 metres, and *Jane's Fighting Ships* put the draught of a *Conqueror*-type nuclear submarine submerged at not more than 18 metres.

Finally, Bonzo in his turn asked a question. 'One thing puzzles me,' he said. 'You Anglo-Saxons are supposed to be so logical. As a mere Latin, I thought that a Total Exclusion Zone must mean that if you were in it, then you got shot at. If you were not in it, you did not get shot at. But if you are going to be shot at in any case, then, tell me, why have a Total Exclusion Zone at all?'

Christopher Wreford-Brown appears to have asked himself the same question. He said that his orders were to attack the *Belgrano* only if she did enter the TEZ. He trailed her for 'over 30 hours' — in fact ever since he read the first faint signatures of the cruiser and her escorts at about 16.00 local time on 30 April, and advised Northwood at once, waiting for instructions. The fact that Lewin had then to ask permission to change the Rules of

General Galtieri addressing a rally in Plazo de Mayo on 6 April 1982

ABOVE LEFT. USS *Phoenix*, later the *General Belgrano*, leaving Pearl Harbor past the burning USS *Arizona* on 7 December 1941, following the initial Japanese air attacks

BELOW LEFT. HMS *Conqueror* returning to Faslane base at Gare Loch

ABOVE. The *General Belgrano*, sinking

RIGHT. Commander Wreford-Brown at Buckingham Palace on the occasion of receiving his DSO

The Jolly Roger flies from HMS *Conqueror* on her return home

HMS CONQUEROR
c o BFPO Ships

From: The Flag Officer Submarines (Vice Admiral
P G M Herbert, OBE)

To: HMS CONQUEROR

1. Your successful attack on BELGRANO pressed
home with determination and precision was in
the highest traditions of the Submarine
Service. The event had the immediate effect
of dissuading Argentinian Surface Forces from
taking any further part in offensive operations,
thereby preventing great loss of life, not only
to UK personnel but Argentinian also.

2. I was also greatly impressed by your determination
throughout the Patrol, and in particular your
penetration of the Gulfo San Matias.

3. You and your Ship's Company can look forward to
a very well earned rest. Congratulations on a
magnificent achievement.

Engagement indicates that the interpretation of both captains, Bonzo and Wreford-Brown alike, was the correct one. Lewin has alleged: 'We warned the Argentines on April 23 that if we met their warships or aircraft they would be considered hostile. So both sides were in no doubt about what would happen if we met up on the high seas.' For most of the 48 hours that the course of the *Belgrano* steered carefully outside the TEZ, both captains assumed that she was safe. Unluckily for Bonzo, who was staking the life of his ship on that assumption, he had never heard the alternative version of the song the brass bands played. The one that goes 'Rule Britannia, Britannia waives the rules . . .'

Aftermath

News of the sinking reached the Argentine Presidency at 18.45 local time, and soon after 19.00 Admiral Anaya informed the Military Committee which had begun discussing the Peruvian peace initiative. President Belaúnde himself did not learn about the loss of the *General Belgrano* until Secretary Haig came on the line from Washington some time after the press conference in which Belaúnde had announced the imminence of a ceasefire. That press conference is valuable, therefore, because it cannot possibly be said to represent some version of events concocted between Peru and Argentina after the British attack. British officials have insisted that Belaúnde did little more than go over familiar ground with Haig that morning, and put forward some tentative suggestions that 'could not possibly be described as "proposals" '.[1] Here are some excerpts from the Peruvian President's own account, given when the survivors of the *Belgrano* were already in their life rafts, and after the nuclear submarine *Conqueror* had shaken off the searching destroyers.

Belaúnde: Before the journalists' first question about this proposal, may I say that it's an instrument by which there would be an immediate end to hostilities. The document is not a capitulation for either party . . . I hope that in the conversations in Buenos Aires that President Galtieri will be presiding at this moment . . . they can make a great advance in deciding the final text.

The proposal which Peru has put forward with the firm support of the US government is to get peace very quickly, if possible tonight . . .

In the palace we're in direct contact with Buenos Aires and Washington, where Foreign Minister Pym has spent the whole day in the State Department.

We've been talking to General Haig, and we have an especially expressive written message from the President of the United States, who thanks us and very decidedly supports our efforts . . .

Journalist: I'd like to go back to the declaration to which you referred a minute ago. Did Peru suggest the basic text? Could you give us a lead in –

Belaúnde: Peru didn't propose it. Really the procedure arose out of a phone call that the US Secretary of State made to us last night. We pushed for it in order to get clear terms. Then he dictated a series of points that he judged interesting. Of course we made comments on these points, and in some cases objected to or modified them before we presented them to Argentina.

After we had had this exchange of ideas, which was very extensive, frank and high-level, then when I talked to General Galtieri I read out to him and he recorded the points I've referred to. [See above, pp. 84–6.] In the course of the morning evidently work was done on this document, and although the Secretary of State didn't say it to me, he did make two or three interjections which did perhaps come from his talks with the British Minister. We've just talked with Mr Costa Méndez, to transmit to him which points General Haig thinks would make the document acceptable to Great Britain . . . in all justice we must give the origin of this document, its editing, and a great part of its content, as being the Secretary of State himself . . .

I can tell you the first point, about which there's no discussion: 'Number One: Immediate Cessation of Hostilities.' . . .

Journalist: Mr President, you mean to say that in spite of the US's attitude we've gone back to trusting Mr Haig's mediation?

Belaúnde: Mr Haig's mediation never stopped because in his statement in the US he said that he would continue with his efforts. Clearly this mediation has reached a climax with the arrival of Mr Pym, because both are in Washington and so he can transmit all the wishes for or possibilities of an agreement from the side of the government of Great Britain . . .

If this attempt fails it will be a tragedy for Latin America and perhaps for the world.[2]

After a few more exchanges, the press conference ended and the AP and UPI agency men sent off their stories to their New York offices. We have already quoted the AP text which reported peace (p. xiv); that text and hundreds of lives had already been blue-pencilled by the *Conqueror*.

In Washington that morning, Haig and Pym had concluded their conversation at noon, and proceeded to lunch at the British Embassy with Ambassador Henderson. According to Henderson's account, just before flying to New York that afternoon, 'Pym received a telephone call from Haig emphasizing the importance of the Peruvian ideas'.[3] Pym had not felt it necessary to report these ideas back to the British government. Reagan, however, lost no time in congratulating Belaúnde and pledging full support for his efforts. Henderson's wording of what happened next is curious: 'It was only at this point that it was *possible* to telegraph a report to London: that telegram was despatched at 17.15 Washington time or 22.15 London time.'[4] (The *Belgrano* had been torpedoed at 15.00 hours Washington time, hours earlier.) Pym would have known how delicately the scales were balanced when he arrived in Washington the day before:

> He was acutely aware that the moment was now approaching when the lines between military and diplomatic action, hitherto wide apart, were beginning to converge and then cross, compounding the high pitch of drama that each had reached. Port Stanley had been bombed by Vulcans that day; other attacks had been made on the islands by Harriers of which one had been lost.[5]

Short of an international telephone strike, combined with the telex and radio facilities of the British embassy both breaking down together, it is difficult to see what made it 'not possible' for Pym to contact London. He was the British channel to Haig, and hence ultimately to Argentina. If there was no hope of peace, then his government needed to know that, in order to push on with its military plans. If there was any hope at all, then it had been present at midday, *before* the sinking, and London might want to know that too, before it accepted what Admiral Lewin called 'the ghastly shock of losses in war'.

Pym flew into Washington 'fully briefed' on the military situation, according to his successor Sir Geoffrey Howe (12 April

1984). So presumably he knew *Conqueror* was trailing *Belgrano* and London favoured using 'more military force'. (See p. 77.) By Sunday, as he has confirmed, the War Cabinet's change in the Rules of Engagement had been reported to him. He did not need much imagination to deduce that a major operation was imminent. Yet, patently, he told Haig nothing of this. Haig, now committed wholly to the new peace bid, would probably have hit the roof had he known what was being prepared. Officially, the British stayed silent. It was Alexander Haig who phoned the British Ambassador at 20.00 that night to tell him of the attack. 'It was the first I had heard of it,' Henderson said.[6]

President Belaúnde phoned Galtieri at 22.30 hours Lima time, 2 May (00.30 next day, Buenos Aires time). The salient passages in the ensuing conversation are as follows:

Belaúnde: Good evening, President, I want to talk to you and I'm rather worried.

Galtieri: I'm more worried than you, Mr President. As you know, in line with what I told you this afternoon, here in Buenos Aires at 19.00 Argentine time, 17.00 Lima, the Military Committee met to deal with the matter of the proposal that your government was making to the Argentine government – after contacts with Washington – to look for peace in the South Atlantic. The contents of the seven points had been analysed in depth, in the time available, and we were going to go on deepening our analysis given that the subject is peace and Argentine sovereignty in the Malvinas and South Georgia. But all that, Mr President, has been tremendously affected and overturned by the British attitude in torpedoing the cruiser *General Belgrano* of the Argentine navy, we say outside the 200-mile zone established by the UK – which we don't accept in any case – and clearly this situation is not only unfavourable, but also the Argentine government will not, in the face of this military pressure, accept any negotiation relating to peace in the South Atlantic in these circumstances. We would rather die on our feet than live on our knees.

Belaúnde: I understand perfectly, Mr President. I was in, and they told me about it in the afternoon, and naturally I understood that this created a very grave situation.

Galtieri: Therefore, Mr President, I should like tomorrow morning to send you the Secretary General of the Presidency, General

Norberto Iglesias. He is my personal delegate, and if it's convenient for you he'll explain the Argentine position to you and to the members of the Armed Forces Commands as broadly as he can – what we have been trying unsuccessfully to agree with Washington from the first moments . . . the first days of April, all the attempts that have been made with the documents, and so as to achieve the utmost understanding of our situation.

Belaúnde: I understand you very well, Mr President, I understand that it was practically a tacit understanding that while there was any possibility of a negotiation, those people would refrain from any warlike act, no? That's something elementary, as I've said to Secretary Haig.

(. . .)

Belaúnde: I'm going to call Secretary Haig. I'm letting you know this because he called me in the afternoon, very mortified, and told me something about the loss of a ship. I naturally expressed my bewilderment, no? And I told him I was waiting for his call and that as soon as I had it I would transmit him your reply, which, I understand, has to be dictated by the circumstances. So we'll suspend all that for now, though I still don't despair that we can do something for peace. Just think, if we'd been able to achieve that peace this morning at 10.00 as I'd hoped, the *Belgrano* would not have been lost. So I know how important hours and minutes are in these things, no? Last night we really thought we were hitting the nail on the head, no? But now one sees the extreme urgency of anything to do with a ceasefire, no? Because so many lives are involved.

(. . .)

Galtieri: It's lamentable, really lamentable, and it's going to cost several decades of American history to rebuild the position of the US government. It's incomprehensible that, with all its capacity and power, the US can't make its influence felt in a delicate situation like this within America.

Belaúnde: Look, I noticed in the course of the day – and this may interest you – a change in General Haig's attitude. He was really almost euphoric in the search for terms which could be accepted by both parties, and it seemed to me that he was ready to impose them on the UK. But evidently this news [the *Belgrano*] and the other news that they are now bombarding the Malvinas and trying to land on them has altered the situation. So he has changed his attitude for one of frustration and he presents Mr

Pym as a man who has no interest in peace but simply in obtaining greater facilities to continue the war, no? And clearly Mrs Thatcher is completely obstinate in this matter . . .

Belaúnde: I'll call Haig now, to tell him that while you were very well disposed to study these points, you've had to put all that aside, in view of what happened this afternoon. That's concretely what I can say, no?

Galtieri: That's so. Beyond the fact that the points, or the seven points, could in some respects be reconsidered and dealt with, Mr President, but I repeat, if we're reconsidering some aspects of the drafting of the seven points, the news of the cruiser *General Belgrano* has thrown aside all study [of the peace proposal] and all reasoning to support it, because of this happening, which is psychologically and politically all-important, going far beyond the military, in its effects upon the people of Argentina.

Galtieri was not utterly rejecting the diplomatic route. Merely from the propaganda point of view, that would have been to hand back to the British the moral high ground which they had just vacated by their decision to escalate the conflict by a leap and a bound and without warning. In fact the Argentine Ambassador to the United Nations continued to discuss possible peace terms with the UN Secretary General, Mr Pérez de Cuéllar, throughout the period from the 2nd to the 19th of May. Hence it cannot be argued that the death of the *Belgrano* put an end to negotiations. What it clearly did achieve was to put an end to the Peruvian initiative for long enough for other events to intervene. It was these events, triggered by the fate of the *Belgrano*, which were to make it more and more difficult for the British themselves to withdraw, or even to halt a while, along the path they had chosen. Once the Argentines too had drawn blood, both sides had their political survival at stake if the dead did not buy victory.

The next step in the war came on 4 May, and was taken by two pilots of the Argentine fleet air arm's Super Etendard squadron, Capitán de Corbeta Augusto César Bedacarratz and Teniente de Fragata Armando Raúl Mayora. The following account was given by their squadron leader, Capitán de Fragata Jorge Luis Colombo:

Attack on the Destroyer Sheffield

The attack was decided for Tuesday, 4 May 1982. It was to be the only one carried out in line with the initial planning [based on the use of spotter aircraft to locate and electronically pinpoint the target], which gave an initial position for the target and its composition, and involved the same spotter aircraft maintaining contact in order to update the target's position immediately before the attack.

The enemy's immediate position was some 100 miles south of Port Stanley and about 380 miles from the Aeronaval base at Río Grande. The Fleet Air Arm Command ordered takeoff at 09.45. Two aircraft took off with a missile apiece, to attack the enemy in a position which had been brought up to date at 09.15 by a Neptune explorer aircraft of the Navy. At 10.04 there was a successful rendezvous for mid-air refuelling, and with the aircraft now 250 miles from target the final phase of the attack began.

At 10.30, in really bad weather conditions owing to the squalls and fog banks common at that season in those latitudes, reducing visibility to 1,000 metres and the ceiling to 150 metres, the aircraft received the target's updated position from the Neptune explorer aircraft. The targets were 115 nautical miles from the attacking aircraft: two medium- and one large-size vessels.

At 11.04 the two aircraft simultaneously launched their two Exocet missiles. They had acquired the targets on their radar screens. Effecting the procedure they had practised so many times before, they managed to launch the missiles without being detected by the enemy, in optimum conditions and at a distance which gave an ample margin to ensure impact on the target. No type of electronic countermeasure was registered, indicating total surprise.

After the launch the two Super Etendards turned and flew back at top speed, skimming the waves, and were not molested. It was conclusive proof that the cautious approach which had been analysed and rehearsed so long and so resolutely had borne its fruit. The aircraft landed without incident at 12.10.

The operation was efficient. It was carried out in a completely professional manner by professional pilots. The partnership of explorer with attacker aircraft thus proved its value, employing a method totally new in naval warfare.

The Argentine Fleet Air Arm thus became a pioneer in these new techniques, never used before by any country in the world. On 4 May 1982 at 11.04, fighting for a noble cause in a lost corner of the South Atlantic, the Argentine Fleet Air Arm opened the eyes of the world to a new chapter in the doctrine of fleet air arm operations in all the modern navies of the West. Let no one doubt it.[7]

Twenty-one men died on the *Sheffield*, in circumstances no less appalling than those suffered by the crew of the *General Belgrano* less than two days before. Some died at once when the missile hit the main engine compartment and exploded, only seconds after it was spotted. Others were killed by the raging fire that broke out, or suffocated in the lethal fumes the fire produced from the PVC covering of the ship's wiring. The full story is told in the Insight Team's book, published soon after the end of the Falklands war.[8] The dead make no distinctions: it would not matter to the sailors who now lie at the bottom of the South Atlantic, less than 200 miles apart, to know that while in one ship one third of the crew were sleeping, and the rest expected no attack, in the other the crew were all at action stations, ready for battle.

On 3 May, Haig had twice met urgently with Henderson. The British action in sinking the *Belgrano* had also had repercussions for the US, who were being accused of complicity in the attack. Public opinion in the West might tilt against the UK, Haig warned. 'People might say that Britain was over-reacting.'[9] Henderson told him that the British government meant to keep up the pressure until Argentina promised to stop fighting and leave the islands, but Haig kept pleading for a ceasefire: 'He did not think that the Argentines could do anything to prevent the British sinking the whole of their fleet. This would bring about the collapse of any authority in Buenos Aires; the whole of Latin America would be alienated.' (This assessment of the likely fate of the Argentine fleet says a great deal about the ability of any of its units to pose any threat to the Task Force: the former commander of the NATO military forces in Europe was dismissing that possibility outright.)

The next move came after the destruction of the *Sheffield*, by land-based aircraft. On 5 May, Haig and Henderson thrashed out some new proposals which London accepted even though they presented 'considerable difficulties'. Henderson relates that: 'The text was transmitted by the United States government to the Peruvians for onward transmission to Argentina, which turned them down.' The conversation between Belaúnde and Galtieri took place late that night, and contained the following exchanges:

Belaúnde: My very cordial congratulations for the military successes you've achieved.

Galtieri: Well, thank you Mr President, in the name of the Argentine people. On the one hand I'm satisfied, but on the other, as a human being, it doesn't really please me. I think they've underestimated us, and I'm not really at all happy to be the cause of these victims that war produces.

Belaúnde: There it is. We all remember that when you occupied the islands you took special care not to cause casualties. [This is certainly not true about Moody Brook Barracks: see pp. 27–8.] . . . Well, the result of this operation [the *Sheffield* attack] has clearly had its psychological consequences. As you know, Great Britain has a different attitude now. She's receptive to the idea of an arrangement and a ceasefire, as you're aware.

Galtieri: Yes, some news of that sort has reached me, though it's not very solid. But if there are leaks, let's say that Argentina's ready for a ceasefire.

  (. . .)

Belaúnde: The reason I'm calling is to let you know the aspirations and ideas of the British government . . . They've let us know them indirectly, it's been via the US, a reaction that they would be ready to consider . . .

Galtieri: I'm listening, Mr President, I'm listening. Go on.

Belaúnde: Look, it's the document I passed on to them when our negotiations were so unfortunately interrupted by the very painful attack on the *Belgrano*. Taking that as a basis, they've reacted to the document. In general, they accept it; they make it a bit more concise, because they reduce it from seven points to six, but they make some changes in editing. They leave the first part, for example – immediate cessation of hostilities. They talk of a mutual withdrawal, but also of a, what they would call a non-redeployment or non-reintroduction – these are rather odd terms – of all forces, that's to say a non-return of the forces during this period. They then go on at once to insist that the Contact Group be those countries originally mentioned – despite the fact that I had been very clear that this was not acceptable to you, above all in one case – and that its mission should be, first, to verify the withdrawal of forces, second, to administer the government of the islands during the provisional period in consultation with the elected representatives of the islands' population – you see how here they want to give prominence to the existing organizations, and make it certain that no action is taken on the islands that contravenes this interim accord – and, third, to ensure that all the other terms of the agreement are respected.

Except for these changes, the rest is practically the same, give or take a word or two, so that this plan we can call structurally the same as the other, though naturally they make some play with their own ideas . . . I have the information that the US would make them accept these accords in a discussion, that's an aspect I want to tell you about so that you can make the appropriate decisions. But there's also a timetable, and it's very tight. It would have 24 hours for giving orders and instructions for the ceasefire, then only 48 hours for the work, but once the ceasefire has started there would be 12 hours to reject or approve the document which would have been presented previously, but to the satisfaction of both parties – which is naturally very difficult. And if there's no agreement then things revert to their prior state. That, along general lines, is what the State Department tells me Britain would accept . . .

Galtieri: . . . You'll understand that in these very tight time lapses that are being chosen, it's really a question of getting agreement between the points of view.

Belaúnde: That's it. Our objective is to get a truce, and once we've got that and obtained a climate of tranquillity – in which we can speak without sinking ships and hostilities – well, to reach this agreement, but it seems that Britain would not accept this procedure. So I want to stress that the Peruvian Proposal as we've made it, which consisted of two periods, the first of peace, and then immediately a period of negotiation – they do not accept that procedure.

Galtieri: I share what you say, Mr President, but they can't put us between the sword and the wall.

Belaúnde: There it is. We have to consider the viewpoints of each party and for the rest the situation is very hard and grave for each party.

Galtieri: I agree with you, and I agree with this last concept and the one before it. If we can't agree on a climate of ceasefire and a truce that can't be of 12 or 24 hours, we can't negotiate such transcendental issues by telephone, Mr President. Each party has got to sit down with the help of two or three agreed friends and talk for 24, 48 or 72 hours.

Belaúnde: That's it, that's it, that's why we asked 72 hours as a minimum. They're ready to give 24 hours as a period in which to give orders and 48 for discussion. I too consider it a bit tight. I know they put great stress on not delaying.

The conversation went on, but with Galtieri refusing to accept the US as a member of the Contact Group, and seeing the tight British deadlines as too brief for real negotiations, the two Presidents agreed that it was time to transfer the problem to the UN and to Pérez de Cuéllar. Galtieri insisted that Argentina had 'lost all belief in the government of the US', while Belaúnde claimed that an American presence in the Contact Group was 'a requirement of the UK'. Belaúnde kept coming back to the need for a negotiated conclusion to the war, while Galtieri peppered the discussion with blustering heroics – 'Hundreds and thousands more Argentines are ready to die . . . we'll wait for Queen Elizabeth and all her fleet . . . there are many Argentines ready to fight to the end.'

Belaúnde was now out of the negotiations, but this particular diplomatic vacuum was filled by Pérez de Cuéllar. The next initiative came from Britain, which made a set of proposals on 17 May, accepting the idea of an interim UN administrator, calling for total withdrawal by the armed forces of both sides within two weeks of a time to be specified, and predicating the agreement on Article 73 of the United Nations Charter, which refers to 'the principle that the *interests* of the inhabitants of [territories whose peoples have not yet attained a full measure of self-government] are paramount'. Argentina presented its counter-proposals on 19 May. The British proposals had omitted the South Georgias and South Sandwich Islands, included in all negotiations on the Falklands between Britain and Argentina ever since 1977; Argentina's new proposal wanted them included again in any new agreement. Argentina was suspicious of the British move to take

Article 73 of the UN Charter as the ruling principle, rather than Resolution 2065; its own proposals omitted any mention of Article 73, because Costa Méndez suspected that it would be used to reintroduce the concept of self-determination. According to Sir Nicholas Henderson, 'the Argentine response . . . was to seek changes designed to pre-judge the outcome of the negotiations, so that they would lead inexorably to Argentine sovereignty and control'. In fact, the Argentine proposals make no direct mention of sovereignty at all. The relevant section reads:

V

1. The Parties commit themselves to commence negotiations in good faith under the auspices of the Secretary General of the United Nations, toward a peaceful and definitive solution of the dispute and with a sense of urgency to complete these negotiations before 31 December of 1982, with the only exception being an extension to 30 June 1983, in order to comply with the United Nations Charter, Resolutions 1514 (XV), 2065 (XX) and all other Resolutions of the General Assembly concerning the issue of the Malvinas Islands. These negotiations will be initiated without prejudice to the rights and claims or positions of both Parties and recognizing that the Parties have conflicting positions relative to the issue of the Malvinas, South Georgias and Sandwich Islands.

But the diplomatic phase was really over by now. Pérez de Cuéllar was still trying to blend the two proposals when Britain attacked on 21 May to establish its beach-head at San Carlos. In the next five days the Argentine air force lost over fifty aircraft in desperate attacks on British ships supporting the beach-head. Four British ships were lost in the same period, and 55 men died on them. On 28 May came the battle for Goose Green, when the 450 men of 2 Para defeated 1,600 Argentines after hard fighting in which the British lost 18, the Argentines some 250 men. An official British account made two points about the battle, in which 2 Para's leader, Lieutenant-Colonel 'H' Jones, was killed. 'First it gave us a chance to assess the fighting qualities of the enemy. Second . . . by their outstanding performance against a numerically superior enemy 2 Para established a pyschological ascendancy over the Argentines which our forces never lost.'[10]

Britain now had the upper hand in the Falklands war on land, as it had had it on sea all along. From here onward there are two main themes in Henderson's account of the diplomatic process. First, the Americans wanted the British to show 'magnanimity': they must not insist on unconditional surrender, and the 'humiliation' of Argentina. Haig's 'anxiety' and 'concern' about this prospect are mentioned again and again: his 'nightmare' is that Argentina may lose the war but still remain in a state of war with Britain, and he tells Henderson that:

> It would be a disaster if the outcome of the Falklands crisis was an intensification of communism and Soviet influence in the American hemisphere. In the long run, the only security for the islands was some agreement in which the United States participated, but it would be impossible to get an American guarantee for a return to the status quo.[11]

Accompanying this theme of acute American anxiety is a second theme, in which Henderson is telling Haig 'on instructions' that the British bridgehead will harden London's diplomatic stance; rubbing it in, 'on instructions from the prime minister and Pym', that the British priority is to repossess the Falklands and reinstate a British administration; informing President Reagan's national security adviser, William Clark, 'at Mrs Thatcher's request', that now the British are back in the islands they are 'not prepared . . . simply to pull out and make way for an umbrella or contact group including countries from Latin America'.[12]

Henderson's is the most comprehensive account of the British diplomatic role in the Falklands conflict to have emerged from any official British participant. (Having retired from the diplomatic service, he wrote his *Economist* article in a private capacity, but it was cleared by the Foreign Office.) We have been compelled to draw upon it at some length, and sometimes to argue with it, because the British government itself has provided no account of its own, and Francis Pym has declined to be interviewed about his own role. Diplomats, even retired ones, choose their phrases with care. It could hardly have been accidental that the only occasions on which Henderson chose to stress that he was acting under orders were those on which the British government's line could have been construed as 'intransigent'.

The war went on. Britain lost two more ships, with a further

50 lives, but the attack on Port Stanley was pushed through to a triumphant conclusion. Robacio's marine battalion fought stubbornly during the final night of 13/14 June, but the Argentine conscripts, ill equipped and poorly led, untrained for war and thoroughly disenchanted with Galtieri and his colleagues, surrendered in their thousands. Their commander, General Menéndez, surrendered to the commander of the British land forces, Major-General Jeremy Moore, at 21.00 local time, 14 June 1982.

After the sinking of the *General Belgrano*, the nuclear submarine *Conqueror* spent two more months at sea, alerted now to the danger from Argentina's Neptune and Tracker aircraft, which carried Jezebel locator buoys and torpedoes. The information from British intelligence was that as many as eight maritime patrol aircraft were looking for the killer of the *Belgrano*, and watch-keeping disciplines began to show a marked improvement. On 4 May *Conqueror* observed an Argentine hospital ship in the region where the *Belgrano* had gone down, and accompanied by a destroyer. No orders came to sink the destroyer, and the submarine headed northward. The following days kept the crew in constant tension. One of the steam generators developed a leak and proved hard to repair, reducing their speed to 15 knots. A Neptune forced them deep when they came up to use the snorkel apparatus at night, and as they headed into the TEZ they learned that Neptune aircraft had been sighted dropping Mark 44 torpedoes on possible submarine locations. The news of the *Sheffield*'s sinking was depressing: to the crew, it seemed as if the Argentines had air superiority and would just pick the Navy off at will. Each time they came to periscope depth, the tension was becoming painful.

From inside the TEZ, *Conqueror* was dispatched northward on 9 May, 100 miles outside it. Air activity reduced when they were sent further north-east to cover some units of the Task Force which included troop-carrying ships. The crew were reassured to learn that British intelligence was intercepting Argentine signals with a success rate close to 100 per cent, and the enemy's intentions were readily accessible. The Argentines realized what had been happening after the war, and Dr Murguizur commented:

Setting aside the indisputable advantage provided by satellite reconnaissance, the British intercepted all our radio transmissions, and almost certainly broke our codes. This may well explain why General Menéndez's (easily locatable) HQ was never attacked, since its destruction would have deprived the enemy of its source of detailed knowledge of the orders promulgated to our troops, their requirements, how they were deployed and the composition of each unit.[13]

However the Argentines themselves were not without intelligence resources. While *Conqueror* was guarding the slow-moving troop-carriers against a possible excursion by the *Veinticinco de Mayo*, she learned that Soviet Bear aircraft had been seen trailing the group, and that *Fearless* had reported sighting a possible Soviet nuclear submarine. Intelligence from both sources may well have reached Argentina.

Conqueror's communications problems persisted, but as long as she was stationed north-eastward of the Falklands, protecting the troop-carriers until they rendezvoused with the rest of the Task Force, she could chance making repairs on the surface. After the landings on the Falklands, everybody expected some intervention from the Argentine navy, still hugging the mainland's twelve-mile limit. On the 23rd, there was intelligence that some ships were refuelling in northern Argentina. That was the day when a diver, Petty Officer Graham Libby, volunteered to go down to free the wire which had been fouling *Conqueror*'s propeller for some days, causing noise which might have been dangerous in battle conditions. (Libby received the DSM for his exploit.) Intelligence reports indicated furious arguments between the Argentine navy and air forces, concerning lack of aggression – by the air force. The hardliner Anaya was making more trouble for his friends than for the enemy. Chilean intelligence gave a false alarm about fleet movements which never materialized, and *Conqueror* received a stream of information about the activities of the Argentine submarine *San Luis*. Neither threat materialized. Reports from Argentina said that the *San Luis* had attacked British surface vessels, but *Conqueror* received no confirmation of these claims from British sources. On 31 May intelligence revealed that Argentine surface ships were headed southward inside the 12-mile limit, and *Conqueror* headed west in the hope that one of these ships might get careless and take a short-cut outside the limit. Signals intercepted from the Argentine naval commander in the Falklands showed that he felt the British now possessed total maritime supremacy; one more Argentine ship sunk should seal their navy in port for the rest of the war. Admiral Woodward asked the Chiefs of Staff to be allowed to operate *inside* the 12-mile limit, but no permission arrived. *Conqueror* was only 20 or 30 miles off the coast by now, and spent two days patrolling at periscope depth, watching merchantmen pass by, but no fighting vessels. A Type 42 destroyer, the *Hércules*, was reported heading southward on 3 June, and on the 5th the submarine lurked outside San José Bay, hoping that the destroyer would cross it, outside the 12-mile limit. They spent the following day in the broad Gulf of San Matías, but never saw the *Hércules*.

In the afternoon of 9 June, trying to confirm the presence of units of the Argentine Task Group 79.2, the *Conqueror* entered Argentina's coastal waters and went within six miles of the mainland along the Gulf of San Matías. The crew were becoming jaded after more than two months at sea, but the visit brought no excitement, and they were a long way from the action now taking place in the Falklands, though regular reports were arriving. Radar picket patrol further south on 11–14 June picked up hardly any Argentine air activity. By now their forces in the Falklands were almost on their own, and news of the surrender reached *Conqueror* early in the morning of 15 June. That day she started for home, and was followed by a telegram next day from Rear-Admiral Woodward, wishing them bon voyage and offering congratulations on their achievement in sinking the *Belgrano*.

After a round-trip journey of over 25,000 miles, the *Conqueror* sailed up the Clyde on 3 July, flying the Jolly Roger, in accordance with service custom after sinking an enemy ship. Royal Navy ships along the Clyde had their companies lined up to greet her, and hundreds of people cheered and waved from the banks. It was a triumphant return. Commander Wreford-Brown later received the DSO for his conduct in torpedoing the *General Belgrano*. It was a proper reward from the British point of view, but a further insult as experienced by the Argentines whose national histories will portray the cruiser's sinking and the deaths of 368 of her crew as British perfidy.

More celebrations took place as the elements of the Task Force filtered home. Somehow the 255 British lives lost came to be represented as a price worth paying for the restoration of British pride and sovereignty. Somehow, too, the conflict came to be regarded as Mrs Thatcher's war. It was she who prosecuted it most fiercely. Her reasoning was stark: Britain must count again in the world. She it was, then, who was caught in the glare of the TV lights, rejoicing in victories, lamenting and wearing black when losses were suffered. And so on 26 July when Falklands veterans marched to a Service of Thanksgiving in St Paul's Cathedral few Britons were surprised that it was their Prime Minister, not the Queen of England, taking the salutes and basking in the glow of military glory. It was not the apotheosis of Margaret Thatcher but it came close to being her coronation.

PART III

8

'Many Lives Were Saved'

In Argentina, the outcome of the war brought immediate re-percussions. Galtieri lost the presidency within a week of the surrender of Port Stanley. The military government which might have survived indefinitely on the strength of regaining the Malvinas was now on borrowed time, and by November 1983 elections were to return a civilian President, Raúl Alfonsín. The Argentine people remained as convinced as they had always been that the Malvinas belonged to Argentina, but they were appalled by the blundering incompetence with which the war had been conducted.

Retired Lieutenant-General Benjamín Rattenbach was appointed by Galtieri's successor, General Reynaldo Bignone, to head a Commission for the Evaluation of the Conflict in the South Atlantic. The Commission was made up of two senior officers from each of the armed services, and Rattenbach made it clear from the beginning that they were not sitting in order either to cover up the facts or whitewash the protagonists of the Falklands war. When the Commission sent for Galtieri on 24 March 1983 the former President and Commander-in-Chief of the Argentine army complained to officials in the Congress building that a plain saloon car had collected him, when it should have been a limousine. When he walked up to the tribunal he simply held out a sheaf of papers to Rattenbach and announced that he was not prepared to answer questions. Rattenbach told him to take the papers away, and informed him that he was to answer whatever the Commission chose to ask.[1]

The Commission broke its investigations and indictments into five main fields: political, strategic, operational, economic and psychological. Some of the questions it asked were:

– Why did the Junta not obey Security Council Resolution 502 at once, by withdrawing the bulk of its troops? It could have left behind an Argentine civil administration and a small police force. Argentina would then have offered the world a brilliant dramatization of the Falklands issue and made it very difficult for the British not to negotiate seriously. The British could hardly have pushed home an attack using thousands of soldiers, sailors and airmen and 113 ships against a small police force of 500 men or so.

– Why did the Junta try both to govern the country and to run the war? That simply meant that it did both jobs badly. It should have appointed a war cabinet to run the campaign under its own overall command. As it was, the war effort showed up a disastrous lack of unity and purpose, bitter inter-service rivalries and fatal operational incompetence. After the Junta withdrew the navy, the air force simply went on fighting its own private war. It could have been decisively more effective if it had been properly coordinated with the navy in joint air-sea assaults.

– Why did General Mario Menéndez, in his short-lived command, spread his land forces around the islands in totally static defensive positions? He should have kept strong mobile reserves, able to move at once to hit any would-be landing force. The Junta was also critically at fault for not *forcing* greater mobility on Menéndez, supplying him with more helicopters, more marines (like Robacio's crack Batallón 5) and close support from more combat aircraft.

– Why did the Junta ignore the use of a psychological warfare executive? Obeying Resolution 502 by withdrawing Argentine troops would have been astute politics, but no one had prepared public opinion for it, nor did anyone stop the *triunfalismo* of the media, which totally distorted the true progress of the war.

– Why did the Junta fail more rapidly to consider, and then accept, Belaúnde's peace proposal? Galtieri had approved it, then the Junta put it aside. The sinking of the *Belgrano* had introduced an emotional factor which ought not to have prevented the Junta from prudently accepting it. Two objectives might have been achieved:

1 An end of the escalating killing war.
2 Serious negotiations with Britain on the sovereignty issue.

Coming from a Commission which had no allegiance to Galtieri, this reference to his acceptance of the Peruvian proposals must carry a certain weight. To have blamed Galtieri for rejecting them would have lost Argentina no propaganda points. The *Belgrano* would still have been sunk outside the TEZ, and in any case Britain might still have rejected Belaúnde's initiative.

The Commission named six men as mainly responsible for the Argentine defeat in the Malvinas. They were the three members of the Junta, plus General Mario Benjamín Menéndez, Economy Minister Roberto Alemann, and Costa Méndez. Costa Méndez was found culpable of a number of grave misjudgements. He had been wrong in assuming that the Argentine landings would not be viewed in Britain as a national humiliation demanding retribution. He had miscalculated the international response to the invasion. He had been too rigid in repeatedly proclaiming that 'sovereignty was not negotiable'.

The Commission saw the offensive phase of the Argentine campaign as well enough planned and executed, but once the British had shown their intention of hitting back, the Junta had proved helpless. They had prepared no strategy for a tough and professional defence. They were left unready and disorganized, with a force unfit for confrontation with a major military power. The Rattenbach Commission considered that all of the men whom it found guilty in the matter of the Malvinas should face trial, and possible execution. President Alfonsín took a risk in indicting the military establishment at the start of his term of office, but the publication of the Rattenbach Report has done a great deal to clear the air.[2] Argentina continues to claim the Malvinas, however, and the issue will not soon lapse again into the obscurity that surrounded it in the years before 1982.

If Argentina was the vanquished country, then Britain must logically be the victor, but it was difficult to stay enthusiastic for very long about the prospect of maintaining 'Fortress Falklands' there in the South Atlantic for the indefinite future, and people began to wonder just what sort of victory it was that they were supposed to have won. It was the stridency of the protestations that hinted that perhaps the claims were being overdrawn, and the first of these claims concerned sovereignty. Britain, according to Pym, was 'not in any doubt about our claim, and never had been'. According to Cecil Parkinson, a member of the War Cabinet, it was a 'rock-solid claim'. Yet as we show in Chapter 1, the British government had felt uncomfortable about its sovereignty in the Falklands ever since Gaston de Bernhardt's memorandum of 1910. The documents withdrawn from the Public Records Office when the war began were not returned when it ended. News was rigorously managed during the fighting; now it seemed that one of the principles on which the war had been fought might be shaky enough to need censoring too.

Then there were the circumstances surrounding the production of the Franks Report. Had the Falklands war truly come 'out of the blue', as Mrs Thatcher claimed, or ought the British government to have realized that Argentina really meant business in 1982? How had it become necessary at all to fight so desperate a war about a place that few Britons could even have located on a map until 1982? In the aftermath of the conflict, Mrs Thatcher reluctantly yielded 'to parliamentary demands for a full-scale investigation into the origins of the dispute and the manner in which successive governments had handled the Falklands question. On 6 July 1982, the Prime Minister announced the appointment of a Committee of Privy Councillors under the chairmanship of Lord Franks, whose task would be:

> To review the way in which the responsibilities of Government in relation to the Falklands Islands and their Dependencies were discharged in the period leading up to the Argentine invasion of the Falkland Islands on 2 April 1982, taking account of all such factors in previous years as are relevant; and to report.

The composition of the Committee was a mirror-image of British Establishment politics in the 17 years which it chose to review. (A longer historical perspective might have raised the awkward question of sovereignty, and given some weight to Argentine impatience.) Franks himself, then 78, was a classical scholar at Oxford before taking on a series of government jobs that included a four-year spell as Ambassador to the United States. Thereafter he served as Chairman of Lloyds Bank from 1954 to 1962, when he returned to Oxford as Provost of Worcester College, a post he held until 1976. He had been created a Life Peer in 1962 and sat as a Liberal in the House of Lords.

Each of Franks's colleagues were appointed to represent the

interests and actions of previous administrators. Lord Watkinson, then 73, was Defence Minister in Harold Macmillan's government. His concern was to represent the views not only of Macmillan but also of Lord Home who, as Sir Alec Douglas-Home, was Prime Minister for a year in 1963–4. This was at a time when Argentina began to actively campaign for the recovery of the Falklands.

Lord Barber, then 62, was Chancellor of the Exchequer from 1970 to 1974. His role was to safeguard the interests of Edward Heath, his former Prime Minister. After leaving politics in the mid-1970s he joined the Standard Chartered Bank as Chairman. Sir Harold Wilson's man was the 69-year-old Lord Lever, a wealthy financier who held various Cabinet posts in two Labour administrations. Wilson's successor as Prime Minister, James Callaghan, had Merlyn Rees, then 62, as his representative. Rees was the second Labour member of the group, a former Cabinet minister and the only Committee member still active in politics. The sixth Privy Councillor, 61-year-old Sir Patrick Nairne, was a retired civil servant who had become Master of St Catherine's College, Oxford. His unwritten brief was to secure the interests of fellow civil servants in the Defence Ministry, the Foreign and Commonwealth Office and other government departments involved.

The credentials of the Committee members were impeccable ones for the task of examining and pronouncing upon the conduct of past and present colleagues who had shared values and a shared commitment to preserve common political privileges and traditions. The Establishment was examining itself. This was no Rattenbach Commission, with a lost war to explain. The victors were going to be magnanimous, at any rate with themselves.

The main conclusion of the Franks Report was that: 'We would not be justified in attaching any criticism or blame to the present Government for the Argentine Junta's decision to commit its act of unprovoked aggression in the invasion of the Falkland Islands *on 2 April 1982*.'[3] The effect is to exonerate British ministers for their natural failure to predict the precise date of the invasion. And since any government must be credited with free will, the rest of the conclusion conveys the truism that the decision to invade was the Junta's, and no one else's.

Yet a careful reading of the full report provides evidence of a rising tide of Argentine frustration with the British failure to implement the recommendations of Resolution 2065. It also shows how many British actions in the years before the invasion could be seen as signals of declining British interest in the Falklands – the Report does point out that the British never really considered how the Argentines might interpret their behaviour. Lastly, the Report shows how during the 30-month period leading up to the invasion a plethora of warnings reached 10 Downing Street which indicated that some sort of confrontation, most likely military, must be expected some time in 1982 – the relevant paragraphs are numbers 75, 77, 86, 88, 90–3, 94–5, 96, 97, 100, 129 and 131, 130 and 132, 138–40, 158 and 159, 169, 182, 187–92, 193–251. Yet in the year before the invasion, from January 1981 until 25 March 1982, the British Cabinet never once discussed the Falklands.

Irrespective of its narrow conclusion, the Franks Report shows beyond question that in the matter of the Falklands successive British governments, but particularly the latest, Mrs Thatcher's, had turned a deaf ear to Argentina's requests and had developed something akin to a paralysis of the will in anything to do with the Falklands. It was an insoluble problem which had always gone away because Britain was the stronger power and could not be *made* to listen. Argentina need not be taken seriously. The Franks Report does not go into the matter of the de facto alliance between Argentina and Britain in supporting US policy in Central America, but the relationship tended to confirm the British view that the Argentines could never be considered as a threat to the British. There is a kind of cultural failure working here: the Latins chattering away and getting quite excited, but all hot air really; the British silent and immobile, but carrying a big stick all the same.

The Franks Report is useful because it shows the continuity of British attitudes right into the Falklands war. A government that felt no need to explain itself, and had very little interest in understanding others, confronts a country – an entire continent – of garrulous foreigners and just cannot take them seriously. It gets on with what it wants to do, and if these people are unable to understand its intentions it lets them suffer the consequences. A similar failure of communications takes place even within the government. Instructions go out from the centre, but nothing comes back to modify them. Before the war, the Cabinet was ignoring both Argentina's signals and the reports and warnings of its own officials; after the war began it declined proposals submitted by Mr Haig and President Belaúnde and refused to be diverted from retrieving British property and from salving the nation's wounded pride.

According both to Mrs Thatcher and Mr Pym, all the time that the Belaúnde initiative was going forward, there was no discussion, no communication by phone or by any other means between Lima and London, or between Lima and London via Washington, or between Washington and London. These two and Cranley Onslow, Minister of State for the Foreign Office, have stated that London never knew what Belaúnde's peace proposal was until 23.15 BST on the night of Sunday 2 May, more than three hours after the *Belgrano* was torpedoed.

Pym's assessment of the proposal is that:

> What Mr Haig outlined to me was, at best, a promising basis for future work. If the Peruvians had prepared a treaty ready for signature on the evening of May 2 they certainly gave us no indication of this in Lima or in London.[4]

Furthermore, it seemed to Pym that this new proposal was not very different from the earlier plan that Argentina had not accepted. Why would the Junta now agree to it? Pym appears to be prejudging the issue here in much the same way as his colleague, Mr Nott, had prejudged the very same issue – the chances of successful negotiations – a month before. It makes no difference that Haig is urging the proposal (as Henderson asserts), or that the British raids on the Falklands may have concentrated Galtieri's mind just as Pym himself had been advising in his press conference the night before. The Foreign Secretary did not contact London till hours later, although he knew how urgent the situation had become. He told the editor of the *Daily Mirror* that he would of course have been ready to discuss Belaúnde's ideas with his colleagues when he got back to London – in two days' time.

Pym acted as if he required a formal treaty to sign, and took the view that there was little substance to the Haig-Belaúnde proposals. Whatever the Peruvians had to say could wait for days – days, at a time when every new hour could see more men killed. For Pym, all that seemed secondary to the major objective:

I flew to Washington on the evening of May 1, not . . . for last-minute talks on the Falklands, but to review with Mr Haig the new situation following Argentina's rejection of Mr Haig's own negotiating efforts and the consequent decision by the US to come down clearly on Britain's side.

The contrast with the mood of Belaúnde in all the conversations we have quoted is perfectly clear. One man is looking for peace, and as fast as humanly possible. The other man is concentrating on military assistance, presumably because he sees little in the revised peace proposals that the Argentines had found acceptable. Additionally Pym, like his Cabinet colleagues, was acutely aware of the vulnerability of the British Task Force. That seemed to be what Haig noticed when he purportedly described Pym to Belaúnde as 'a man who has no interest in peace but simply in obtaining greater facilities to continue the war'.

Yet the alleged absence of communications on that day remains widespread. The Peruvian Prime Minister, Manuel Ulloa, claimed he rang Haig in the morning while Pym was with him, and begged for a 24-hour or even a 48-hour truce. Henderson maintained that he never got to hear of it.[5] Nothing reached London from the British Embassies either in Washington or Lima about any of the intense diplomatic activity which went on over the weekend of 1–2 May, according to Mrs Thatcher's government. So the British account says, and although diplomats both in Peru and the US have told these writers that they are convinced there was close and regular contact with the Foreign Office from both embassies, the British still stand by their story.

Most of the British accounts of the reasons behind the sinking of the Belgrano are flawed or contradictory. This is what Rear-Admiral Woodward says:

Early on the morning of 2 May, all the indications were that 25 de Mayo, the Argentine carrier, and a group of escorts, had slipped past my forward SSN barrier to the north, while the cruiser General Belgrano and her escorts were attempting to complete the pincer movement from the south, still outside the Total Exclusion Zone. But Belgrano still had Conqueror on the trail. My fear was that Belgrano would lose the SSN as she ran over the shallow water of the Burdwood Bank, and that my forward SSN barrier would be evaded down there too. I therefore sought, for the first and only time throughout the campaign, a major change in the Rules of Engagement to enable *Conqueror* to attack *Belgrano* outside the exclusion zone. This was achieved in remarkably short order, reputedly in the entrance porch at Chequers, with the result that a successful attack was completed. That the sinking of the *Belgrano* would have such a dramatic effect on those surface forces could not be foreseen but the submarines did effectively bottle up the Argentine surface fleet for the rest of the war.[6]

Lord Lewin said in a radio interview on 'The World This Weekend':

What confuses people is that they think nothing could be attacked unless it was in the exclusion zone. We warned the Argentines on April 23 that if we met their warships or aircraft they would be considered hostile. So both sides were in no doubt about what would happen if we met up on the high seas.[7]

Taking these accounts point by point:

1 The *25 de Mayo* and her escorts had been called home the previous night at 20.07 (Lombardo said just past midnight) by an order confirmed at 01.19 on 2 May. British interception and decoding were penetrating almost all enemy traffic, but even if they had missed all the signals these orders generated, the carrier was nevertheless homeward-bound.

2 *Belgrano* and her escorts were heading homeward too, and *Conqueror* had been following them up and down for long enough to know that they were patrolling outside the TEZ.

3 The Burdwood Bank at its shallowest leaves room and to spare for a nuclear submarine, especially when following a target at periscope depth, as *Conqueror* would have had to do in any case, if *Belgrano* had turned north.

4 Woodward did in fact seek a second change in the Rules of Engagement, to attack inside the Argentine 12-mile limit. The request was refused.

5 The warning of 23 April had mentioned ships or aircraft which 'could amount to a threat to the task force'. If this 'possible' threat really meant something merely imaginable sooner or later, then *Conqueror* could have opened fire the

previous day, when the cruiser and her escorts were refuelling. In any case, why change the Rules of Engagement if
they already permitted unprovoked attacks? (Henderson:
'You have a tenable point there.')[8] And why bother to have a
TEZ at all, as Captain Bonzo asked, if you were going to
open fire no matter where the target was?

Other official accounts claimed that the *Belgrano* had actually
been closing on the Task Force (false), heading towards the TEZ
(false), had been heavily armed (false), and had been sunk not
long after sighting (false).

The fact that ministers were compelled at various times to
amend their explanations as new evidence surfaced raised doubts
not only about the accuracy of Woodward's version but about
the ambiguities in the British announcements about conditions
for attacking enemy shipping, and what would constitute a
threat. Again it seemed that the British were not bothering about
reaching any understanding with the Argentines. If they got hold
of the wrong end of the stick, it was their hard luck. Henderson
referred to their 'endemic unawareness'.

Lord Lewin's approach was quite straightforward. He told
television interviewers that he would have recommended attacking the cruiser even if he had known it was heading for home.
'She was still at sea, she was still a warship, and she was still
capable of attacking our forces,' he said.[9]

This pragmatic reasoning of Lewin's would not have surprised
his fellow-admiral, Horacio Zaratiegui, commander of the
Southern Naval Region during the Falklands conflict. He gradu-
ated from the Royal Naval Staff Course in Britain in 1971, the
only Argentine admiral with that qualification on active service.
Anaya, with typical incompetence, gave him no active role in the
fight against the British, and asked him for no advice. Zaratiegui
achieved fame and a year's arrest when on 20 September 1982 he
circulated a document in which he rejected the authority of the
naval C-in-C and fiercely criticized both Admiral Anaya and his
successor, Admiral Rubén Franco.

Interviewed in his suite at the Naval Dockyards' Detention
Centre in Buenos Aires, where treatment of senior officers is not
too harsh, Zaratiegui advanced his own theory on why Mrs
Thatcher had authorized the sinking of the *Belgrano*, whatever
the ship's course and location. 'The British were looking for a

way to give us a really low blow,' he suggested, 'as they have done so often in history – trying to blunt our aggressiveness for fighting at sea. When they make war they always take out their monocle first. This was a simple action which could help save many British casualties, if by it the British could lock up our fleet. Sinking the *Belgrano* had other advantages. It was the first resounding victory for the British in the Malvinas area. It dealt a real psychological blow to Argentine public opinion. It sent a clear message about the determination of the British to carry the conflict through to its ultimate consequences. It was also a deliberate, though indirect, revelation of the importance of satellite information at the Royal Navy's disposal and it was designed to create a sense of impotence in our fleet.'[10]

If Zaratiegui is right, then Mrs Thatcher might just as well have announced a South Atlantic Exclusion Zone and had done with it. That would have advertised British intentions from the beginning, and helped to further concentrate the mind of Argentina on the severe predicament the country faced. She never made that announcement, any more than she phoned Galtieri before the invasion of the Falklands, or (officially) asked Pym early on 2 May whether there was news of any softening in the Argentine attitude. Had she done so while he and Haig were in conversation, he might have had to answer Yes. After all, only two days before the Argentines had been 'intransigent' and Haig had tilted; now Haig was back in negotiation and Belaúnde had Galtieri taking peace proposals to the Military Committee.

As it was, the many changing versions of the *Belgrano*'s course and intentions, and the reasons for sinking her, drew the attention of the Labour MP Tam Dalyell. From the start of the British–Argentine crisis Dalyell had argued against the need for armed forces in settling the dispute. In that stance he found himself at odds not only with the government but also with majority opinion in the Parliamentary Labour Party, to the point of being dismissed as a member of the Shadow Cabinet. He charged that Mrs Thatcher's leadership would have been at risk if she had compromised with the Junta and the Task Force had been left to straggle home without a military victory. The obvious embarrassment of the government roused the suspicions of Dalyell, a tenacious pursuer with a nose for inconsistencies. He went so far as to accuse the Prime Minister of 'coldly and deliberately [giving] the order to sink the Argentine cruiser,

General Belgrano, in the knowledge that an honourable peace was on offer and in the expectation that HMS *Conqueror*'s torpedoes would scupper the Peruvian peace plan then under way'.[11] Mrs Thatcher scorned the charges.

Pym in the BBC's Newsnight programme on 2 June 1983 denied any link between the two events:

> All that happened that day was that there was the beginnings of an outline of a possible future basis for negotiations which Mr Haig outlined to me, but that is all that it was, as I made clear in that article [in the *Daily Mirror* of 20 May]. There was no connection between the two things, and it's quite wrong to suppose that there is.

Haig was cautious when interviewed. 'Don't forget, the issues were being hastily handled that weekend,' he pointed out. 'There was no way of assessing the prospects of achieving an immediate Argentine consensus on the proposal. We found it difficult to know if Galtieri's acceptance would have been accepted by the whole Junta.' Recalling that previous agreements with Galtieri had been frustrated by subsequent vetoes, sometimes by a single member, Haig recalled: 'We had been hopeful that a basis for settlement would emerge but there was no confirmed agreement, no final approval by the Junta as such. Our communications with London did not suggest that we were on the verge of a breakthrough.' Having protected Mr Pym, and contradicted the account he gave to Belaúnde in the process, Haig could not be less chivalrous to Mrs Thatcher. Asked if he believed that she had sunk the Peruvian peace proposals deliberately, he said: 'I would have to know a lot more about the timing of the orders, but I would say now those suggestions amounted to a bum rap.'[12]

There was no point in asking Haig whether the proposals might not have been simply immaterial to the British Prime Minister – hence her failure to inquire whether there was anything hopeful happening across the Atlantic, and Pym's casual manner when Haig raised the possibility. Haig's whole mediating function had been bound up with representing Mrs Thatcher in as creditable a light as possible, and that meant that he could not admit the existence of a British intransigence. It was partly as a result of protecting British interests that he had lost his job as US Secretary of State, sacrificed to the restoration of US–Latin

American relations. It would be pointless to tilt back again so late in the game, and utterly in conflict with Haig's whole career, in which loyalty – even to a President like Richard Nixon – once given, has stayed given.

British MPs pressing to learn more about the case for sinking the *Belgrano* and the progress of diplomacy that weekend faced an unyielding Mrs Thatcher. Their scope to address parliamentary questions to members of her War Cabinet was quickly reduced – as Dalyell noted publicly – by retaining in exposed ministerial office only one of its four elected members. William Whitelaw, formerly Deputy Prime Minister, was elevated to the peerage after the General Election of 9 June 1983. John Nott, Defence Minister, quit politics in December 1982 and was knighted. Following the June 1983 election, Francis Pym found himself deprived of the office of Foreign Secretary; he refused the Prime Minister's proposal that he should become Speaker of the House of Commons – and so for ever gagged – and was dropped. Only Cecil Parkinson, Chairman of the Conservative Party and reputedly one of the hawks in the War Cabinet, remained in office, but as Trade and Industry Secretary he could not take questions on the Falklands, and in October 1983 he was to remove himself permanently from Cabinet circles.

In delving for the whole truth about the *Belgrano*, MPs critical of the government's record built up a long series of questions which needed answering. John Morris, a member of the Callaghan Labour Cabinet and former Defence Minister, crystallized their anxieties and suspicions when the newly elected House of Commons assembled in mid-1983. He pinpointed more than a dozen issues in need of clarification:[13]

– Why did John Nott tell the Commons that the *Belgrano* 'was close to the total exclusion zone and was closing on elements of our task force, which was only a few hours away'?[14] Later evidence showed that she was 'on a course away from the islands and our ships – on which part of the Task Force was she closing?'

– When was the *Belgrano* sighted? Was it, as the incumbent Chief of the Defence Staff, Sir Terence Lewin, claimed, only a few hours before the attack on 2 May? Or was it earlier that day, as the government White Paper (Cmnd. 8758) first and Fleet Commander Sir John Fieldhouse later claimed? Or was it, as Commander Wreford-Brown announced, more than 30 hours before she was torpedoed?

– Why did John Nott tell the House of Commons that 'the actual decision to launch a torpedo was clearly one taken by the submarine commander'?[15] Was that correct or did the War Cabinet authorize the launching?

– Who was concerned that the *Conqueror* might lose the *Belgrano* as she ran over the Burdwood Bank shallows as the Commons was told on 29 November 1982? How could this concern have been relevant given the fact that the *Conqueror* could easily have navigated through those shallows?

– Was there any evidence to suggest that the *Belgrano* might suddenly head for the Burdwood Bank, remembering that she was sunk 45 miles to the south-west and on a course pointing homewards?

– In advance of the decision to attack *Belgrano* had anyone in London been informed that an Argentine decision on withdrawal was pending? Or that the Argentine fleet had been ordered home? When did details of these developments reach British ministers?

– Just how much of the Peruvian–American peace proposals was known to Pym? Did Britain's Ambassador to Peru communicate at all with Pym, or with the Foreign Office in London, about those peace proposals? Was he aware that the Peruvians had prepared a peace document which he and the Argentine Ambassador might possibly have been asked to sign on the night of Sunday, 2 May?

– Did Haig speak, or in any way communicate, with Mrs Thatcher on 1 or 2 May?

– When Mrs Thatcher insisted that news of the Peruvian plan reached London only after the attack on the *Belgrano*, did she mean that London knew nothing whatsoever of developments in Lima?

– Mrs Thatcher referred to the Peruvian proposals as 'a sketchy outline' while Haig thought 'we had a formulation that provided hope that a settlement could be reached'. How could those two statements be squared?

– What reasons were there for the Prime Minister's assertion that major Task Force ships would have been at risk if the *Belgrano* had been spared? Was it not a fact that she was at least nine but probably 14 hours away from those ships, and anyway heading homewards?

– If as suggested by Wreford-Brown the *Belgrano* was spotted early on 1 May sailing *towards* the Task Force, why were orders not issued to sink her there and then instead of waiting over 30 hours, when she was less of a threat?

– Were there any intercepts of Argentine High Command signals ordering all fleet units home on the night of 1 May? If so, were those intercepts decoded successfully?

– What reasons were there for Pym to say on 1 May in Washington that 'no further military action is envisaged at the moment, except to keep the exclusion zone secure'? Had the Foreign Secretary been consulted in any way, and specifically on whether the *Belgrano* should be attacked? Were not his views of paramount importance? Was he informed that the cruiser was being trailed?

– Finally, if the British warning of 23 April was valid, that all ships risked being attacked, even outside the exclusion zone, why was a change in the Rules of Engagement necessary?

These questions of Morris's have remained officially un-answered. Our own researches answer some of them directly, and strongly suggest a coherent interpretation of many of the others. Considering the effect of the Falklands war both at home and abroad; the continuing state of war in the South Atlantic; the enormous financial and strategic burden that the Falklands now represent; and, most of all, the lives which have been lost, both Argentine and British, in producing a society which cannot now survive without far more than its own numbers in soldiers, sailors and airmen, Great Britain badly needs to answer as many of those questions as possible, and some others which the rules of the House made it impossible for Morris to ask.

9

Grounds for Inquiry

The British government's counter-invasion of the Falkland Islands was never properly examined in Parliament because neither the Labour party nor the Liberals nor the new-born SDP opposed it. However, in their speeches at the time and since, British ministers put forward three main principles which were at stake and had to be upheld. Britain had the right and duty to defend the Falklands because they were sovereign British territory; the wishes of the islanders in deciding their own future were paramount – they had the right of self-determination; and finally, Britain was fighting on the side of law and order – the occupation could not be allowed to succeed because Argentina's landing constituted an act of international aggression which had to be resisted for the sake of a stable world.

About the first principle, sovereignty, Mrs Thatcher had 'absolutely no doubt' in the debate of 3 April 1982, although her faith was not shared by the Foreign Office, as we have seen, and doubt had been endemic there for more than 70 years. Nor was it shared by the United Nations, whose Resolution 2065 of 16 December 1965 accepted that the Islands' sovereignty was in dispute. For a century neither Britain nor Argentina had been ready to go to international arbitration, and Britain's own negotiations with Argentina had appeared to accept that the question was open. The British were angry when US Ambassador to the UN Jeane Kirkpatrick pointed out that if the islands really did belong to Argentina, then they were not being 'invaded' at all, but as she saw things it was a fair account of the unresolved legal situation.

Because of its publicly inadmissible misgivings about the sovereignty principle, the British government had for half a century been shifting its case towards the unrelated principle of self-determination. Because it is obviously not feasible simply to deposit enough of one's citizens upon some disputed piece of land to manufacture a majority, and then to take a moral stand on the wishes of those deposited, the notion of prescription was introduced. The Islanders' wishes must be respected because they had been in continuous occupation for so long. Yet Argentina might be forgiven if it did not take the British government's respect for self-determination with the seriousness that the principle seemed to demand. There had been a number of episodes which showed the British ready to override it.

In the case of Banaba, the 3,000 inhabitants of that Pacific island were resettled against their will in Fiji in 1948, to make way for the profitable mining operations of the British Phosphate Commission. The Banabans sued for compensation in a British court, and were awarded £3 each in 1976. Public pressure forced the then Foreign Secretary, Dr David Owen, to make them an ex gratia award of £6.5 million – about one tenth of the value of the phosphates exported, and the equivalent of £200 to each islander for every year of exile. They had not wished to go, and had not wished to see their home made almost uninhabitable by mining operations after their eviction.[1]

In the case of Diego García, a British island dependency 1,000 miles south-south-east of the Indian subcontinent, and politically part of the Mauritius group, the US wanted to integrate the island into its global nuclear defences. In the late 1960s, with Conservative support, the Labour government of Harold Wilson removed the 1,400 Diego Garcians, leased their island to the United States, and shipped them upwards of 1,000 miles away, to Mauritius. In 1982, the Diego Garcians were awarded £4 million in compensation, but are unable to go home. It cost the UK government about £2,200 apiece to override their wishes in perpetuity.

Philanthropy is not the business of governments, however, and Britain is not alone in its treatment of the inhabitants of small islands. The US did not consult the people of Bikini atoll before holding H-bomb tests there in 1946–58 (having first evacuated the islanders). The people of Kwajalein, in the Marshall Islands, have had their lives reluctantly transformed by the bases the US established there after the Second World War. The nonsense of self-determination as an absolute principle would not need insisting on, had it not been harped upon so often by British spokesmen. Thus Sir Nicholas Henderson has stated that what was at issue in the Falklands was 'whether, in the American hemisphere, differences were going to be settled by force, and whether the principle of self-determination, which the United States had pioneered, was going to be overthrown'.[2] In none of the cases discussed above were the islands' inhabitants white.

One of the difficulties about self-determination as a principle is to know which group to apply it to. It has been pointed out by Anthony Barnett that it was this same principle to which Adolf Hitler appealed in 1938 when he backed the wishes of the two million ethnic Germans living in the Sudetenland, disputed territory owned by Czechoslovakia. They asked to be affiliated to Germany, and the British and French governments jeopardized the existence of Czechoslovakia and the peace of Europe by agreeing to let Germany take over. As Barnett remarks: 'It is clear today that whatever local, community self-government the Sudeten Germans should have been allowed, they should not have been granted "self-determination" when this meant their affiliating to the sovereignty of their "kith and kin".'[3] That is, principle has to be modified both by the realities of geo-political practice, and by rights and other principles which may be in conflict.

The issue is posed in a particularly uncomfortable way, from the British point of view, by the case of Hong Kong, whose five million inhabitants are bound to fall under Chinese control again by 1997, when the New Territories' 99-year lease runs out and they revert to China. On 17 November 1983, the Liberal leader, David Steel, asked in the House of Commons: 'Would the wishes of the people of Hong Kong be paramount to a greater or lesser degree than those of the Falkland Islands?' (It is felt by the British that most of the five million would rather stay independent, and failing that, that they might wish to remove themselves to their parent country, which is Britain.) Mrs Thatcher's answer was concise: Steel was missing 'one very fundamental point. The Falkland Islands is freehold; Hong Kong is leasehold.' Here the wheel comes full circle. Self-determination is not paramount (or the British might have to fight the mainland Chinese); it is ownership – sovereignty – which is paramount. Yet this is the very point at issue, the one which Britain is unready to submit to arbitration. It nevertheless takes precedence over the islanders' wishes, no ruling principle in the view of the British Prime Minister.

Resisting aggression, supporting the rule of law, the most noble of the three asserted principles, is also the least observed by most of the world's governments, including the British. A past British government did not resist when Turkish invaders seized one third of Cyprus in 1974, although Britain was treaty-bound to intervene in defence of the constitution and territorial integrity of that Commonwealth republic. No Task Force defended the black majority in Rhodesia when Ian Smith took over the country in 1965. It is estimated that 200,000 men, women and children died, mainly of starvation, during the chaos that followed the Indonesian takeover of East Timor in 1976. Either of the former two countries would have been easier to reach than the Falkland Islands. East Timor was a genocidal disaster next to which the Argentine invasion of the Falklands cannot decently be put at all. No government intervened because no vital interests were at stake in any of these instances. The rule of law was a lofty slogan, but it did not account for the role of the British in the Falklands conflict of 2 April–14 June 1982.

The House of Commons debate of 3 April exemplified a number of the energies which did drive the Task Force down to San Carlos, Goose Green, Fitzroy, Mount Longdon, and to the location of 55 degrees 27 minutes south, 61 degrees 25 minutes west. The Commons set up a roar of shame, fury, indignation and wounded amour-propre that woke the sleeping Drake in the British right out of his hammock. Mr Powell told Mrs Thatcher that the time had come for her to show her metal, and she nodded in agreement. The Senior Service, smarting under the government's cuts, took up the same challenge and threw in its fate with Mrs Thatcher's.

Even before the advent of the Falklands crisis, the Prime Minister's position had been under severe attack. Her party had occupied a galling third place in the public opinion polls since the previous summer. At that rate, according to Simon Jenkins, 'it is probable that pressure from within and outside the government would by late summer have driven Mrs Thatcher into a major reflationary package or into resignation'.[4] One of the principles that may have influenced her was sheer self-preservation. Her party, notoriously, does not love losers.

Of the options which faced her, one must be dismissed at once. She might, with sadness and cutting invective, have denounced the impertinence of Argentina in stealing a piece of British territory, but at the same time have had to confess that the risk of attempting repossession was far too high. That could have worked if the invasion had really come out of the blue, as she later claimed. But her government had not so much as discussed the stream of warnings which had reached it; she had sent her own envoy, Cecil Parkinson, to shake hands with Galtieri's fore-runners; she had sent no warnings to the Junta, and made no protective moves, until it was far too late. Argentina might have stolen the islands, but it was the British who had left the door open. Just to have let them go would have brought Mrs Thatcher instant oblivion, and she felt she had a role to play – a role, furthermore, which happened to involve a vision of national greatness compounded of inflexible will, embattled courage and military clout.

With hardly a voice raised against the second option, there was more to be said for it than the survival of Mrs Thatcher as Prime Minister. Britain's annual military expenditure is huge, predi-cated as it is on opposing the USSR. If the British could not tackle even a country with half their population and a vastly inferior industrial and technological base, their entire defence posture was in doubt. The money would seem to be buying no security. The government had been gambling on a change of alignment in British politics, a rightward move that would break the approxi-mate consensus of the 1950s and 1960s. This new Conservative militancy could be catalysed into a real national change if it was seen as a necessary toughness, a Churchillian belligerence. Con-servative conferences have always flown the Union Jack as if it were their party's.

But in between the dispatch of the Task Force and its arrival came an interval which needed to be filled. As Sir Nicholas Henderson explained, it was now up to the diplomats to occupy the vacuum. With the help of Alexander Haig, Britain gained the backing, first tacit then explicit, of the one country which it really needed in order to pull off its Falklands gamble. Britain presented itself as the injured party – though injured in its sovereignty only to the extent that Argentina had been injured for the past 150 years. It also portrayed Argentina as the intransigent challenger in the mediations organized by Haig, who saw that Mrs Thatcher was bent on total victory, and who knew his country would find it easier to mend its fences with the Latin Americans after an Argentine defeat than to lose its mainstay in Western Europe after a British one.

One instance of the effectiveness of British diplomacy was shown by the myth of Argentine time-wasting. It was the British, not the Argentines, who needed to waste time. They could bring no pressure to bear until the Task Force arrived, but if they could keep negotiations in play and the Junta guessing, then they might be able to reach the battle area before the Argentines were quite sure that battle was the order of the day. That was how things turned out in fact. The Super Etendards did not sally out to attack the British fleet before it could fire a shot, nor did the Argentine air force send the waves of Skyhawks and Daggers, because the Junta was unsure. It had no plans for a real occupation, and had not prepared to resist a counter-invasion. Yet Henderson writes of the period in mid-April 1982, before the Task Force was much past Ascension, that 'the Argentines may well have been spinning out negotiations to gain time'.[5]

Our own investigations show a different pattern. Haig stood pat on the British provisos – withdrawal, British administration, the paramount wishes of the Falklanders. The Argentines kept trying to draw the British out – though not themselves prepared to make vital concessions either – hoping perhaps for some face-saving formula, or perhaps that the British would not have the stomach for a war, as Anaya is said to have believed. However there is no doubt that they were genuinely flabbergasted when Haig performed his 'tilt'. Although they had been warned that their mediator's other hat was actually a bowler, they were manoeuvred, with the help of their own wishful thinking, into believing that things would stop short of bloodshed.

Haig's role is crucial here, and has to be seen in the light of Galtieri's experience of the United States. Argentina had been helping them in Central America, where President Reagan was expressing loud alarm about the communist menace. Galtieri's own predecessors had taken the same short way with the communist menace, and any other kind of dissidence, that the US seemed prepared to countenance in El Salvador and Guatemala. The Argentina Junta felt that it was in good odour. Before taking over the Presidency, Galtieri had been the US favourite for the job. During official visits in September and November 1981 he had been accorded the most cordial receptions. Defence Secretary Caspar Weinberger, for instance, referred to him as a 'magnificent person'; the former National Security Adviser, Richard Allen, dubbed him 'an impressive general'.

Sir Nicholas Henderson inclines to the view that the influence of the 'pro-Latinos' – he means people like Thomas Enders and Jeane Kirkpatrick, but perhaps also the section of the Pentagon represented by General Walters, with eyes on a less deferential Panama, and a safe route round Cape Horn – 'may well have encouraged the Argentines in their intransigence, just as it may have emboldened them to take their impetuous decision to invade'.[6] Argentine sources confirm that the Junta felt, mistakenly or not, that it could rely on benevolent neutrality from the US, and perhaps something more. For it is very hard to believe that what British intelligence knew for certain only on 31 March had been a mystery to the Americans till then. Latin America has been under the American umbrella ever since the enunciation of the Monroe Doctrine in 1823. Although the American role in destabilizing Allende's Chile drew unwelcome attention to the CIA's activities there, in Argentina things had run smoothly enough since the latest series of Juntas, starting with General Videla. After the Falklands war began, US intelligence had channels all the way to the ruling Military Committee. These cannot have been established overnight. It is not far-fetched to suppose that at least a part of the American government may have hoped to see its ambitions for a new strategic air and naval base fulfilled by a fast Argentine success, and so kept quiet about what it knew.

The Argentines carried over a residual feeling that the US could not drop them flat, right up to 30 April, when Haig tilted and the British Total Exclusion Zone came into effect. Haig, their old ally's consigliero, had led them up an alley and then run for it. The next day the British were bombing Stanley airstrip, Harriers were strafing Argentine troops, and ships were bombarding their shore defences. Francis Pym said that the intention was to concentrate the minds of the Junta, and that is what happened. The Argentines gave orders to withdraw their entire fleet to its bases, and an overwhelming majority of the country's generals informed Galtieri, in a state of near-panic, that they did not want open war. Galtieri knew only too well that he had made no plans for such a war, but he was on the tiger's back. Like Mrs Thatcher, a defeat would finish him. He was puzzled by the mess he had got himself into, and welcomed the helping hand of President Belaúnde, whose phone call found him still awake in the Casa Rosada, truculent but anxious.

Belaúnde's role is transparent. He was desperate to arrange a peace. He saw as well as Haig did that the British must win an all-out war, but he did not see what Haig had known for some time, that is that the US could not afford to offend the British Prime Minister, and that she for her part viewed anything short of complete British victory as a personal defeat. This view had impressed itself powerfully on Francis Pym and Henderson alike, and each of them reveals it in the same way. In writing about the Belaúnde proposal, Henderson remarks that it was not very different from Haig's own scheme (the Memorandum of Agreement of 27 April) 'which had just been totally rejected by Argentina'. As we make clear (see pp. 71–2, and Appendix 3B), Costa Méndez had by no means 'totally rejected' the US démarche, but for the British, anything short of their own terms – as represented here by Haig – was so much beneath consideration that it might as well be a rejection. This state of mind is even more strikingly expressed by Pym, when in his letter to the *Daily Mirror* of 20 May 1983 he declares: 'If the Peruvians had prepared a treaty ready for signature on the evening of May 2 they certainly gave us no indication . . .' Apparently if the Peruvian proposals were not so precisely formulated – and so totally acceptable to the British – as merely to need a signature, then even though they paralleled the Haig Memorandum which the British had been ready to accept less than a week before, they need not be taken seriously.

So although Pym spoke of 'concentrating the minds' of the Junta, and although Henderson mentioned the 'high pitch of drama' after the British attacks on the Falklands throughout Saturday, 1 May, neither of them saw an Argentinian readiness to negotiate, even when backed by Haig, and pressed upon Galtieri by his ally, Belaúnde, as proof enough of the requisite concentration.

Unfortunately Haig does not seem to have retained his former

employer's procedures, and we know practically nothing of
what went on between him and the British Foreign Minister on
the morning of 2 May, after the Cabinet had decided to sink the
Belgrano, but before the order had been carried out. All that
Henderson could say about his own former chief and the Peruvian proposals was: 'It's certainly true Haig commended them
strongly to Pym in a telephone conversation before Pym left for
New York. If there was any detailed discussion of them, or if
Galtieri's acceptance of them in principle was conveyed to Pym
during his two-hour tête-à-tête with Haig, I certainly was not
told. Ask Pym.'[7]

Mr Pym has revealed few details, except to insist that he was
not visiting Haig for last-minute peace talks. Why not? If Belaúnde's version was correct Haig dropped his guard in telling
the Peruvian President that Pym showed 'no interest in peace but
simply in obtaining greater facilities to continue the war'. Later,
and more diplomatically, he would only say what he must also
have said to Pym, namely that there was 'no confirmed agreement, no final approval by the Junta as such'. Since the Junta as
such was not due to meet until later that evening, Pym could
hardly take their refusal for granted. But we have reached the
point where the official British version insists that the Argentines
were playing for time – even though the Task Force had only just
reached the TEZ, and could afford to spend, say, three days after
its introductory assault, before deciding that the Junta was not
paying attention.[8]

There must also be a questionmark over Haig's own function
during his morning meeting with Pym. Prime Minister Manuel
Ulloa of Peru claimed to have phoned Haig asking for a one- or
two-day truce between Britain and Argentina, while the meeting
was in progress. Henderson was not aware of any such request,
and said that it had never come up during any of his extensive and
frequent talks with Haig and Pym.[9] Whether Pym did not hear,
or Haig chose not to pass on a request which stood no chance of
acceptance, it is not possible to say. If Ulloa's own memory is at
fault, it nevertheless coincides with Belaúnde's mention to Galtieri of a 'tacit agreement', words using during an urgent conversation which can hardly be seen as a charade staged in aid of an
Argentine disinformation campaign timed to begin after the
defeat they had not yet suffered. Pym would not need to tell
Henderson anything about the government's secret war aims,

and would see no point in passing on to Henderson news which was not going to make any difference to the programme for achieving them.

What may safely be said about the whole *Belgrano* weekend is that no single British official seemed actively to be looking for peace following the lesson supposed to have been inflicted on the Junta on Saturday 1 May. The imperturbable Pym, sitting with Haig while he talked to Belaúnde, and making no commitment for or against whatever Haig was conveying, represents the whole of the UK's official diplomatic effort. Mrs Thatcher had a contact with Lima in the person of Lord Thomas, a fluent Spanish speaker and born-again Conservative, but Thomas has refused to be interviewed on the subject of his role in Falklands diplomacy.[10]

A final clue from Henderson, who recalls how: 'To me in private Pym spoke to me about the very tough mood at home'. In his view:

> Even if . . . British ministers had been told that discussions had been going on between Washington, Lima and Buenos Aires . . . I do not think that they would on that account have refrained from a decision they thought necessary for the security of British forces . . . It was widely thought that, if negotiations were going to lead to anything, this would only be as a result not of conciliatory noises but of direct and heavy military pressure.[11]

He can hardly come closer to saying that he believes that the only word on the British agenda was War, and that any other noises were likely to be ignored. As for British forces, they were not at risk from the *Belgrano*, chugging homeward at less than 13 knots, and trailed by a submarine which could catch and sink her wherever she went.

Lord Lewin had left Chequers with his orders about 13.00 BST (08.00 Washington). 'Here was an opportunity to knock off a major unit of the Argentine fleet; and that was enough for him, despite his acknowledgement on the Panorama programme of 16 April 1984 that the cruiser *Belgrano* 'was not an absolutely immediate threat to our surface ships, and Woodward knew where she was. . . .'

According to Henderson, the British 'knew of an Argentine

plan for a coordinated attack on the Task Force to be conducted by aircraft from the mainland, from carrier-based aircraft, and from surface ships equipped with Exocets.'[12] It was
not the destroyers with Exocets that *Conqueror* was to be told to
sink, but here, clearly, is the source of the pincer movement
notion – bogus, as by early 2 May the entire Argentine surface
fleet was running for cover. Also according to Henderson, the
Belgrano and her escorts 'provided useful air guidance for
Argentine air attacks on British forces'. This story is about on a
par with the fanciful Burdwood Bank one. No Argentine air
attacks had been reported for 2 May, and aircraft from Río
Grande headed for the Falklands would have passed about 100
miles north of the position she was sunk in. Since she also saw no
British ships all day (not even *Conqueror*), the only 'air guidance'
she could provide would have been to tell stray planes to head
north-eastward.

Lewin's duty was to sink enemy ships, especially if the man on
the spot was reporting them as a threat. Woodward acknowledged that he was anxious to move into action as soon as
possible. To some fellow officers he sometimes appeared tense,
impatient and dismissive of the ideas of others almost to the point
of arrogance according to the *Sunday Times* Insight Team (p.
141). They also suggest that his judgement was occasionally
suspect. For instance in April he described the successful recapture of South Georgia as 'an appetizer', then went on to say:
'Now this is the heavy punch coming up behind. My battle
group is properly formed and ready to strike. This is the run-up
to the big match which in my view should be a walkover. We
were told they [the Argentines] were a tough lot but they were
quick to throw in the towel.' Within 48 hours London made him
recant. He 'clarified' his thoughts on 28 April by telling journalists on board his flagship, HMS *Hermes*, that there would be 'no
simple, short, quick military solution to re-establishing British
administration on the Falklands while the Argentinians resist us'.
He later confided to associates that his 'walkover' prediction was
his way of signalling to the Junta that there was still time for them
to think again. It appears that from 1 May onward their time was
up. Woodward was eager to land his heavy punch.

The decisive factor in making sense of the military situation is
the British capability to intercept and decode enemy signals. The
men on the *Conqueror* developed a considerable respect for this

ability, and felt that the Argentine signals were practically an open book to the British. Dr Murguizur agrees (see pp. 128–9). Officials in London have also confirmed to the writers that the British were reading all Argentine traffic, though a Defence Ministry spokesman asked to expand on the subject said: 'It has long been our practice not to comment on intelligence matters generally.'

However, we can say that the procedure worked more or less as follows. The four Nimrod surveillance planes based on Ascension Island carried high-frequency receivers, as did various British ships including the carriers *Hermes* and *Invincible*.[13] These were tuned in to listen to the Argentines' tactical signals, transmitted by voice, and also to those highly secret operational orders coded and sent in Morse. These listening techniques are so highly developed that a Royal Navy vessel parked 1,000 miles off the Argentine coast would have been able to pick up literally hundreds of signals coming in simultaneously. If an important message could not be decoded on the spot, it was referred immediately to the British government's Communications Headquarters at Cheltenham, the centre of a worldwide Signals Intelligence (SIGINT) network. Throughout the 10-week campaign, teams of specialists worked round the clock there to monitor, analyse and decode thousands of Argentine operational and other messages.

These arrangements were augmented by periodic references to a composite signals station known as Two Boats, manned by 50 Britons on Ascension, where listening systems were also installed. Ascension also accommodated an American satellite tracking station (designated DSCS 11). This, along with several other American–British joint satellite services, provided the British with facilities to maintain voice-links secure against Argentine interception, as well as to carry out photographic surveillance of enemy military movements. The Task Force was able to communicate instantaneously with its home-based High Command and to record visual evidence of military activity in the Falklands proper, the mainland and on the sea. The Argentine navy transmitted two 'come home' signals to all surface vessels of the fleet at 20.07 on 1 May and again at 01.19 on 2 May – about 20 and 15 hours respectively before the *Belgrano* was sunk. 'It's inconceivable that both messages would have been missed,' a British authority on SIGINT operations remarked. 'And once picked up, the contents of the messages would have been decoded and circulated to the proper authorities in London very, very soon indeed.'

The SIGINT network operates in partnership with the US National Security Agency (NSA), whose headquarters are at Fort George Meade, Maryland. The NSA is reputed to have more than 100,000 employees on its books around the world, with costs running into billions of dollars, much of this spent on the computer technology which has replaced most of the old-style human cryptographers. For its part, Cheltenham's concealed budget is said to exceed £200 million annually. Up against Argentine code techniques instead of Soviet, the task was not strenuous.

We do not know if Lewin told Mrs Thatcher that the Argentine fleet had been called home. His own language – 'We could not wait' – suggests that he knew that the 'opportunity' might not come again. All the accounts except Lewin's own agree that the War Cabinet reached its decision with little ado. According to two participants in the discussions who asked not to be identified, it was Mrs Thatcher personally who transmitted to Lewin, her Chief of Defence Staff, the authority he had requested.

There was no need for a quick decision. At 12.00 BST (08.00 Argentine) the *Belgrano* was still about 15 hours out from Argentine coastal waters. The War Cabinet could have sent Argentina an ultimatum – negotiate or we sink some ships of yours in eight hours' time. If they did not already know that the *Belgrano* was going home, they could have decided to tell the Argentines to get her home and not let her out again, because the British intended to change their Rules of Engagement – the change was not announced until 7 May, and the fact that it was announced at all constitutes a further argument, if one is needed, against the claim that the Argentines knew already that their ships outside the TEZ were in jeopardy just by being there.

The abundance of contradictory statements about the *Belgrano*'s sinking is what drew the attention of Tam Dalyell, and led him to conclude that what was being concealed was a deliberate decision to scupper the Belaúnde initiative. Our own researches have produced no firm evidence to confirm Dalyell's suspicions, but nor do they enable us to dismiss them. Authoritative sources in Lima have assured us that Ambassador Charles Wallace was keeping London in touch with President Belaúnde's progress from hour to hour on the weekend in question. Sir Nicholas Henderson insists, on the other hand, that Wallace saw Foreign Minister Arias Stella on 1 May without learning anything substantive, and was not told of the exchanges with Buenos Aires and Washington until 18.30 on 2 May – more than four hours after *Conqueror*'s attack.[14] Supposing that Wallace was in fact sending regular dispatches, and that Henderson himself might have sent some sort of news from Washington – for total silence is hard to imagine at so critical a juncture – this question arises: what messenger would have dared to tell the War Cabinet that there were more negotiations in prospect, at a moment when its mind was set on making its 'demonstration'?

Our own conclusion is that whether or not Mrs Thatcher and her War Cabinet were informed about the Belaúnde proposals, it did not matter very much. The indications suggest that Argentina was to be taught a lesson by the sternest military means, and the *Belgrano* happened unfortunately to be the first target. To scupper the proposals, the British only needed to say No, and to pick on some point of real or imagined Argentine intransigence. Haig would have confirmed whatever it was. But Mrs Thatcher and her ministers appeared bent on total victory.

All the changing statements revolve around the Chief of Staff's claim that the *Belgrano* was a threat. That is what he said he told the War Cabinet, and he does not seem to have been questioned about it on the morning of 2 May. Later on, when the questioning began, the nature of the threat the cruiser posed required substantiating. A rationale had to be presented. The shifting explanations suggest that they were produced in haste by people not used to having to explain themselves. Politicians would have done a better job.

However, this conclusion merely pushes the problem back one step. Mrs Thatcher and her Cabinet had been asked for permission to sink an enemy ship, rather than just warning it off– an option readily available to the British, who had known that the *Belgrano* was patrolling between Tierra de Fuego and the TEZ since 30 April, possibly from the Chileans, possibly from a US spy satellite. Whatever threat the *Belgrano* might represent, the War Cabinet knew that for the moment she was outside the TEZ and some way from the Task Force. Consequently there was no immediate danger to the Task Force, which was somewhere south-east of Port Stanley, out of Argentine fighter-bomber range. Yet Lewin was bound to ask to sink the enemy ship – that was his job. And Mrs Thatcher was bound to consider whether it was the proper political and ethical decision – that was hers. Mrs Thatcher is known to respect the military and to subscribe to the armed services' maxim that says 'leave it to the man on the spot' – in this case, Admiral Woodward. But in the circumstances of the Falklands war and of the challenge it presented to her own position, it is difficult to think of a consideration that might have stopped her giving Lewin what he had requested.

Argentina had committed a crime, and retribution must follow. In Mrs Thatcher's world-view, governments that sin should not complain if they are punished. The Prime Minister seems to have developed an exhilaration for the challenges of war – for her a new experience. Less than two weeks after the loss of the *Sheffield* she told the Scottish Conservative Party in Perth on 14 May that: 'When you've spent half your political life dealing with humdrum issues like the environment . . . it's exciting to have a real crisis on your hands.' Perhaps she might have withheld the order to sink the *Belgrano* had there been evidence of an imminent enemy surrender but anything less was unacceptable.

If Mrs Thatcher could contemplate nothing less than an Argentine surrender, it seemed that there was no other member of the War Cabinet to gainsay her. The absent Francis Pym said he was not consulted – nor expected to be – even though there was time to do so. William (now Lord) Whitelaw, John Nott and Cecil Parkinson, according to our information, shared the view that the advice of the Chief of the Defence Staff had to be accepted. And so a change in the Rules of Engagement permitting the attack on the *Belgrano* was swiftly authorized with little debate:

From the discussions I have had subsequently I do not believe that any of those who were responsible for the decision to attack the *Belgrano* hesitated about it at the time or have had any regrets about it since, except of course for the loss of life inseparable from war.[15]

The last clause was Henderson's gesture of compassion. The compassion of others was implied rather than stated. According to the official account of the Falklands war:

> Our nuclear-powered submarines (SSN) played a crucial role. After the sinking of the *General Belgrano* the Argentine surface fleet effectively took no further part in the Campaign.[16]

In other words the destruction of the cruiser with 368 crewmen actually *saved* many more lives because the bottling up of the enemy fleet headed off even bigger and bloodier naval encounters. This, at any rate, was the theme of messages received by *Conqueror*, and the argument used by government spokesmen, in attempts to mitigate a widespread feeling of revulsion against the toll of casualties – to many it was like the Second World War revisited. Not all of the crew of the *Conqueror* were persuaded. Some thought that the warning to the Argentines to stay within their 12-mile limit, not issued until 7 May, would have had the effect of saving lives if it had been given earlier; and if, after being given it had been defied, then the *General Belgrano* or any other major Argentine warship could have been attacked in good conscience.

Speaking at the Lord Mayor's Banquet at the Guildhall, London, on 14 November 1983, the British Prime Minister promised:

> We will do everything possible to reduce the risks of war, and to avoid the misunderstandings which increase those risks. Britain is ready to pursue, in the right circumstances, a sensible dialogue . . .

The speech continued: '. . . with the Soviet Union and the countries of Eastern Europe.' Britain did none of those statesmanlike things in the Falklands. It did nothing until it was too late to reduce the risks of war – not so much as an eleventh-hour phone call from Mrs Thatcher to Galtieri. Its behaviour before the war sent a spate of signals which led to greater Argentine misunderstandings, and even its TEZ warnings were so ambiguous (though not to Captain Bonzo and the Argentines) that later attempts to justify them turned into semantic quibbles.

HMS CONQUEROR
c o BFPO Ships

FROM: Commander-in-Chief Fleet (Admiral Sir John
Fieldhouse, GCB)

TO: HMS CONQUEROR

1. The sinking of the BELGRANO was fundamental to
the success of Operation Corporate and took the
heart out of the Argentinian Navy. Your long
patrol was conducted throughout to my complete
satisfaction. Well done."

From: Commander-in-Chief Fleet

To: UK Forces in the South Atlantic

1. I have had the honour to receive the following
message from Her Majesty the Queen and pass it
to you all with pleasure:

"I send my warmest congratulations to you and all
under your Command for the splendid way in which
you have achieved the liberation of the Falkland
Islands. Britain is very proud of the way you
have served your country.   Elizabeth R.   "

The Falklands war cost Britain and Argentina up to 1,250 dead, more than 3,000 casualties and billions of pounds in material losses. Bills are still coming in, and will keep doing so for years. The lives of the Falklanders have been disrupted, perhaps for ever. Argentina's initial resort to force was a cynical manipulation of the people by the Junta, conducted in haste. Had it been only the Malvinas they wanted, they might have waited two more years before attacking. Reason alone should have told them that Britain, having disengaged from most of its imperial ties, would in time yield up what Horace Walpole called this 'morsel of rock that lies somewhere at the very bottom of America'. The Junta had no time.

If the war proved anything it was that in manpower and armament the British were far superior – a conclusion that could have been reached by anyone who could count and read. One commentator summed up the irony of the Falklands conflict by remarking that it:

> must represent one of the very few wars in history in which one nation had no real intention of invading and the other fought for territory which it had spent twenty years saying it did not really want.[17]

According to Kevin McNamara, speaking in the House of Commons on 17 November 1983, the annual cost of maintaining the present garrison on the Falklands, with all its men, ships, planes and provisioning, is £684 million (£380,000 per islander) per year – a cautious estimate. The islands have been converted into one vast intensive care unit for a patient which cannot survive on its own. A government which otherwise asserts the iron rule of market forces, and has watched dispassionately as hospitals and factories were closed in the name of a fitter economy, saw no paradox in the policy of 'Fortress Falklands'. It accorded 'paramountcy' – effectively a veto – to the wishes of the 1,800 islanders, defying its habitual logic and to satisfy a dubious concept of national pride. Only in a community which exists, according to Lord Shackleton, in a 'near feudal state of dependency'[18] could such a situation appear to make sense.

The war had some beneficiaries. Inevitably the arms merchants have hurried to replace lost ships, aircraft and weaponry.

The complicated gadgetry of electronic warfare garnered hundreds of millions of pounds in contracts placed not only by the combatants but by interested onlookers in South America who decided that their own countries' security had better be strengthened as the defeated Argentines embarked upon a crash rearmament programme. Even before hostilities ceased (and in January 1984 they had not been formally ended by either side) the manufacturers of certain missiles – Exocets among them – had placed advertisements in specialist military journals extolling the virtues of their wares and using the catchline 'proven in battle'.

Another group whose fortunes rose what the Falkland Islands Company, which went on trading with the enemy during the occupation, asserting later that it could hardly have refused to do so. That was a short-lived secondary gain. A longer-term advantage resulted from the Fortress Falklands policy. It brought not only an immeasurable enhancement of land and property values but also a transformation of the islands' infrastructure, even though this was geared primarily to meet the needs of the big new garrison. Roads and bridges were built; telephone and other services extended; housing, administrative, land, sea and shipping services doubled then redoubled. The company-owned stores began to cater for a triple-expanded consumer public, and for Coalite Limited, the parent firm, the boom looked guaranteed. This was the programme of public works which the government had abjured in the UK, now lavished at an enormous per capita rate. Observers have not been slow to point out that most if not all the islanders would willingly have left the Falklands to the sheep and the Argentines merely for one year's costs of Fortress Falklands divided among them.

Mrs Thatcher and the Conservative party were beneficiaries too. Tables 1 and 2 (below) show how the politics of war helped transform imminent failure into instant victory.[19]

Table 1   Party ratings from January to June 1982(%)

Party	January	February	March	April	May	June
Conservative	27½	27½	31½	31½	41½	45
Labour	29½	34	33	29	28	25
Liberal	13	14½	11½	11	9½	10
SDP	26½	21½	19½	20½	13½	15

Table 2   People in the sample were asked to indicate if they were satisfied with the leadership of the three parties; the answers were (%):

	January	February	March	April	May	June
Mrs Thatcher	32	29	34	35	44	51
Michael Foot	18	19	21	23	18	14
David Steel	59	59	58	63	64	62

The image of combative resolution became the hallmark of a Prime Minister revitalized by the war and faced with a Labour party whose divisions were in part caused by the war. Defence became an issue in the election which Mrs Thatcher called in mid-1983, and it was impossible for the Labour party to outbid the Conservatives after so formidable an exhibition of tough realpolitik. Having limped on the heels of the Conservative party militants, Michael Foot failed to regain the voice of sturdy prudence. During the election campaign he appeared as a waverer – clamorous enough about the Falklands, but timorous on the issue of the nuclear deterrent. He could not match the shining confidence of Margaret Thatcher speaking to the faithful:

> When the demands of war and the dangers to our own people call us to arms – then we British are as we have always been – competent, courageous and resolute . . . We have to see that the spirit of the South Atlantic – the real spirit of Britain – is kindled not only by war but can now be fired by peace.
>
> We have the first prerequisite. We know we can do it – we haven't lost the ability. That is the Falklands Factor.[20]

It was not only the British who were caught up in the whirl of tabloid hype and splendid self-assurance. After the speech (quoted on p. 53) in which Mrs Thatcher accepted the Churchill Award for services to the North Atlantic Alliance, a letter was read out from President Ronald Reagan to Prime Minister Margaret Thatcher. It said in part:

> World affairs today demand the boldness and integrity of a Churchill. In his absence I know he would want us to look to you as the legendary Britannia – a special lady, the greatest defender of the realm.

That perhaps was Reagan's apology for the remark he made to
Haig during his shuttle diplomacy, and which was leaked to the
world press on 16 April 1982. What the President said then, as the
British stood firm on sovereignty and self-determination was:
'Maggie wants a skirmish.'[21]

Few Britons would have denied that Mrs Thatcher's personal
performance and self-belief were integral to her party's landslide
victory. The government's failure to avert the Falklands conflict
was erased. Doubts about the *Belgrano* and the Prime Minister's
sincerity in seeking a negotiated peace were made to look ungra-
cious or obsessional, as in the case of Tam Dalyell, who was
refusing to let the subject drop. Yet although the voters' salute
brought the Conservative party a great increase in seats, its total
vote actually fell by two per cent compared with 1979. After the
victory parades, the honour redeemed, the electoral strategy of
Cecil Parkinson, that vote was something less than an unquali-
fied national endorsement.

In Argentina the Junta fell, and elections late in 1983 produced
a civilian President after years of military rule. Raúl Alfonsín
received a message of greeting from Mrs Thatcher on the occasion of his inauguration on 10 December 1983, and in an interview published in the *Observer* next day he revived the idea of
leaseback. It looked as if a thaw was on the way, although when
government leaders learned of this response they fell to stressing
sovereignty and paramountcy all over again. The familiar old
pattern was restored.

Having poured £2,000 million annually from 1978 to 1981 into
arms imports, Argentina spent more than £1,000 million on new
foreign weapons in the year following the war.[22] These figures
take no account of domestic arms production. Britain was angry
with President Reagan when, on 8 December 1983, he lifted the
ban on arms sales to Argentina which former President Jimmy
Carter had imposed because of the Videla Junta's violations of
human rights. However, lingering Argentine resentment over
the US role in the war inhibited the new regime from hurrying
into the American arms market. Not that this diluted Mrs
Thatcher's patent irritation – irritation, incidentally, heavily
laced with irony. For the British government itself had by late
1982 made some significant contributions to Argentine rearmament. They took the form of permitting the sale of Rolls-Royce
engines, gear and radar systems for four modern frigates and six

corvettes then being built in West German yards for Argentina.[23] Some of the contracts predated the Falklands conflict, but after the fighting commercial considerations re-emerged.

The Falklands war raised the military temperature throughout Latin America and the Caribbean. It touched off a dangerous new arms race among those countries with frontiers still disputed or ill-defined. Brazil, competing with Argentina for leadership in the region, set out to modernize and expand its air, land and sea power despite its huge foreign debts. More ominous internationally, Vice-Admiral Castro Madero, President of Argentina's Atomic Energy Commission, announced that his country intended building one or more nuclear-powered submarines; he also reaffirmed Argentina's refusal to adhere to the world non-proliferation treaty which aims to check the spread of nuclear weapons.

Brazil had moved with Argentina well along the way towards a nuclear weapons capacity. Its political, military and scientific leaders were stirred to accelerate their faltering programme when Argentina disclosed in November 1983 that it had mastered the technique of uranium enrichment. The main by-product of this process is plutonium – usable in the manufacture of nuclear explosives. While British authorities privately professed concern at these developments it emerged that the British themselves were indirectly helping the Argentine programme. Their assistance took the form of enabling Argentina to purchase more than 100 tonnes of heavy water – vital in a number of nuclear manufacturing processes, both civil and military – from West Germany in early 1983.[24]

Even before these controversial transactions the South Atlantic situation had been invested with a nuclear dimension. The British were accused by Argentina and Panama of having introduced atomic weapons into the nominally nuclear-free Latin American region. Tangled international arrangements formed the background of their charge. In 1967, countries of South America signed the Treaty of Tlatelolco, which bound participants to keep nuclear weapons out of the area. Since Argentina had signed but not ratified the pact, it had no real right to complain. Britain is pledged to observe the Treaty provisions in respect of its own colonial territories in Latin America. However, it claimed that its obligation was limited only to keeping nuclear weaponry out of its colonies and their territorial waters.

The British declined either to confirm or deny whether any Task Force ship carried such weapons into the South Atlantic during the war.

These were developments which could threaten a record cited with pride by Thomas Enders, former Assistant Secretary of State for Inter-American Affairs. In late 1982 he told a Congressional subcommittee meeting in Washington:

> In the world as a whole some four million persons have lost their lives in armed action between states since the Second World War. Including the toll in the South Atlantic fewer than 4,000 of them have died in the Western Hemisphere. The countries of Latin America spend less of their national resources for arms than any other area in the world. Their military expenditures come to only 1.4% of Gross National Product – a quarter of the average in the Third World as a whole.[25]

His own government was the next to increase the casualty list when it invaded the Commonwealth state of Grenada in November 1983, calling its intervention 'Operation Urgent Fury'. President Reagan had learned that it was possible after all to bring force to bear in South America. He did not consult with Mrs Thatcher before toppling Queen Elizabeth's government in Grenada and evicting several hundred Cubans. British officials suggested that he was playing tit-for-tat in retaliation against her own failure to consult the US before sinking the Belgrano.

Defeat in the Falklands may have hastened the demise of military dictatorship in Argentina; victory certainly contributed to Mrs Thatcher's mid-1983 reelection. What the war did not achieve was an enduring solution of the islands' disputed future: if anything, it dimmed prospects of a rational settlement indefinitely. For Argentines the reality was that, by their invasion, they had forfeited any goodwill or sympathy they may have had among Falklanders who now were invested by Mrs Thatcher with rights to veto whatever compromise a future British government might fashion. For the British, victory brought an open-ended commitment to defend the distant territories at a cost which in 1983–4 alone approached £400,000 for each of the 1,800 islanders.

Even before their military rulers were swept from power the

Argentine people seemed determined to face up to the tragedies of the past as well as to the challenges of the future. Raúl Alfonsín, a benign Social Democrat, was elected President on campaign pledges to judge and punish the crimes of the dictators and to pursue the nation's objectives at home and abroad by consent and in peace. One of his first acts on being inaugurated in December 1983 was to accept the findings of General Rattenbach's Commission which investigated the origins and conduct of the war with Britain and which blamed political misjudgements, strategic blunders and operational incompetence for the loss of an unjustifiable conflict. Alfonsín also quickly empowered civil courts to investigate and bring to trial key members of yesterday's Juntas, and their subordinates, accused of violence and murder. Leaders once unassailable were interrogated or arrested in the search for retribution for the torture and death endured by long-vanished opponents. More than half Argentina's generals, admirals and brigadiers were struck off the active list in a purge of the armed forces. The new regime also moved toward reconciliation with an old antagonist by conceding Chile's claim to the three bleak disputed islands in the Beagle Channel.

The road ahead for Argentina was as rocky as its past was painful. At the start of 1984 the national debt exceeded US$43 billion, the inflation rate was above 400 per cent annually, and ousted military rulers were waiting in the wings. On the Falklands, the President's prospects of achieving progress were circumscribed by two related difficulties; on the one hand by Mrs Thatcher's blank refusal to negotiate over sovereignty against the 'wishes' of the islanders and on the other hand by the certainty that his own authority would decline, and the influence of the military would revive, the longer a solution eluded him. His government therefore lost little time in calling publicly for a transfer of sovereignty, but coupled the request with the offer of a special statute that would guarantee the interests of the Falklanders. Alfonsín and his ministers went further with suggestions that the sovereignty issue could be skirted for a while, possibly by reviving some sort of leaseback arrangement. In his interview with the *Observer* the President floated the idea that if Mrs Thatcher would suspend construction of the new Port Stanley airport and reduce the 150-mile exclusion zone around the islands 'that would take us a long way down the road to a solution'.

The British Prime Minister, in her 1984 New Year's message,

re-emphasized that the sovereignty of the Falklands was not negotiable. Policy remained embedded in the concrete being poured into the military installations that made up the concept of 'Fortress Falklands' as Mrs Thatcher argued that Britain could not yield in negotiations what its soldiers had won in battle. Whether or not this was only a public posture, there was evidence of accumulating pressure for a British shift towards compromise. A vote in the UN General Assembly on 16 November 1983 showed 87 countries (including the US) in favour of British-Argentine negotiations; nine countries voted against the resolution while 54 abstained, including Britain's nine European Community partners. Mrs Thatcher's response, that she would 'carry on as before to honour the wishes of the Falkland islanders',[26] was better rhetoric than political realism. The US decision to lift its ban on arms sales to Argentina was another sign of Britain's growing international isolation on the issue of sovereignty.

National support for the indefinite maintenance of the expensive Falklands life-support system had begun to wane by the start of 1984. The true cost of fighting and winning the war, and of defending and developing the islands for the five years ending 1987 became a subject of dispute. Estimates varied from about £3 billion to £8 billion. Editorials in serious newspapers and journals, public opinion polls and statements from politicians of all parties reflected a growing realization that the huge price of keeping the Falklands British did not match their strategic or symbolic value, especially at a time of high unemployment and retrenchment at home, hospital closures, cutbacks in education, road-building and social spending, and other manifestations of domestic travail.

There were further problems. One related to the effects on the Falklanders themselves of the presence of a British garrison outnumbering the inhabitants by at least two to one. Some of the islanders have said the changes had ruined what they valued most about their way of life – its serenity and isolation. Others employed by the Falkland Islands Company had their hopes dashed of being able to acquire their own bits of land through a mandatory breakup of the company's vast holdings. A second consideration concerned Britain's attitude toward an Argentina freed from the rule of the military. Given that Argentina's reborn democracy was something to be nurtured, the British would be risking international wrath if they were to persist in a churlish refusal to meet the civilian regime of Buenos Aires halfway.

It was plain that military defeat in no way dispelled or diluted the Argentine obsession with recovering the islands somehow, some day. Capitán Robacio, commander of Argentina's 5th Marine Battalion and holder of his country's highest decoration for military valour, remarked that if his people had been able to wait 150 years to regain their heritage, they probably could wait a little longer if asked. 'If there are no negotiations,' he said matter-of-factly, 'then there *will* be another war. If not for me, then for my son. If not for my son, then my grandson.'[27]

President Alfonsín's signals to the British in December 1983 suggested that he was ready to consider a compromise that would fall short initially of a transfer of sovereignty. In a situation of resumed negotiations, the concept of leaseback would acquire a new relevance. Rural Argentina has Scottish, Welsh and Afrikaner communities who have managed to preserve their ethnic identities since the nineteenth century despite being out-numbered by considerably larger Spanish and Italian groups. Falklanders and Argentines could become natural partners in any coherent programmes to develop the fishery resources of the South Atlantic or the minerals of the Argentine continental shelf and Antarctica.

On some levels Argentina moved further than Britain towards confronting the blunders committed before and during the 1982 war. Perhaps the stings of defeat induced a process of soul-searching. The Rattenbach Commission looked into the political and military conduct of the conflict as well as its causes; in contrast Lord Franks and his Privy Counsellors were barred by their terms of reference from examining events that followed Argentina's invasion. Where Rattenbach identified key Argentine culprits and was free with his criticisms, the Franks Report found nobody to blame.

The dispassionate judgement of Rattenbach's Commissioners was exemplified by their observations on the sinking of the *Belgrano* just when Peruvian mediation seemed likely to succeed. The Commission conceded that the sinking 'constituted an emotional factor which conditioned the rejection of the [peace] proposals'. But then, recognizing that defeat was the inevitable result of rejection, it concluded with a combination of icy logic and hindsight that the Junta had acted imprudently. 'Keeping in mind the negotiations which could have led to a ceasefire and the achievement of the proposed objectives,' the Rattenbach Report said, 'the most rational and productive course would have been to accept the proposal in spite of the sinking of the *General Belgrano*.'[28]

These strictures on the judgement of the Junta did not mean that Rattenbach was absolving Britain of culpability; or that British responsibility was diminished for an act portrayed as being as cold as it was unjustified. 'Beyond all sentimental considerations, it remains for the UK – winner of this contest – objectively to analyse its conduct which simply was not consistent with its stature as a major power of the Western and Christian world,' the Rattenbach Report reflected. 'This conclusion undoubtedly will be borne out by a recognition of Britain's undeniable responsibility for the sinking of the *General Belgrano*, an action intrinsically cruel because it was so unnecessary.'[29]

The British government, for its part, used the blanket of official secrecy to cover up some of the more controversial actions in the war; and notably questions relating to the assault on the *Belgrano*, at the very moment when a basis for a settlement was deemed to be within grasp by all the parties concerned excepting British ministers and diplomats. (Several unanswered questions, addressed to Admiral Woodward, appear in the epilogue.) Other political mysteries remain to be unravelled. Did Francis Pym, for instance, try genuinely to transform the Belaúnde initiative into an acceptable basis for compromise or did he not have the opportunity? Why was Commander Wreford-Brown not ordered to sink either, or both, of the escorting destroyers known to have been carrying Exocets, rather than the *Belgrano* which was not, to minimize the loss of life? What were Mrs Thatcher's reasons for refusing to publish the log of the *Conqueror*, thereby resolving the controversy over the course of the *Belgrano*, if the Defence Chiefs and War Cabinet had been so sure of their case?

The sinking of the *Belgrano* embittered an already anxious Junta, leading it into a precipitous rejection of Peru's promising peace initiative. We share the Rattenbach conclusion that Argentine interests would have been better served if, despite the sinking, the search had been continued for a ceasefire and a rational basis for compromise. But at the same time our researches have uncovered no real necessity for Britain to destroy the *Belgrano*, and with it about one-third of all the lives lost in the Falklands war. In the absence of thorough and consistent answers, the performance and motives of war cabinet ministers and the military judgement of their defence advisers have been assailed both inside and outside Parliament. Any linkage between Britain's dubious diplomatic tactics and the operational imperatives which preceded the attack on the cruiser can be investigated best under the procedures laid down in the Tribunals of Inquiry (Evidence) Act of 1921. Democracies, unlike dictatorships, do not normally open fire without fair warning unless every conceivable alternative has been explored.

We take the view that Mrs Thatcher's war cabinet decided in principle on the use of force the day Argentina occupied the Falklands, and that only unconditional surrender by the Junta could have prevented a killing war. The phase of phantom negotiations through April served only to fill the 'diplomatic vacuum' until the Task Force could be brought to bear. It then went into action at once and the attack on the *General Belgrano* escalated the confrontation. If the assessment is correct that British leaders were never really seriously interested in negotiating, there would be little to choose in terms of opportunism between the hawks of London and those of Buenos Aires. We find it hard to avoid the suspicion that the crews of both ships, the *Conqueror* as well as the *General Belgrano*, were used in a cynical politico-military machination which most Britons would want to see exposed.

Epilogue

We approached the Ministry of Defence on 26 June 1983 with a request for interviews with Admiral Lord Lewin, Admiral Woodward and Commander Wreford-Brown in order 'properly and fairly to represent Britain's position' about key aspects of the Falklands war. The Directorate of Public Relations advised us eight days later that the request for meetings with Woodward and Wreford-Brown 'will be investigated by Defence Promotions and Facilities' but Lewin, who had left the Service, should be approached directly.

The investigation by Defence Promotions and Facilities went on for more than three months; in mid-October we were advised that Woodward would answer written questions and that a meeting with Wreford-Brown was still being considered. Our questions were submitted on 25 October 1983. In early December, the Ministry advised us, Woodward's were received in the Ministry and were being studied for clearance – meaning that they required to be reconciled with previous ministerial and other statements.

At that point our publication deadline was approaching. Through December and half of January we pressed for a speedup of the process of clearance but were told that the matter was 'with the Minister'; in fact John Stanley, Minister for the Armed Forces. Ministry officials acknowledged to us they thought the delay in responding had been 'inordinate'.

Finally on 16 January 1984, the day our book was going to press, the Directorate of Public Relations called to say that 'the minister has decided not to supply Admiral Woodward's answers'. No explanation was offered but we understand that Stanley's decision was taken against the advice of his officials.

We print the questions addressed to Admiral Woodward with regret that Stanley has vetoed the answers provided by the former commander of the Task Force.

1 You told the Royal United Services Institute in a lecture on 20 October 1982 that 'all the indications' suggested that the Argentine carrier 25 de Mayo and escorts in the north, and the General Belgrano in the south, were attempting to complete a pincer movement against Task Force units. Can you say on which part of the Task Force the Belgrano was moving?

2 HMS Conqueror was, of course, under Northwood command but can you, nevertheless, say when she first sighted the Belgrano? Was it, as the incumbent Chief of the Defence Staff (Admiral Lewin) originally claimed, a matter of hours before the attack? Or was it, as Sir John Nott, the Defence Ministry White Paper and Fleet Commander Admiral Sir John Fieldhouse, all subsequently reported, on 2 May? Or was it, as Commander Christopher Wreford-Brown disclosed, more than 30 hours before she was torpedoed? Or finally, was she detected at approximately 16.00 hours local time on Friday 30 April, as some members of the Conqueror's crew have conveyed to us informally?

3 In your RUSI lecture you said you had been concerned that the Conqueror might lose the Belgrano if the cruiser were suddenly to run over the Burdwood shallows. How do you reconcile that concern with the fact that the Conqueror could easily have navigated through those shallows?

4 If, as Commander Wreford-Brown has said, the Belgrano was heading toward the Total Exclusion Zone when first sighted and consequently considered a threat to the Task Force, why was she not torpedoed at once instead of much later at about 16.00 on 2 May?

5 The official British warning of 23 April gave commanders on the spot discretion to attack any Argentine ship or plane if it displayed hostile intent. If this warning was valid as Ministers have argued why, then, was it necessary to seek a change in the Rules of Engagement even though the Belgrano was well outside the Total Exclusion Zone?

6 Bearing in mind that the *Belgrano* had a cruising speed of about 18 knots and that she was about 45 miles south-west of the Burdwood Bank and heading homewards, is it not a fact that she was about 13 to 14 hours sailing time away from the main body of the Task Force? And, furthermore, that she could have been sunk at almost any time of Wreford-Brown's choice if suddenly she were to have turned northwards?

7 If Argentine High Command signals were being intercepted and decoded, as we have been assured they were, were you not informed as Task Force Commander that all Argentine fleet units had, on the night of 1 May, been ordered home? If you had been aware of this order would you still have asked for a change in the Rules of Engagement permitting the *Belgrano* to be destroyed?

8 Were you totally uninformed that strenuous efforts were under way in Lima, Washington and Buenos Aires for a political settlement that could have included an Argentine withdrawal from the islands?

9 Do you know of any reason why no disclosure was made of the fact that the Argentine destroyer *Hipólito Bouchard*, one of the *Belgrano*'s escorts, also was torpedoed 20 minutes after the *Belgrano* was hit? (The torpedo struck but did not explode or exploded away from the hull.) Was this an action by the *Conqueror*?

Falklands Chronology

1833   *3 January.* British warships *Clio* and *Tyne* evict Argentine settlers from the Falkland Islands. Captain James Onslow of the *Clio* strikes the Argentine flag.

1910   Gaston de Bernhardt submits 49-page analysis of British Falklands claim to Foreign Office. It casts doubt on British sovereignty.

1940   Foreign Office produces draft (now in closed file), of 'Proposed offer by HMG to reunite Falkland Islands with Argentina and acceptance of lease'.

1965   *16 December.* UN General Assembly passes Resolution 2065 (see Appendix 1), calling on the British and Argentine governments to negotiate a peaceful Falklands settlement, in the context of ending 'colonialism in all its forms'.

1977   Labour Foreign Secretary David Owen sends nuclear submarine and two frigates to Falklands, in reaction to Argentine sabre-rattling against slow UK negotiating tactics.

1979   *September and November.* Lord Carrington and Joint Intelligence Committee report high risk of Argentina resorting to force if negotiations fail.

1980   *2 December.* Fierce House of Commons reaction against Nicholas Ridley's mention of the leaseback option.

1981   British announce plan for early withdrawal of lone guard ship HMS *Endurance* from Falklands.
       October. New UK Nationality. Bill sets provisions to deprive one-third of Falkland Islanders of British citizenship; government refuses to grant Falklanders exemption.

1981   *December.* New Junta takes over in Argentina. President Galtieri agrees with Admiral Anaya that Junta will move against Falklands. (The formal decision came on 6 January 1982.)

1982	*January*. Argentine media start dropping heavy hints that the Junta means business in the Falklands.
19 March	Argentine scrap merchants land at Leith, in South Georgia, and hoist Argentine flag.
20 March	HMS *Endurance* dispatched from Port Stanley to remove scrapmen.
28 March	RFA *Fort Austin* leaves Gibraltar for South Atlantic, carrying SAS and SBS men.
29 March	Nuclear submarine HMS *Spartan* leaves Gibraltar for South Atlantic.
31 March	Defence Minister John Nott informs Cabinet of Argentine invasion plans. Mrs Thatcher asks President Reagan to intervene with Galtieri.
1 April	Reagan phones Galtieri when Operation Rosario, the taking of the Falklands, is already under way.
2 April	Argentina occupies the Falkland Islands.
3 April	UN passes Resolution 502. Emergency sitting of the House of Commons endorses dispatch of Task Force.
4 April	HMS *Conqueror* sets out from Faslane.
5 April	Lord Carrington resigns as Foreign Secretary. First Task Force ships set out.
7 April	Haig appointed mediator. UK announces 200-mile maritime exclusion zone round Falklands.
8 April	*Conqueror* passes Madeira. Haig flies to London.
9 April	*Conqueror* passes Canary Islands. Haig flies to Buenos Aires.
10 April	*Conqueror* passes Cape Verde Islands.
12 April	*Conqueror* crosses Equator. 200 mile exclusion zone comes into effect. Haig flies to London.
13 April	Haig returns to Washington.
15–17 April	Argentine fleet, including the cruiser *General Belgrano*, puts to sea.
17 April	Task Force at Ascension Island.
19 April	Haig leaves Buenos Aires after second visit. *Conqueror* reaches South Georgia.
23 April	British government 'warns Argentina that any approach by Argentine warships or military aircraft which could amount to a threat to the task force would be dealt with appropriately.'
25 April	British forces recapture South Georgia.
26 April	UN Secretary General Javier Pérez de Cuéllar announces that Resolution 502, asking forces to withdraw from Falklands, applies to UK too.
27 April	Haig sends his Memorandum of Agreement to British and Argentine governments.

28 April   *Conqueror* leaves South Georgia area for the Falklands.

29 April   Haig indicates UK ready to consider his plan; Costa Méndez asks for changes. US Senate brands Argentina the aggressor, urges US support for Britain.

30 April   Haig 'Tilt' statement: US to back Britain. *Conqueror* picks up distant signatures of *Belgrano* and two destroyer escorts in the afternoon.

1 May   Task Force attacks on Falklands: Vulcan, Sea Harriers, naval bombardment. Argentine navy ordered to attack, 15.55. Instruction rescinded and withdrawal ordered, 20.07. Francis Pym flies in to Washington in the evening. Generals tell Galtieri: 'We don't want open war.' *Conqueror* trails *Belgrano* group all day.

2 May   01.30 Buenos Aires time, President Belaúnde of Peru calls Galtieri with new proposals devised with Haig. Galtieri promises swift answer. 13.00 London time (08.00 Washington), British War Cabinet orders attack on the *Belgrano*. 10.00–12.00 Washington, Pym confers with Haig, who informs him of Belaúnde proposals. 10.00 Argentine (09.00 Washington), Belaúnde calls Galtieri, who hands negotiations to Costa Méndez, starting triangular exchanges, Lima–Washington–Buenos Aires. London advised (?). 16.00 Buenos Aires time (15.00 Washington, 20.00 BST), *Conqueror*'s two torpedoes hit *Belgrano* outside TEZ. 17.00; *Belgrano* sinks. 368 killed. 17.15 Washington (18.15 Buenos Aires) Pym contacts London, mentions Belaúnde approach. 17.00 Lima (19.00 Buenos Aires), Belaúnde press conference reports ceasefire and agreement imminent and discloses message of thanks from Reagan for peace efforts.

4 May   British destroyer HMS *Sheffield* hit by Exocet missile. 21 killed.

7 May   British government 'warns Argentina that any Argentine warships and military aircraft over 12 miles from the Argentine coast would be regarded as hostile and liable to be dealt with accordingly'.

17 May   Britain submits new proposals to Argentina via UN.

19 May   Argentina counters with proposals of its own.

21 May   Beach-head established at San Carlos bay. HMS *Ardent* lost. 15 Argentine aircraft destroyed. Peace negotiations lapse.

23 May   HMS *Antelope* crippled (sinks on 24th); 10 Argentine aircraft destroyed. 24 killed on *Ardent* and *Antelope*.

24 May   18 Argentine aircraft destroyed.

25 May   HMS *Coventry* lost, 19 killed; SS *Atlantic Conveyor* hit by

Exocet (sinks on 28th) 12 killed; 8 Argentine aircraft destroyed.

28 May   British troops capture Darwin and Goose Green.

30 May   Major General Jeremy Moore takes command of all land operations.

8 June   RFAs *Sir Galahad* and *Sir Tristram* hit at Fitzroy, 51 killed; 10 Argentine aircraft destroyed. Ronald Reagan in London reaffirms US support for Britain.

11-12 June Shore-based Exocet hits HMS *Glamorgan*, 13 killed.

11-14 June Advance on Port Stanley. Argentine commander, General Menéndez, surrenders to General Moore at 21.00 on 14 June.

1 July   General Bignone new President of Argentina.

3 July   *Conqueror* returns to Faslane.

26 July   Mrs Thatcher takes salute at Falklands Thanksgiving march-past.

1983

January   Franks Report says that British government could not have known that Argentina would invade the Falkland Islands on 2 April 1982.

9 June.   Thatcher government returned with increased majority in General Election.

16 Nov.   UN General Assembly votes 87–9 in favour of British–Argentine negotiations. US votes against Britain. 54 countries abstain.

10 Dec.   New President Raul Alfonsín, a civilian, inaugurated in Buenos Aires. Pledges peaceful pursuit of Argentine claim on Malvinas; Thatcher insists British sovereignty over Falklands not negotiable.

Appendix 1

UN General Assembly Resolution 2065,
16 December 1965

The General Assembly,

Having examined the question of the Falkland Islands (Malvinas),

Taking into account the chapters of the reports of the Special Committee on the Situation with regard to the Implementation of the Declaration on the Granting of Independence to Colonial Countries and Peoples relating to the Falkland Islands (Malvinas), and in particular the conclusions and recommendations adopted by the Committee with reference to that Territory,

Considering that its resolution 1514 (XV) of 14 December 1960 was prompted by the cherished aim of bringing to an end everywhere colonialism in all its forms one of which covers the case of the Falkland Islands (Malvinas),

Noting the existence of a dispute between the Governments of Argentina and the United Kingdom of Great Britain and Northern Ireland concerning sovereignty over the said Islands,

1 Invites the Governments of Argentina and the United Kingdom of Great Britain and Northern Ireland to proceed without delay with the negotiations recommended by the Special Committee on the Situation with regard to the Implementation of the Declaration on the Granting of Independence to Colonial Countries and Peoples with a view to finding a peaceful solution to the problem, bearing in mind the provisions and objectives of the Charter of the United Nations and of General Assembly resolution 1514 (XV) and the interests of the population of the Falkland Islands (Malvinas);

2 Requests the two Governments to report to the Special Committee and to the General Assembly at its twenty-first session on the results of the negotiations.

Appendix 2

The Argentine Peace Proposal of 19 April 1982

(This proposal was submitted to Haig at 16.00, not long before he left Buenos Aires. A comparison with Haig's own Memorandum of Agreement, Appendix 3A, shows how much of the Argentine text he incorporated in his own proposal. The text below is the authors' unofficial translation of the Spanish text printed in full in Cardozo, Kirschbaum and van der Kooy, *Malvinas, La Trama Secreta*, 1983.)

On the basis of United Nations Security Council Resolution 502, and the desire of the Argentine Republic and the United Kingdom to resolve the controversy which has arisen between them, renouncing the use of force, both governments agree on the following steps, which form an integrated whole:

1 Effective on the signature of the present agreement by both governments, an immediate cessation of hostilities will come into effect.

2 With effect from 0000 hours on the day after the day on which this agreement is signed, the Argentine Republic and the United Kingdom will neither deploy nor introduce any forces into the zone (hereinafter called 'Zones') defined by circles of 150 nautical miles in radius from the following coordinates:

   A) LAT. 51° 40' S, and LONG. 58° 30' W.
   B) LAT. 54° 20' S, and LONG. 36° 40' W.
   C) LAT. 57° 40' S, and LONG. 26° 30' W.

2.1 Within 24 hours from the signature of this agreement, the United Kingdom will annul its exclusion zone and Argentina will carry out no operations in that zone.

2.2 Within 24 hours from the signature of this agreement, the United Kingdom and Argentina will start withdrawing their forces in accordance with the following details:

2.2.1 Within seven days from this agreement, Argentina will have withdrawn half of its military and security forces present in the zones at the date of this agreement, including their equipment and related armament.

In the same period the United Kingdom will have effected the withdrawal of all its forces from the zones, and its naval task force will remain at a distance of at least two thousand nautical miles from any of the coordinates.

2.2.2 Within fifteen days from the date of this agreement, Argentina will have withdrawn all its forces, equipment and armament remaining in the zones. In the same period, the United Kingdom task force units and submarines will have returned to their bases or usual areas of operation.

3 From the date of this agreement, the two governments will take measures to end simultaneously, and without delay, the economic and financial measures adopted in relation to the present conflict, including decisions relating to voyages, transport, communications and transfer of funds between the two countries. The United Kingdom will without delay ask the EEC and third countries which have taken similar measures to end them.

4 Argentina and the United Kingdom will each designate a representative to constitute the Special Interim Authority which will provide observers to verify the execution of the obligations contained in this agreement. The United States has indicated its agreement to designate a representative for the same object.

5 Until a definitive arrangement is reached, all the decisions, laws and regulations which the local administration of the islands adopts in the future shall be submitted to the Special Interim Authority and rapidly ratified by it, except when the SIA judges that such decisions, laws and regulations are incompatible with the aims and dispositions of this agreement or its execution.

5(a) The traditional local Administration will continue through the executive and legislative councils which will be expanded in the following manner:

The Argentine government will designate two representatives who will serve in each council; the Argentine population whose residence is equal to that of others who have the right to representation will elect representatives, there being at least one representative in each council. The local police will continue to be under the administration of the councils, with representation of the resident Argentine population, and will be subject to the supervision of the SIA. The national flag of each constitutive member of the SIA shall be flown in its headquarters.

5(b) Until a definitive arrangement is achieved, no government shall carry out any action incompatible with the aims or dispositions of this agreement or its execution.

6(a) Until a definitive arrangement is achieved, travel, transport, the movement of people, and, in relation to them, residence, property, the disposal of property, communications and trade between the mainland and islands will be promoted and aided on a basis of equality. The SIA will propose the adoption of measures appropriate to such questions, including possible arrangements for compensation for islanders who do not wish to remain in the islands. The two signatories undertake to act promptly in regard to these proposals. The SIA will control the application of all these proposals.

6(b) Until a definitive arrangement is achieved, the rights and guarantees that the inhabitants of the islands have enjoyed till now will be respected on a basis of equality, particularly the rights relating to freedom of opinion, religion, expression, teaching, movement, property, employment, family, customs and cultural links with the countries of origin.

7(a) 31 December 1982 will end the period of transition, during which the signatories will conclude their negotiation on ways of eliminating the islands from the list of Non-Autonomous Territories according to Chapter XI of the UN Charter, and on mutually agreed conditions for their definitive status, including due consideration of the rights of the inhabitants and the principles of territorial integrity in this dispute, in accordance with the aims and principles of the UN Charter and Resolutions 1514 (XV) and 2065 (XX) and in the light of the pertinent resolutions of the General Assembly on the issue of the Malvinas Islands (Falklands).

The above-mentioned negotiations shall start within 15 days of the signature of the present agreement.

7(b) The US government has indicated that, at the request of the two governments, it would be ready to help in negotiating a mutually satisfactory accord by the dates set in sub-paragraph (a).

8 From 1 January 1983 and until the accord on definitive status is effective, the head of government and administration shall be exercised by an official designated by the Argentine government.

Appendix 3

(A) The Haig Memorandum of Agreement, 27 April 1982

Preamble

On the basis of United Nations Security Council Resolution 502, and the will of the Argentine Republic and of the United Kingdom to resolve the controversy which has arisen between them, renouncing the use of force, both Governments agree on the following steps, which form an integrated whole:

Paragraph 1

1 Effective on the signature of this Agreement by both Governments, there shall be an immediate cessation of hostilities.

Paragraph 2

2 Beginning at 0000 hours local time of the day after the day on which this Agreement is signed, and pending a definitive settlement, the Republic of Argentina and the United Kingdom shall not introduce or deploy forces into the zones (hereinafter, 'zones'), defined by circles of 150 nautical miles' radius from the following coordinate points (hereinafter, 'coordinate points'):

A) LAT. 51° 40' S
   LONG. 59° 30' W
B) LAT. 54° 20' S
   LONG. 36° 40' W
C) LAT. 57° 40' S
   LONG. 26° 30' W

2.1 Within 24 hours of the date of this Agreement, the United Kingdom will suspend enforcement of its 'zone of exclusion' and Argentina will suspend operations in the same area.

2.2 Within 24 hours of the date of this Agreement, Argentina and the United Kingdom will commence the withdrawal of their forces in accordance with the following details:

2.2.1 Within seven days from the date of this Agreement, Argentina and the United Kingdom shall each have withdrawn one-half of their military and security forces present in the zones on the date of this Agreement, including related equipment and armaments. Within the same time period, the United Kingdom naval task force will stand off at a distance equivalent to seven days' sailing time (at 12 knots) from any of the coordinate points, and Argentine forces that have been withdrawn shall be placed in a condition such that they could not be reinserted with their equipment and armament in less than seven days.

2.2.2 Within fifteen days from the date of this Agreement, Argentina shall remove all of its remaining forces from the zones and redeploy them to their usual operating areas or normal duties. Within the same period, the United Kingdom shall likewise remove all of its remaining forces from the zones and shall redeploy such forces and the naval task force and submarines to their usual operating areas or normal duties.

2.3 In accordance with its letter of acceptance of even date, the United States shall verify compliance with the provisions of this paragraph, and the two Governments agree to cooperate fully with the United States in facilitating this verification.

Paragraph 3

3 From the date of this Agreement, the two Governments will initiate the necessary procedures to terminate simultaneously, and without delay, the economic and financial measures adopted in connection with the current controversy, including restrictions relating to travel, transportation, communications, and transfers of funds between the two countries. The United Kingdom at the same time shall request the European Community and third countries that have adopted similar measures to terminate them.

Paragraph 4

4 The United Kingdom and Argentina shall each appoint and the United States has indicated its agreement to appoint, a representative to constitute a Special Interim Authority (hereinafter 'the Authority') which shall verify compliance with the obligations in this Agreement (with the exception of paragraph 2), and undertake such other responsibilities as are assigned to it under this Agreement or the separate Protocol regarding the Authority signed this date. Each representative may be supported by a staff of not more than ten persons on the islands.

Paragraph 5

5.1 Pending a definitive settlement, all decisions, laws and regulations hereafter adopted by the local administration on the islands shall be submitted to and expeditiously ratified by the Authority, except in the event that the Authority deems such decisions, laws or regulations to be inconsistent with the purposes and provisions of this agreement or its implementation. The traditional local administration shall continue, except that the Executive and Legislative Councils shall be enlarged to include:

(A) two representatives appointed by the Argentine Government to serve in the Executive Council; and

(B) representatives in each Council of the Argentine population whose period of residence on the islands is equal to that required of others entitled to representation, in proportion to their population, subject to there being at least one such representative in each Council. Such representatives of the resident Argentine population shall be nominated by the Authority.

The flags of each of the constituent members of the Authority shall be flown at its headquarters.

5.2 Pending a definitive settlement, neither Government shall take any action that would be inconsistent with the purpose and provisions of this Agreement or its implementation.

Paragraph 6

6.1 Pending a definitive settlement, travel, transportation, movement of persons and, as may be related thereto, residence and ownership and disposition of property, communications and commerce between the mainland and the islands shall, on a non-discriminatory basis, be promoted and facilitated. The Authority shall propose to the two Governments for adoption appropriate measures on such matters. Such proposals shall simultaneously be transmitted to the Executive and Legislative Councils for their views. The two Governments undertake to respond promptly to such proposals. The Authority shall monitor the implementation of all such proposals adopted.

6.2 The provisions of paragraph 6.1 shall in no way prejudice the rights and guarantees which have heretofore been enjoyed by the inhabitants on the islands, in particular rights relating to freedom of opinion, religion, expression, teaching, movement, property, employment, family, customs, and cultural ties with countries of origin.

Paragraph 7

7 December 31, 1982 will conclude the interim period during which the two Governments shall complete negotiations on removal of the islands from the list of Non-Self-Governing Territories under Chapter XI of the United Nations Charter and on mutually agreed conditions for their definitive status, including due regard for the rights of the inhabitants and for the principle of territorial integrity, in accordance with the purposes and principles of the United Nations Charter, and in light of the relevant Resolutions of the United Nations General Assembly. The negotiations hereabove referred to shall begin within fifteen days of the signature of the present Agreement.

Paragraph 8

8 In order to assist them in bringing their negotiations to a mutually

satisfactory settlement by the date stipulated in the preceding paragraph, the Authority shall, after consultation with the Executive Council, make specific proposals and recommendations as early as practicable to the two Governments, including proposals and recommendations on:

8.1 The manner of taking into account the wishes and interests of the islanders, insofar as islands with a settled population are concerned, based on the results of a sounding of the opinion of the inhabitants, with respect to such issues relating to the negotiations, and conducted in such manner, as the Authority may determine;

8.2 Issues relating to the development of the resources of the islands, including opportunities for joint cooperation and the role of the Falkland Islands Company; and

8.3 Such other matters as the two Governments may request, including possible arrangements for compensation of islanders, or matters on which the Authority may wish to comment in light of its experience in discharging its responsibilities under this Agreement.

8.4 The Governments have agreed on the procedure in subparagraph 8.1 without prejudice to their respective positions on the legal weight to be accorded such opinion in reaching a definitive settlement.

Paragraph 9

9 Should the Governments nonetheless be unable to conclude the negotiations by December 31, 1982, the United States has indicated that, on the request of both Governments, it would be prepared at such time to seek to resolve the dispute within six months of the date of the request by making specific proposals for a settlement and by directly conducting negotiations between the Governments on the basis of procedures that it shall formulate. The two Governments agree to respond within one month to any formal proposals or recommendations submitted to them by the United States.

Paragraph 10

10 This Agreement shall enter into force on the date of signature.

(B) Reply to the Haig Memorandum by the Argentine Foreign Minister, 29 April 1982

Dear Mr Secretary of State:

We have carefully reviewed the document you sent us and have compared it with our previous proposals and with the viewpoints we have maintained in our various meetings. From that review, significant differences have emerged, some of which give rise to difficulties that it is essential to overcome.

As my Government has already stated to you, the objective the Argentine Government has set is recognition of its sovereignty over the Malvinas Islands. This central element of our discussions is the ultimate justification of the actions taken by my country, and as I have had occasion to tell you many times, constitutes for us an unrenounceable goal.

Along with the question of sovereignty, the current crisis gives rise immediately to the need to establish a provisional regime for administration of the islands, as an essential step in the process of separating the two military forces and as a reasonable pause in the face of the logical impossibility of formalizing their final fate at this time.

The conversations we have held have been based primarily on these two questions – recognition of sovereignty and a provisional administrative regime. Solution of the remaining problems will be simpler if there is agreement on the two points that I have just mentioned.

The one certain thing is that the two are intimately connected to each other. To the extent that the provisions relating to the recognition of our sovereignty are imprecise, for us it is necessary – if we do not want to return to the frustrating situation that prevailed before April 2 – to establish mechanisms that give us broader powers in administration of the islands.

On the other side of the coin, if it were clear that Argentina's sovereignty would be recognized in the end, then we could be more flexible regarding the matter of temporary administration.

The document sent by the Secretary of State falls short of Argentine demands and does not satisfy its minimal aspirations for either of the two points. To the contrary, unfavourable changes have been made to both. The number of Argentine representatives involved in administration of the islands has been decreased, and the opportunity of expanding my country's control in the event that negotiations on the basic issue go on endlessly without a solution has been barred. Thus we are faced with the real possibility of establishing a predominantly British administration with no fixed expiration date.

As concerns the matter of sovereignty, the concept of territorial integrity has been stripped of all meaning. Further, the new element of a virtual referendum to determine the 'wishes' of the inhabitants has been introduced in open opposition to United Nations Resolution 2065 and the unwavering position sustained by Argentina.

The Secretary knows that we cannot accept these changes. In my opinion, other formulas must be found. For this effort, we will always be at the disposal of the Secretary. These formulas should provide for the balance that I referred to above in order to weigh properly the data relating to the matter of sovereignty against the provisions regulating temporary administration of the islands. These provisions should have a fixed term and include gradually larger Argentine participation or, in lieu of this, the provision should be made precise enough to offer security for recognition of Argentina's rights within a specific period.

If Argentina's position were encompassed, agreement would be facilitated enormously and the final text of the document would not pose any insurmountable problems.

Thank you once again for your arduous and difficult negotiations.

Accept, Mr Secretary, the renewed assurances of my highest consideration.

NICANOR COSTA MENDEZ

Appendix 4

The Haig 'Tilt' Statement, 30 April 1982

The South Atlantic crisis is about to enter a new and dangerous phase, in which large-scale military action is likely. I would like to bring you up to date on what we have done, why, and what we must do now.

We have made a determined effort to restore peace through implementation of UN Security Council Resolution 502. That Resolution calls for an end to hostilities, the withdrawal of Argentine forces from the Islands; and a diplomatic settlement of the fundamental dispute.

The United States made this extraordinary effort because the stakes in human lives and international order required it. From the outset, the United States has been guided by the basic principle of the rule of law and the peaceful settlement of disputes. The collapse of that principle could only bring chaos and suffering.

We also made this effort because the crisis raised the vital issues of hemispheric solidarity at a time when the communist adversaries seek positions of influence on the mainland of the Americas, and latent territorial disputes in much of the Hemisphere called for unity and the resolute defense of principle. We acted as well because the United States has the confidence of the parties. The United Kingdom is our closest ally, and Prime Minister Thatcher's government looked to us to pursue a peaceful solution. We have also recently developed a better relationship with Argentina as part of our success in revitalizing the community of American states. President Galtieri also requested our involvement.

Under the direction of President Reagan, I participated in many days of intense discussions with the parties in the search of a framework for implementing UN Security Council Resolution 502. Our initial aim was to clarify the position of the parties and to offer suggestions on how those positions might be reconciled. We took no position on the merits of either the British or Argentine claims to the Islands. As the prospects for more intense hostilities arose, we put forth an American proposal. It represented our best estimate of what the two parties could reasonably be expected to accept, and was based squarely on our own principles and concern for the rule of law.

We regard this as a fair and a sound proposal. It involves a cessation of hostilities, withdrawal of both Argentine and British forces, termination of sanctions, establishment of a United States–United Kingdom–Argentine interim authority to maintain the agreement, continuation of the traditional local administration with Argentine participation, procedures for encouraging cooperation in the development of the Islands, and a framework for negotiations on a final settlement, taking into account the interests of both sides and the wishes of the inhabitants.

We had reason to hope that the United Kingdom would consider a settlement along the lines of our proposal, but Argentina informed us yesterday that it could not accept it. Argentina's position remains that it must receive an assurance now of eventual sovereignty or an immediate *de facto* role in governing the Islands which would lead to sovereignty.

For its part, the British Government has continued to affirm the need to respect the views of the inhabitants in any settlement.

The United States has thus far refrained from adopting measures in response to the seizure of the Islands that could have interfered with our ability to work with both sides in the search for peace.

The British Government has shown complete understanding for this position. Now, however, in light of Argentina's failure to accept a compromise, we must take concrete steps to underscore that the United States cannot and will not condone the use of unlawful force to resolve disputes.

The President has therefore ordered the suspension of all military exports to Argentina, the withholding of certification of Argentine eligibility for military sales, the suspension of new Export-Import Bank credits and guarantees, and the suspension of Commodity Credit Corporation guarantees.

The President has also directed that the United States will respond positively for requests to materiel support for British forces. There will, of course, be no direct US military involvement.

American policy will continue to be guided by our concerns for the rule of law and our desire to facilitate an early and fair settlement. The United States remains ready to assist the parties in finding that settlement. A strictly military outcome cannot endure over time. In the end, there will have to be a negotiated outcome acceptable to the interested parties. Otherwise, we will all face unending hostility and insecurity in the South Atlantic.

Appendix 5

Falkland Islands Inquiry

As part of its inquiry into the future of the Falkland Islands the Foreign Affairs Committee of the House of Commons set out to examine prospects for a negotiated settlement of the British-Argentine dispute 'in the light of the establishment of a democratic regime in Buenos Aires and in the light of previous failures to secure such a settlement'. Ten days after publication of *The Sinking of the Belgrano* the Committee invited the writers to submit a memorandum as part of their inquiry. Its text follows with two appendices attached.

Introduction
    1 The terms of reference governing the inquiry undertaken by the Foreign Affairs Committee include an examination of 'the prospects for a negotiated settlement in the light of . . . previous failures to secure such a settlement'. In this context a special relevance attaches to the circumstances in which the peace initiative launched by the government of Peru (with US backing) collapsed on May 2, 1982.
    2 The Peruvian formula for a settlement differed from previous peace proposals in content. It made no mention of sovereignty. Administration of the Falkland Islands was not to be shared nor restored to Britain but vested in third parties. British insistence on rights of self-determination for the islanders was omitted. There was to be simultaneous and mutual withdrawal of forces. These terms were not likely to have been hailed as a triumph by the Prime Minister's followers in Parliament.

3 It was distinctive in two other respects – in mode of presentation and in timing. The plan was formulated (with US help) by a country strongly supportive of Argentina; through April the proposals placed before the Junta by former Secretary of State Alexander Haig had proved unacceptable not only in substance but also because Haig was deemed to be acting in Britain's interests. The factor of timing was all-important. On the day it was transmitted telephonically to Leopoldo Galtieri by fellow-President Fernando Belaúnde Terry the bombs had begun to fall and the guns to fire on Argentine positions wreaking a toll of 56 casualties. It was on that day too that Argentina's top generals and senior officers had called on Galtieri to sue for peace because the nation's armed forces were in no position to wage all-out war against the British.

4 On the evidence of Haig and Belaúnde, playing the role of umpires, it was the first time an agreement seemed to be within sight since Argentina invaded. Galtieri himself, Nicanor Costa Mendez' Foreign Ministry and the Junta's key Working Group of senior Navy, Army and Air Force officers found the terms acceptable and expected the full Military Committee to endorse it that evening. Pym's initial reaction, he has since disclosed, was sceptical; the outline he regarded as being too 'sketchy' did not, for instance, meet Mrs Thatcher's condition according paramountcy to the 'wishes' of the Falklanders. But by May 7, with some of the terms revised, Pym indicated in Parliament that a basis of agreement did exist. But then it was too late.

5 On the night of Sunday, May 2, the Peruvian initiative foundered. What, until a few hours before, had been a controlled confrontation between British and Argentine forces suddenly escalated into fullscale conflict which only ended six weeks and more than 1,000 deaths later.

6 There had been two developments:

a At 16.01 Argentine time (19.01 GMT) the nuclear-powered submarine HMS *Conqueror* torpedoed the Argentine cruiser *General Belgrano* with the loss of 368 lives. *Belgrano*, due for retirement after 44 years' service, was outside the Total Exclusion Zone and homeward bound at the time. The decision authorizing the attack had been taken by Prime Minister Margaret Thatcher's war cabinet at Chequers seven hours earlier. Mrs Thatcher and her ministers subsequently insisted first word of the Peruvian proposals reached London only three hours *after* the *Belgrano* went down. Cecil Parkinson, at the time a member of the War Cabinet, told a Panorama TV interviewer on April 16, 1984, he and his colleagues knew about the Belaúnde initiative *before* they changed the Rules of Engagement to permit the *Conqueror* to attack the *Belgrano*.

    b News of the *Belgrano's* destruction reached members of the Junta soon after 19.00 (22.00 GMT) while they were considering the recommendations calling for approval of the Peruvian proposals. Angry uproar greeted Admiral Jorge Isaac Anaya's announcement of the sinking. With passions aroused and pride committed the Junta suspended further discussion on the option for peace and resolved instead that the fight must go on.

    7 Authorities in Washington, Lima and Buenos Aires have at no time seriously questioned the proposition that the sinking of the *Belgrano* gravely jeopardized, if it did not actually destroy, prospects for the success of Peru's attempt to arrange a negotiated peace. Pym has argued that the incident had no such effect. Other British politicians and officials have, in addition, suggested that there was no certainty the Junta would have accepted the proposals if the *Belgrano* had not been attacked. Equally, there could have been no certainty that a rejection would have been inevitable in those circumstances.

    8 What appears to be beyond argument, however, is that the sinking turned out to be the pivotal event of the South Atlantic crisis. Before it took place peace always seemed possible; afterwards it was all-out war. On a political level the incident transformed world opinion. Britain, regarded initially as the innocent victim of aggression by an unpopular authoritarian regime, was seen as the power responsible for escalating the conflict disproportionately. The huge casualty toll evoked memories of the Second World War. As a consequence the government defensively fell back on a series of rationalizations in attempting to justify the attack. As each cover story fell away under challenge a new one was advanced. The effect was to intensify controversy. Controversy generated speculation. Speculation fed suspicion.

    9 This memorandum examines official British claims that no word of the Peruvian initiative reached the government until Francis Pym's account came in after the sinking. It scrutinizes some of the dozen or so varying official explanations offered in defence of the action. And it assesses whether there was a real or

imagined linkage between the attack on the *Belgrano* and the breakdown of Peru's initiative. However no attempt has been made to analyze the US role in the affair because that would seem to stretch the Committee's terms of reference. By way of background it nevertheless should be noted that (a) Haig at the start of his mediation admitted his mission had little hope (b) US concern was focused less on the South Atlantic and more on the Mideast where the Americans knew Israeli plans were evolving for the intervention against the PLO in the Lebanon. That situation commanded greater attention from President Reagan's administration than the Falklands dispute.

Transatlantic Silence

10 A phase of intensive diplomacy followed the ending of US mediation in the Falklands dispute on April 30, 1982. The Peruvian initiative was at the centre of exchanges which also involved the United States, Argentina and, depending on which version one accepts, possibly the United Kingdom. A detailed account of those exchanges is attached to this memorandum as Appendix A.

11 A conflict of evidence has arisen over precisely when the British government first learned about the existence and content of the Peruvian peace proposals – whether before or after the *Belgrano* was sunk. The issue is one of considerable importance. It raises the question of whether the War Cabinet authorized the attack knowing there still was a prospect of peace however slender; or whether it was truly ignorant of what had been happening in Lima and Washington from early Saturday, May 1, onwards.

12 If members of the War Cabinet took the decision knowing peace talks were under way it would imply that Parliament and the people have been misled and that the logic of their military advisers was permitted to transcend the political judgement of ministers. If they were in fact ignorant of the peace talks it would imply that the British embassies in Washington and Lima had failed to keep London properly informed and that Francis Pym was, to say the least, slow in reacting to the significance of what he was being told by Haig at their Sunday, May 2, meeting and over their lunch that day.

13 The clearest and most recent Prime Ministerial statement on the matter was contained in Mrs Thatcher's April 4 letter to

Denzil Davies: 'Ministers agreed to the proposed change in the Rules of Engagement at about 1pm (12.00 GMT) London time on May 2. Orders were sent immediately to HMS *Conqueror*, which attacked the *Belgrano* at 8pm London time (19.00 GMT). Because of the indications that the *Belgrano* posed a threat to the task force, her precise position and course at the time she was sunk were irrelevant. The first indications of the possible Peruvian peace proposals reached London from Washington at 11.15 London time (22.15 GMT) and from Lima at 2am London time (01.00 GMT) on May 3.'

14 Cecil Parkinson, then a member of the War Cabinet who was at Chequers, appeared to contradict Mrs Thatcher when he told an interviewer for BBC's Panorama programme broadcast 12 days later: 'We knew that all sorts of people were . . . people who wanted to see a peaceful solution, which we wanted to see, which the prime example is . . . was President Belaúnde, trying to take up where General Haig had left off but we couldn't . . .'

15 Pym had flown into Washington by Concorde around 18.00 (22.00 GMT) Saturday, May 1 'fully briefed' on the military situation, his successor Sir Geoffrey Howe told Labour MP Tam Dalyell in a letter on 12 April 1984. That suggested he knew the *Belgrano* was in *Conqueror*'s sights; and also that he knew the government intended using 'more military force' and wanted the carrier *25 de Mayo* destroyed. If that were so it is not easy to understand why he told journalists on arrival that the day's military activity was intended to 'concentrate Argentine minds' on the need for a peaceful settlement. He added reassuringly: 'No further military action is envisaged for the moment other than making the Total Exclusion Zone secure.'

16 In the Foreign Secretary's absence Sir Anthony Acland, permanent under-secretary for foreign affairs, attended the Chequers meeting. Parkinson and Admiral of the Fleet Lord Lewin, then Chief of the Defence Staff, both told Panorama Acland kept in regular contact with Pym and advised him about the change in the Rules of Engagement. 'I have no reason to believe that he [Pym] didn't agree with that decision,' said Parkinson.

17 Pym confirmed he did not disagree and accepted the fact that, being away, he could not be consulted on the decision to sink the *Belgrano*. He told the Foreign Affairs Committee of the House of Commons on 11 June 1984 his talks with Haig had

ranged over all aspects – economic, military and strategic – of the
situation in the South Atlantic. He said he had not been especially
impressed by Haig's account of the Peruvian plan – it required a
lot more work. That is why he felt no need formally to report to
London until later in the day even though, between his tête-à-tête
with Haig at the State Department and their subsequent lunch at
the British Embassy, he was with Ambassador Sir Nicholas
Henderson for about an hour. He thus had time either to
telephone or dictate a despatch advising his War Cabinet colleagues about what Haig had told him.

18 After his two-hour session with Pym, Haig received a
confirmation from the Peruvians that Galtieri had accepted the
peace proposals in principle, subject only to ratification by the
whole Junta that evening; also that arrangements were being
made for immediate implementation. This led him to call Pym at
the British Embassy for the purpose of impressing on him the
importance the US attached to those proposals. One has to
assume Haig made that call because he felt that the Foreign
Secretary needed prodding. Whatever the reason, Pym decided
against speaking to Haig; instead he instructed Henderson to
telephone the Secretary back and emphasize that Pym, indeed,
did regard the Peruvian proposals and significantly any *other*
peace plan very seriously. He since has explained he declined
Haig's call because he did not want to miss his flight to New York
even though there is a regular air shuttle between the two cities.
The incident raised eyebrows as well as a key question: behind
the excuses did Pym refuse Haig's call because he could not, in
good conscience, speak directly with his close ally without
telling him that the destruction of the *Belgrano* was imminent?
There can be little doubt that if he learned at that crucial moment
the British were about to mount a major operation Haig would
have hit the roof. Pym, a seasoned politician, would have known
that.

19 Publicly and privately Haig, Belaúnde, Peruvian Prime
Minister Manuel Ulloa and Arias Stella have said they were
convinced British ministers were made fully aware of the progress then being made as the Peruvian initiative gained momentum. On 30 November 1983 a former member of Haig's staff
reported that the Secretary of State's office was equipped with a
secure direct telephone line to 10 Downing Street and that each
development was relayed thus to London. Ulloa and Arias Stella

have claimed they kept Wallace closely informed at all stages of
the Peruvian exchanges with Buenos Aires and Washington.
Wallace disputes this.

20 These things, taken together with information that has
filtered through confidentially from other War Cabinet ministers,
make it extremely difficult to avoid the conclusion that those
present at Chequers knew before the decision on the *Belgrano* was
taken that a Peruvian peace initiative was under way.

Cover Stories

21 The ever-changing cover stories advanced by British
ministers and officials to explain the circumstances surrounding
the sinking of the *Belgrano* appeared to conform with the traditional ambivalence which has characterized the approach to the
Falklands dispute followed by successive governments. These
shifting versions reflected not only what seemed to be ministerial
discomfiture over a controversial episode but also the government's failure to get its act of presentation together. Some aspects
of the affair have had to be discarded under challenge in the
House of Commons or by investigative journalists. Others have
remained in doubt because they have been disputed by various
participants including Haig, Belaúnde, Ulloa and Arias Stella.
The details are too numerous to incorporate in this memorandum. They are, therefore, attached as Appendix B.

22 We acknowledge that in times of war or national emergencies governments have to function under a variety of constraints.
Truth usually becomes an early casualty. Military and political
misjudgements are bound to occur. Intelligence reports are not
always assessed accurately and in any case may be mistaken. The
prime responsibility of a nation's leaders has always to be to
safeguard the lives of their servicemen in the drive for victory.

23 With all that said we suggest it would not be asking too
much to expect any government in this democratic country to
take the nation into its confidence and openly acknowledge any
blunders that may occur. Such a course would command respect
rather than contumely. A policy of consistent concealment
would, conversely, generate doubt, mistrust, cynicism.

24 From the first announcement of the reasons for the attack
on the *Belgrano* until today governmental efforts to justify the
action have been variable and therefore dubious. In turn leaders
of the opposition parties – Labour, Liberal and Social Democratic

– with differing degrees of vigour urged the need for an inquiry into the affair to reconcile disparate versions even though the issues involved are hardly vote-winners.

25 We call the attention of the Foreign Affairs Committee to two specific situations which display the sort of confused and contradictory perceptions that certainly should be avoided if future negotiations for settlement are to succeed:

a The record shows that Pym and Haig, men who were presiding over the conduct of their countries' foreign policies, had diametrically opposite understandings of what they had been discussing and of the conclusions they had reached. Haig thought they were 'down to words, single words and specifically in two paragraphs of the six points' relating to a text of the peace plan. Pym dissented, insisting 'no text [was] discussed between us, no actual words.' Again, Haig said he telephoned Pym on Saturday night, soon after his arrival, about the initiative. Pym had no memory of that. Haig maintained that the Peruvian plan 'gained acceptance in principle' from Britain and Argentina. Neither Pym nor his cabinet colleagues confirm that.

Flowing from those misunderstandings Mrs Thatcher's claim warrants study that first word of the Peruvian proposals reached London at 22.15 GMT 2 May when it was too late to undo the attack on the *Belgrano*. On the assumption that she was correct it seems fair to ask why the Washington and Lima embassies failed to keep London adequately informed. Literally thousands of lives were at stake in a war-or-peace situation. The Foreign and Commonwealth Office has always prided itself on the efficiency and competence of its operations. What went wrong?

b In writing to Denzil Davies the Prime Minister retracted past governmental claims that the *Belgrano* was spotted only a few hours before being torpedoed and that she was 'closing in' on the Task Force. Instead she acknowledged the accuracy of the information in our book, *The Sinking of the Belgrano*, saying that *Conqueror* first detected the cruiser on Friday, 30 April and sighted her early next day. In other words *Conqueror* had been trailing her for more than 30 hours before the attack. Mrs Thatcher then went on to repeat the discredited theory that *Belgrano* 'posed a threat' to the Task Force because the 'indications' (intercepts?) were that she was part of a hostile pincer movement. And so because she 'posed a threat' Mrs Thatcher asserted the *Belgrano*'s position (outside the Total Exclusion Zone) and her course (homeward for nine hours) were 'irrelevant' meaning it did not matter if she was steaming toward, or away from, the Task Force. If the Prime Minister's version was correct it would have made better military sense to have eliminated the 'threat' of the *Belgrano* much earlier when, at times, the cruiser was nearer to the Task Force.

26 The theory had been discredited at various times by officials of Mrs Thatcher's own government. '[The *Belgrano*] was not an absolutely immediate threat to our surface ships,' Admiral of the Fleet Lord Lewin told the Panorama interviewer. The former Chief of the Defence Staff added: 'She didn't become an immediate threat because we sank her.' She was, in other words, a potential threat. Lewin here seemed to be out of tune with his Prime Minister and it was not the only time. Mrs Thatcher told BBC's Newsnight programme on June 2, 1983, just before the election, that the British found and lost the Argentine carrier *25 de Mayo* twice. But Lewin told Panorama there had never been contact with the carrier and so there had been no chance to sink her. The admiral, who sallied into television studios and newspaper headlines frequently after retiring, was in no doubt that the *Belgrano* had been directing air attacks on the Task Force. Asked by Panorama's interviewer how he had got his information he replied that he had read it in the book by Max Hastings and Simon Jenkins entitled *The Battle for the Falklands*.

27 On May 5, 1982, John Nott as Defence Secretary and a member of the War Cabinet told Parliament: 'The actual decision to launch a torpedo was clearly one taken by the submarine commander.' He knew otherwise because he attended the War Cabinet meeting which authorized *Conqueror* to torpedo the *Belgrano*. From that time on British ministerial and official statements have swerved and slithered. The government's credibility became suspect. It needs restoration before any new negotiations for a settlement begin.

Linkage

28 The Thatcher government has maintained that the sinking of the *Belgrano* and the failure of Peru's peace initiative were parallel but unconnected events. It has insisted that purely military considerations motivated the attack because the cruiser posed either an immediate or, as Lewin says, a potential threat to the

Task Force. Pym told BBC's Newsnight on June 2, 1983: 'There was no connection between the two things and it's quite wrong to suppose that there is.'

29 This explanation has been challenged. Specific charges have been made inside and outside Parliament that the *Belgrano* was destroyed precisely in order to wreck the then promising prospect of a compromise settlement initiated by Peru with US help. Neil Kinnock added his authority to this sense of disquiet when, in an analysis of shifting governmental statements, he said on June 1, 1983: 'The Falklands may not be, and should not be, an election issue. The judgement and credibility of the Prime Minister is. Since she and her government have drawn credit from their conduct of the Falklands conflict they should be eager to demonstrate through a public inquiry into the sinking of the *Belgrano* that their orders were not given before all prospect of negotiated peace on acceptable terms was absolutely exhausted. Without such a thorough and impartial investigation the feeling will continue to exist that the *Belgrano* was sunk before the means of securing a bloodless defeat had been fully exploited.'

30 Leaders of the Liberal and Social Democratic parties supported the calls for a public inquiry into the affair. The controversy remains alive even now in mid-1984.

31 It follows, therefore, that even if the government is right in claiming that the two events were not connected when they took place, some sort of linkage has evolved since and does exist whether it is imagined or merely suspected. Factors that have contributed to such a belief include the inconsistencies in official explanations of the attack; contradictions between Britain's perceptions of the progress achieved by the Peruvians and the perceptions of US, Peruvian and Argentine governments; differing ministerial statements on the key question of whether the War Cabinet did or did not know that a last-ditch attempt at a compromise was under way.

32 There are two other considerations, one circumstantial, the other speculative:

    a On the cause-and-effect concept, only the British of the four governments involved has disavowed the idea that the sinking gravely harmed if it did not actually wreck the prospects for the success of the Peruvian initiative.

    b On timing, British ministers have failed to explain why they withheld authority for an earlier attack on the *Belgrano* when at times it may have been nearer, and therefore more of a danger, to the Task Force. The day-long delay in issuing the order has aroused speculation that ministers in reality were kept informed about developments in the peace talks but anticipated failure; and when prospects brightened they realized they would have to face stiff American, and general international, pressure to settle for something less than they were prepared to accept and they therefore acted in the way they did.

Conclusions

33 All the *prima facie* evidence on public record and additional information made available to us confidentially by qualified authorities in four capitals suggest the general content of the Peruvian peace proposals reached British ministers through informal channels *before* the Rules of Engagement were changed. General Haig and President Belaúnde both believe that Pym, on behalf of the British government, had accepted the plan in principle, as Galtieri had done, subject to later confirmation.

The credibility of the British government has not been enhanced by the constantly amended rationalizations offered during and since the South Atlantic conflict on the sinking of the *Belgrano*.

The attack on the Argentine cruiser was linked to the breakdown of the Peruvian peace initiative at least a) in cause-and-effect terms and b) in its timing immediately ahead of the Junta's crucial meeting when the *Belgrano* posed less of a threat than at most moments since being sighted on the morning of May 1.

Arthur Gavshon   London
Desmond Rice   June 10, 1984

Appendix 6

A Chronicle of Diplomatic and Military Developments from
April 30 to May 2, 1982

April 30:

In Washington at 11.30 (15.30 GMT) Haig announced the end
of his mediation mission, imposition of sanctions against Argentina, an offer of material support for Britain. He added: 'The
United States remains ready to assist the parties in finding that
(early and fair) settlement. A strictly military outcome cannot
endure over time.'

In Buenos Aires Nicanor Costa Méndez, then Foreign Minister, assailed the US action as 'unjustified and inopportune' and
observed it seemed to have been 'scheduled to fit in with the
operational plan of the British fleet.' On that day main elements
of the Task Forces were being deployed for action within the
newly-declared 200-nautical-mile Total Exclusion Zone around
the Falklands.

In Lima about three hours after Haig's announcement Javier
Arias Stella, incumbent Foreign Minister, telephoned US
Ambassador Frank Ortiz and expressed his government's fear
that a dangerous military situation was building up; he proposed
a determined new effort for peace citing Haig's readiness to go on
trying. Ortiz responded positively and immediately contacted
the State Department. So began the late, desperate Lima-
Washington bid to head off war with officials of both countries
working urgently to produce a set of new proposals.

In London ministers decided on the use of 'more military

force' and ordered the 'destruction' of Argentina's lone carrier, the 25 de Mayo. Signals reporting this were sent to nuclear-powered submarines attached to the Task Force. The carrier at the time was north of the islands in an area being patrolled by HMS *Splendid*: *Conqueror* was ordered to locate the *Belgrano* and by 16.00 (19.00 GMT) had picked up her group's signals.

May 1:

The pace of consultation quickened as the British launched air and sea strikes on Argentine positions in the Falklands exacting 56 casualties. Argentine authorities mistakenly assumed the naval bombardment, plus sudden shore forays by SAS and SBS units, were the start of a full-scale counter-invasion. This by mid-afternoon led the Argentine Naval High Command to order its ships at sea to search and destroy British vessels but by nightfall the order was countermanded when it was realized that the 'counter-invasion' had been no more than a feint. By about midnight all Argentine ships were called back to their home ports.

Meantime the diplomats and politicians were hard at work. From 09.00 to 14.00 (14.00 to 19.00 GMT) Peruvian President Fernando Belaúnde Terry and his ministers worked intensively with the Americans (including Haig personally) on the first draft of a new peace plan that seemed closer to Argentine than to British ideas for a settlement. Haig, broadly, was reflecting British terms while Belaúnde was speaking up for the Argentines. British embassy officials remained in touch with their State Department colleagues; Peruvian ministers insist they kept both the Argentine and British Ambassadors (Charles Wallace) closely informed of all developments. By Saturday night the draft plan had been completed after a long Haig-Belaúnde telephone talk (in the absence of President Reagan).

Belaúnde undertook to transmit the new proposals to Galtieri and did so by midnight Lima time. Haig said he would pass them on to Pym who meanwhile had flown into Washington for talks with the Secretary of State next day. Haig recalled later that he had telephoned Pym on Saturday night; Pym said he does not remember talking with Haig that night.

Pym on May 20, 1983, wrote in a letter to the *Daily Mirror* that the purpose of his visit was to discuss the consequences of the US decision to support Britain in the conflict; in other words to arrange for Britain's material needs. He gave a different version to the BBC's Panorama programme broadcast April 16, 1983: it was to make a final effort to reach a negotiated settlement.

Galtieri's first reaction to the new proposals read to him by Belaúnde were cautious but generally favourable. He had been shaken by two developments during the day. The first was the severity of the initial British air and sea attacks. The second was a demarche by the overwhelming majority of Argentine generals urging the Junta to sue for peace because the country's armed forces were simply in no state to take on the British.

May 2:

By dawn about all surface units of Argentina's high seas fleet were homeward bound, the *Belgrano* included, according to British as well as Argentine information. Exchanges between Lima and Buenos Aires and Lima and Washington went on continuously. By the middle of the day Galtieri's acceptance in principle of the Belaúnde-Haig proposals was confirmed; the ratification by the Junta was expected that night because a meeting had been set for 19.00 (22.00 GMT).

When a second confirmation of Galtieri's acceptance in principle reached Haig he took the trouble to call Pym at the British Embassy to stress what he perceived to be the significance of the situation as it then existed. Haig, as he was to confess in his memoirs two years later, knew that his job was on the line in the outcome of his role over the Falklands. If he pulled off a peace he would, for an indefinite time, be secure against the attempts of his rivals in the administration to oust him; but if he failed his number was up. That, perhaps, was one of the factors that caused him to put so much into the Peruvian effort the administration was backing. At all events Pym decided against taking Haig's call. The reason now appears plain. He had been advised of the War Cabinet's decision to change the Rules of Engagement and take out the *Belgrano*. Knowing these things he could not discuss peace prospects with his closest ally at a moment when peace prospects were about to be jeopardized by the decision of the War Cabinet. So he had Henderson call Haig back on his behalf.

While all this was going on HMS *Conqueror* was positioning herself to fire off her torpedoes against the doomed cruiser. At 16.01 (19.01 GMT) the action began. Within an hour the *Belgrano* was beneath the icy South Atlantic waters and the fate of the peace plan was sealed.

Appendix 7

A Catalogue of Inconsistencies

Official UK Position

Contradictions

On the Use of Force

First British attacks on Argentine positions on 1 May 1982 were intended to 'Concentrate Argentine minds' on the need for peace. 'No further military action is envisaged for the moment other than making the Total Exclusion Zone secure.'
(Foreign Secretary Francis Pym, Press Conference, Washington, 1 May 1982)

A Northwood signal on 30 April 1982 told Commander Wreford-Brown that the government had decided to use 'more military force' and had ordered the 'destruction' of the Argentine carrier *25 de Mayo*.
(30 April 1982 excerpt from diary of crew member of HMS *Conqueror*.)

When the Belgrano was detected

'The next day, 2 May, at 8am London time, one of our submarines detected the Argentine cruiser *General Belgrano*, escorted by two destroyers.'
(John Nott, former UK Defence Minister, House of Commons, 4 May 1982. Hansard Col. 29–30.)

'We located her on our passive sonar, and sighted her visually on the afternoon of May 1. We took up a position astern and followed the *General Belgrano* for over 30 hours. We reported that we were in contact with her.'
(Wreford-Brown, *Our Falklands War*, Geoffrey Underwood, 1983, p. 16.)

Official UK Position

'I was informed of the *Conqueror*'s signal, that she was in contact with the *Belgrano*, at around 9 or 10 on the morning of Sunday, May 2.'
(Lord Lewin, former Chief of Defence Staff, *Sunday Telegraph*, 8 April 1984.)

The Belgrano *as 'Threat'*
'This heavily armed surface attack group was close to the Total Exclusion Zone and was closing on elements of our Task Force, which was only hours away . . .'
(John Nott, ibid.)

'According to my recollection, that signal reported the *Belgrano* heading towards the Task Force.'
(Lord Lewin, ibid.)

'We were told that the *Belgrano* posed a threat, that it had the capacity within a time of about 6 hours of steaming towards our fleet, getting within range of it . . .'
(Cecil Parkinson MP, ex War Cabinet member, *Panorama*, 16 April 1984.)

Contradictions

'HMS *Conqueror* . . . detected an Argentine oiler auxiliary which was accompanying the *Belgrano* on 30 April. She sighted the *Belgrano* for the first time on 1 May . . .'
(Mrs Thatcher's letter to Denzil Davies MP, 4 April 1984.)

'Continuing passage to an area where the threats are from the cruiser *Belgrano* – an ancient ex-US 2nd World War ship with no sonar or ASW capability, two Allen Sumner Class destroyers – equally decrepit – and an oiler . . .'
(30 April 1982 entry, *Conqueror* diarist.)

'When torpedoed, we were pointing straight at the Argentine coast on a bearing we had been following for hours.'
(Captain Bonzo, *Belgrano* commander, 4 April 1983.)

'Absolute nonsense. The nearest British surface ship must have been 250 miles off. I'd have needed 14 hours to catch it at my top cruising speed of 18 knots, provided it stopped dead in its tracks.'
(Captain Bonzo, 3 June 1983.)

'They spent the night meticulously paralleling the

Official UK Position

Contradictions

Exclusion Zone about 18 miles
to the south of it.'
(*Conqueror* diarist, 2 May
morning 1982.)

'Six hours is a danger . . .
We all changed the Rules of
Engagement to enable a ship
which was a danger to our
Task Force to be sunk.'
(Mrs Thatcher, Newsnight, 2
June 1983.)

'She was not an absolutely
immediate threat to our surface
ships.'
(Lord Lewin, Panorama, 16
April, 1984.)

Who Pressed the Button?

'The actual decision to
launch a torpedo was clearly
one taken by the submarine
commander.'
(John Nott, House of Com-
mons, 5 May 1982, Hansard,
Vol. 23, Col. 156.)

'I went straight to Chequers
and called the War Cabinet into
a side-room and told them the
situation. I said we could not
wait. Here was an opportunity
to knock off a major unit of the
Argentine fleet. The cabinet
said go ahead. [Mrs Thatcher]
was superb . . .'
(Lord Lewin, *Sunday Mirror*,
11 Sept 1900.)

Was the Haig-Belaúnde Peace Plan Ready?

'All that happened on that
day [2 May 1982] was that
there were the beginnings of an
outline of a possible future
basis for negotiations which
Mr Haig outlined to me, but
that is all that it was.'
(Pym, Newsnight, 2 June
1983.)

'I most thoroughly disagree
that our 7-point peace proposal
was at all vague or general or
not ready to be put into effect
at once. It was the result of
very intensive negotiations
mainly with Haig whom we
always took to be speaking for
Britain. We thought that we
had worked out a completely
practical proposal which had a

Official UK Position

Contradictions

fair and balanced text completely consistent with the rulings of Security Council Resolution 502.'
(Arias Stella, ex Foreign Minister Peru, *Observer,* 12 June 1983.)

'There was no text discussed between us on Sunday, no actual words. We discussed ideas and the headings . . .'
(Pym, Panorama, 16 April 1984.)

'We [Haig, Belaúnde, Galtieri, Costa Méndez] had progressed rather well on the telephone. We were down to words, single words . . .'
(Haig, Panorama, 16 April 1984.)

Belaúnde: 'With the sole exception of this word wishes which the UK has just insisted on, the rest is acceptable?'

Costa Méndez: 'Correct.'
(Telephone conversation 12.00 Argentine time (15.00 GMT) 2 May 1982.)

'There was no actual piece of paper with a text being altered – there was nothing like that . . .'
(Pym, Panorama, ibid.)

'The State Department will have the two texts, English and Spanish . . . at the hour that you can give your reaction.'
(Target 10.00 Washington 2 May)
(Belaúnde to Galtieri, 01.30 Argentine time (04.31 GMT) 2 May 1982)

Who accepted Peru's Peace Plan?
'I would of course need to discuss any new proposal with

'We reduced the proposal to five simple points. [Belaúnde] gained acceptance in principle

Official UK Position

my colleagues on my return. Mr Haig fully agreed that more time and more detailed work were needed.'
(Pym, *Daily Mirror*, 20 May 1983.)

Contradictions

from both parties and on 2 May sent an official . . . to Buenos Aires with the new paper. But while the Junta was . . . considering it, the submarine HMS *Conqueror* sank the Argentine cruiser *General Belgrano* outside the blockade zone . . . The Argentinians, reacting angrily to the bad news, rejected the peace proposal.
(Haig, *Caveat*, Weidenfeld and Nicolson, 1984, p. 293–4.)

'These words were critical and it was critical to know whether or not they would be acceptable to the British government . . . basically, we arrived at some articulations that appeared that they might be.'
(Haig, Panorama, ibid.)

When did London learn of the Peace Plan?

'A thorough investigation of the records confirms that an outline of the American-Peruvian framework proposals was first communicated to London in a telegram despatched from Washington at 22.15 GMT on 2 May, over three hours after the attack on the *Belgrano*.'
(Cranley Onslow, then Minister of State FCO, House of Commons, 13 May 1983, Hansard Col. 1062.)

Cecil Parkinson MP: 'We knew that all sorts of people . . . wanted to see a peaceful solution . . . which the prime example was President Belaúnde . . .'

Panorama Presenter Emery: 'You knew that on Sunday 2 May?'

Parkinson: 'We knew all the time that there were continuing processes . . .'

Official UK Position	*Contradictions*
'The first indications of the possible Peruvian peace proposals reached London from Washington at 11.15pm London time (22.15 GMT) and from Lima at 2am London time (01.00 GMT) on 3 May.' (Mrs Thatcher's letter to Denzil Davies MP, 4 April 1984.)	. . . Anthony Acland was there. I'm sure that everybody expected that his job was to report to the Foreign Secretary what occurred at the cabinet meetings . . .' (Lord Lewin, Panorama, ibid.)
'Wallace [Charles Wallace, then British Ambassador in Lima] told Panorama that it was Sunday evening before he heard anything.' (Emery, Panorama, ibid.)	'I was in constant phone contact from about midday that Saturday until well into Sunday 2 May 1982 with both the Argentine Ambassador in Lima and the British, Charles Wallace, whom I know very well. I phoned each several times from my office to their homes, advising them of every step in our peace plan negotiations. Wallace, a conscientious man, gave me the clear impression that he was referring back to London all the time.' (Arias Stella, telephone interview, January, 1984.)

Notes

Prologue

1 The text quoted is the authors' free version of a Spanish original which runs as follows:

> CABEZA BELAUNDE MALVINAS
>
> LIMA 2 (AP) – EL PRESIDENTE FERNANDO BE-LAUNDE TERRY DIJO HOY QUE GRAN BRETANA Y ARGENTINA ANUNCIARAN ESTA NOCHE EL CESE DE TODA HOSTILIDAD EN SU DISPUTA POR LAS ISLAS MALVINAS.
>
> EL DOCUMENTO BASE FUE REDACTADO POR EL SECRETARIO DE ESTADO NORTEAMERICANO ALEX-ANDER HAIG Y TRANSMITIDO AL GOBIERNO ARGEN-TINO POR MEDIO DEL PRESIDENTE PERUANO.
>
> DIJO QUE LOS CONTACTOS PERMANENTES Y PRO-LONGADOS ENTRE LAS DOS PARTES SE INICIARON AYER, PROSIGUIERON ANOCHE Y ESTA MADRUGADA Y SERAN DADOS A CONOCER ESTA NOCHE.
>
> BELAUNDE DIJO QUE NO PODIA ADELANTAR LOS PUNTOS DEL ACUERDO CON LA EXCEPCION DEL PRIMERO, SOBRE EL CUAL NO HAY DISCUSION: CESA-CION INMEDIATA DE LAS HOSTILIDADES.
>
> AP-NY-05-02 2244GMT

2 The *Conqueror*'s own announcement gave the position as 55°30′ S, 60° 40′ W; the Argentine UN representative's on 3 May as 55° 24′ S, 60° 32′ W. The latter figure coincides with that given to the authors by Captain Bonzo of the *Belgrano*.

Chapter 1

1   The word 'again' appears to prejudge the issue, but in using it the
    authors are echoing the Foreign Office file dated 1940, not to be
    opened until the year 2015, and whose title is 'Proposed offer by
    His Majesty's Government to *reunite* Falkland Islands with Argen-
    tina and acceptance of lease' (our emphasis). It is quoted in Latin
    America Bureau, *Falklands/Malvinas. Whose Crisis?* (1982), p. 36. It
    appears that leaseback is not a new solution to the Falklands
    problem.

2   Quoted in Peter J. Beck, 'The Anglo–Argentine Dispute Over
    Title to the Falkland Islands: Changing British Perceptions on
    Sovereignty since 1910', *Millennium: Journal of International Studies*,
    vol. 12 no. 1 (Spring 1983), p. 18. The authors are indebted to Dr
    Beck for much of their material on the sovereignty of the Falkland
    Islands.

3   Latin America Bureau, op. cit., p. 35.

4   See Beck, op. cit., p. 12.

5   Quoted ibid., p. 13.

6   Ibid., p. 16.

7   Ibid., p. 15.

8   Julius Goebel, *The Struggle for the Falkland Islands* (New Haven,
    1982 ed.), p. 468.

9   Beck, op. cit., p. 21.

10 Quoted by Martin Walker, *Guardian*, 19 June 1982.

11 Beck, op. cit., p. 17.

12 *The South American Handbook 1977* (Bath, 1976), p. 125.

13 Latin America Bureau, op. cit., p. 6.

14 Quoted ibid., p. 17.

15 *Falkland Islands Review*, Report of a Committee of Privy Counsel-
    lors under the Chairmanship of Lord Franks (henceforward re-
    ferred to as Franks Report), Cmnd. 8787 (1983), p. 94.

16 Franks Report, paras 52–7.

17 Ibid., paras 17, 16.

18 Ibid., para 23.

19 Ibid., para 60.

20 Ibid., para 61.

21 Martin Walker, *Guardian*, 19 June 1982.

22 Franks Report, para 66.

23 Ibid., para 148.

24 Ibid., para 75.

25 Ibid., para. 77.

26 Interviewed on 13 July 1983.

27 Franks Report, para. 112.

28 Ibid., para. 108.

29 Ibid., para. 100.
30 Ibid., para. 291.
31 William Wallace, 'The Franks Report', *International Affairs*, vol. 59 no. 3.

Chapter 2

1 League of Nations figures quoted in A. R. Carranza, *El Terrorismo en la Historia Universal y en la Argentina* (Buenos Aires, 1980).
2 Interviewed in Buenos Aires, 15 April 1983.
3 Taking unit prices in 1970 as 100, Argentina's export price index had risen to 247.1 by 1982. Her *import* price index shot up to 534.5 in the same period. Every dollar earned by imports in 1982 bought less than half – 46.2 per cent – of what it had bought in 1970. Information from *Clarín*, 17 April 1983.
4 Main sources are various interviews in Buenos Aires in July 1982 and April 1983.
5 A. A. Pineiro, *Crónica de la Subversión en la Argentina* (Buenos Aires, 1980).
6 Quoted in *La Nación*, 6 August 1980.
7 Sir Nicholas Henderson, 'America and the Falklands', *Economist*, 12 November 1983, p. 50. Strictly speaking, Argentina had no troops in Central America but followed the American tradition of 'military advisers', mainly in El Salvador, some 100–110 in all. The Argentines also trained between 40 and 50 anti-Sandinista officers for the Nicaraguan guerrilla in January and February 1982 and made a large sale of automatic rifles and pistols to the anti-Sandinistas at the same time. For the 'rapprochement with the United States from the time President Reagan's administration took office', see Franks Report, para. 276.
8 The efforts of General Walters to interest Argentine military leaders in the SATO project, or something like it, were reported to the authors by officials in the Pentagon and State Department, Washington, and by Argentine officials in Buenos Aires. They asked not to be identified.
9 *Clarín*, 17 April 1983.
10 See Sunday Times Insight Team, *The Falklands War* (1982); Latin America Bureau, *Falklands/Malvinas. Whose Crisis?* (1982), pp. 80–1; Franks Report, paras 274–5.
11 Franks Report, paras 129–32.
12 The Franks Report denial is made in para. 66 and reiterated in paras 148 and 329, as well as on p. 91. When approached by the authors about the discrepancy, James Callaghan declined to go into detail in advance of publishing his own account of the affair.

13   Henderson, 'America and the Falklands', p. 54.

14   Franks Report, para. 316.

15   Interview with one of the writers, London, July 1981.

16   Franks Report, para. 321.

17   'Informe Secreto', article in *Siete Días*, Buenos Aires, 30 March 1983, p. 43.

18   Costa Méndez was interviewed on 13 and 19 April 1983.

19   Galtieri interview, 11 August 1982. *Clarín*, 2 April 1983.

20   'Informe Secreto', p. 41.

21   Franks Report, para. 262.

22   Ibid., para. 201.

23   For more details on Astiz and his role, see *The Falklands War*, pp. 68–9; *Falklands/Malvinas. Whose Crisis?* pp. 78–9.

24   Franks Report, para. 195.

25   Ibid., para. 209.

26   The National Union of Seamen later sent an official protest to the Ministry of Defence over the way the *Fort Austin*'s crew had been treated. 'The crew were totally misled by those in authority,' the Union wrote.

27   Franks Report, paras 216, 222, 243.

28   Ibid., paras 233–4.

29   *Daily Express*, 26 July 1982.

30   *Official Report*, 26 October 1982, col. 885.

31   *Official Report*, 3 April 1982, col. 667.

32   *La Nueva Provincia*, Bahía Blanca, issues of 2 April 1982 and 2 April 1983.

33   Interviewed on 30 March 1983 at Joint Chiefs of Staff HQ, Buenos Aires.

34   Dr J. C. Murguizur, 'The South Atlantic Conflict, an Argentinian point of view', *International Defense Review* 2 (1983), p. 135.

35   Ibid.

36   Interviewed in Buenos Aires, 15 July 1982.

37   Murguizur, 'The South Atlantic Conflict', p. 137.

38   Interviews of 13 and 19 April 1983.

39   Murguizur, 'The South Atlantic Conflict', p. 135.

Chapter 3

1   *Official Report*, 3 April 1982, vol. 21, col. 668 (emphasis added).

2   These observations were made in a conversation with a serving British admiral who asked that his name should not be used. Other serving officers confirmed what he said.

3   Franks Report, paras 152–3.

4   Ibid., para. 273.

5 Third Report from the Defence Committee of the House of Commons: 'The Future Defence of the Falkland Islands'; HC-154, 12 May 1983, p. XLIII. Task Force ships were given servicing and victualling facilities during the conflict by Senegal and Gambia; payments were made under the cloak of Britain's Overseas Development Aid Programme.

6 SIPRI, *The Falklands/Malvinas Conflict – a Spur to Arms Build-ups* (1983), p. 9.

7 Institute for Strategic Studies, London, quoted in *La Nueva Provincia*, Bahía Blanca, 2 April 1982.

8 Dr J. C. Murguizur, 'The South Atlantic Conflict, an Argentinian point of view', *International Defense Review* 2 (1983), pp. 138, 140–1.

9 SIPRI, op. cit., p. 9.

10 *Economist*, 1 May 1982.

11 Total made up of 16 Miragos (*Statesman's Year-Book 1981–82*, p. 90) and 42 Daggers (Latin America Bureau, *Falklands/Malvinas. Whose Crisis?* (1982), Table 10, p. 133). Together with Argentina's 68 Skyhawks and 5 Super Etendards, this gives a total of some 131 front-line attack aircraft, 29 more than in the SIPRI account. However the latter concerns major armaments directly involved in the war, so there is no necessary contradiction.

12 *Statesman's Year-Book 1981/82*, p. 90.

13 Press conference, Buenos Aires, 8 July 1982.

14 Sunday Times Insight Team, *The Falklands War* (1982), p. 194.

15 Murguizur, 'South Atlantic Conflict', p. 139.

16 Captain Pablo Marcos Carballo (Squadron Commander), *Dios y Los Halcones* (*God and the Falcons*, dealing with the Argentine air force's war). Quoted in *Siete Días*, 30 March 1983, p. 20.

17 *Falklands War*, p. 196.

18 *Dios y los Halcones*, quoted in *Siete Días*, 30 March 1983, p. 20.

19 *The Falklands Campaign: The Lessons*, Cmnd. 8758 (December 1982), Annex C.

20 Interview with Captain Raúl Galmarini, ex-commander Aeronaval, Espora 21 July 1982.

21 Article in the Centro Naval's Bulletin of October–December 1982.

22 Interviewed in Bahía Blanca, 14 April 1983.

23 Murguizur, 'South Atlantic Conflict', p. 136.

24 Major-General Moore was delivering a lecture on 'The Falklands Experience' alongside Admiral Sir John Woodward, at the Royal United Services Institute, London, 20 October 1982.

25 See *The Falklands Campaign*, Cmnd. 8758, p. 25.

26 Ibid., p. 6.

27 Sir Nicholas Henderson's disclosure was made during an interview with one of the writers on 13 July 1983.

28 Sir Nicholas Henderson, 'America and the Falklands', *Economist*, 12 November 1983, pp. 53, 54.

29 The Right Honourable Margaret Thatcher, speaking at the Winston Churchill Foundation Award Dinner, British Embassy, Washington, 29 September 1983.

30 Félix Luna, 'Habla El Presidente del Peru', *Todo Es Historia*, Buenos Aires, no. 191, April 1983.

31 This interview with Galtieri of July 1982 is quoted in *Clarín*, Buenos Aires, 2 April 1983.

32 In addition to the five nuclear submarines, the Oberon-class diesel-electric submarine *Onyx* participated not only in patrols and protection but also in landing raiding and scouting parties on the Falklands. She was refuelling at Ascension on 12 May, and did not reach the Falklands till around the 24th.

Chapter 4

1 Franks Report, para. 235.

2 Interviewed on 13 July 1983.

3 Takacs and Costa Méndez were interviewed in Buenos Aires on 12 April and on 13 and 19 April 1983 respectively.

4 Sir Nicholas Henderson, 'America and the Falklands', *Economist*, 12 November 1983, p. 50.

5 Ibid., p. 53.

6 Ibid., p. 50.

7 *The Falklands Campaign: The Lessons*, Cmnd. 8758 (December 1982), pp. 37, 39.

8 *La Nueva Provincia*, 2 April 1983.

9 Details of vessels from *Jane's Fighting Ships 1981–82*.

10 Composition of Argentine Task Force 79 from Mark Hewish, 'The Falklands Conflict: Naval Operations', *International Defense Review* 10 (1982), p. 1340.

11 Telephone interviews with the commander of the *General Belgrano*, Captain Hector Bonzo, 3 June 1983.

12 Henderson, 'America and the Falklands', p. 54.

13 Ibid.

14 José García Enciso, Personal Assistant to General Norberto Iglesias, Secretary General of the Presidency, interviewed in Buenos Aires on 7 April 1983.

15 Dr Kiracofe was interviewed in Washington at various times between 22 April and mid-May 1983. He had visited Buenos Aires

on 19 May 1982, and took copies of key parts of the five Argentine peace proposals.

16   Henderson, 'America and the Falklands', p. 54.
17   Interview of 11 August 1982, quoted in *Clarín*, 2 April 1983.
18   Henderson, 'America and the Falklands', p. 55.
19   Ibid., p. 60.
20   Interviewed at Brooks's Club, 22 November 1983.
21   *Congressional Record*, Senate, 29 April 1982, S.4316.
22   Henderson, 'America and the Falklands', p. 54.
23   Interviewed on 7 April 1983.
24   Quoted in H. H. Rodriguez, 'Special Report', *Convicción*, Buenos Aires, 10 February 1983.
25   Quoted in Henderson, 'America and the Falklands', p. 53.
26   Ibid., p. 54.
27   According to the article by H. H. Rodriguez, quoted in note 24 above, some time after the sinking of the *Belgrano* Senator Helms contacted Jeane Kirkpatrick, who that morning had told the press – at Haig's suggestion – that she intended to resign. When she was informed about Kiracofe's report of the five undisclosed peace proposals, she changed her mind about resigning. She told Helms that she had had a memo from Haig saying that: 'All we can expect from the Argentines is a mind set against negotiation.' One of Helms's contacts in the Pentagon told him that Haig had never mentioned the five proposals there either, and President Reagan's aides said that he too had been kept in the dark. According to Helms, Reagan then asked Haig for the proposals, which he had no option but to hand over. Reagan commented: 'This is much more reasonable than what Haig told us. Haig has lost his grip.' All this was going on in early June 1982. On 26 June Reagan asked for and received Haig's resignation. During his incumbency the Secretary of State had been at the centre of several controversies.
28   Interview of 22 November 1983.
29   Henderson, 'America and the Falklands', p. 60.

Chapter 5

1   Dr J. C. Murguizur, an Argentine military expert with access to the High Command, has written about the Falklands war casualties that: 'The British loss figures, no doubt fudged by the British government, ought to be at least comparable with ours. The author is personally convinced, however, that British losses were considerably higher.' Of naval losses, he asserts: 'It is quite evident that the British are concealing the true scale of their losses; it is highly likely that other ships were sunk and their loss will be

announced later.' 'The South Atlantic Conflict', *International Defense Review* 2 (1983), p. 136.

To highups in Britain's Ministry of Defence Dr Murguizur's account reflected either poor research or fanciful self-delusion. We asked the Ministry whether three British landing attempts on the Falklands were repulsed on 1 May 1982, as the Argentine historian claimed. A spokesman replied: 'The only landing attempt which British forces made was the successful one on 21 May. Special forces did begin to infiltrate the Falklands from 1 May onwards but there were no hostilities between them and the defenders until after the main landing with the exception of the raid on Pebble Island on 15 May.' Were 'several British warships, including the *Hermes* hit?' The spokesman's reply: 'In Argentine air attacks on 1 May no *serious damage* was caused to any ships of the Task Force. *Hermes* was not hit and, despite repeated Argentine assertions to the contrary, neither carrier was damaged at all during the entire course of the conflict.' The spokesman then went on to offer this general observation:

> The Argentine failure to come to terms with the untruths which their propaganda machine generated about damage to or sinking of the carriers is very profound. To refute it one has only to look at the pictures of the warships returning to the UK. The badly damaged ships (HMS *Glamorgan*, HMS *Argonaut* and others) carried visible scars. There was no comparable damage to the carriers.

Murguizur's estimate that 'at least 38 British ships . . . including the two aircraft carriers' had been either lost or damaged was brushed aside with equal emphasis. 'It's fanciful to suggest that we have concealed the true scale of our ship losses,' the spokesman said. 'The loss of a ship simply cannot be concealed indefinitely from a democratic society. The total number of Task Force ships, including merchant ships, lost or damaged was 19.' Finally the charge by Murguizur and others that British casualty figures had been fudged was put squarely to the Ministry. 'It's an absolutely baseless allegation,' the spokesman insisted. 'The figures – 255 dead, 777 injured – have been given repeatedly in public statements.'

Task Force ships lost or damaged were HMS *Sheffield, Coventry, Ardent, Antelope, Glasgow, Antrim, Glamorgan, Argonaut, Brilliant, Broadsword, Plymouth, Arrow*; Royal Fleet Auxiliaries (RFA) *Sir Lancelot, Sir Galahad, Sir Tristram*, and *Sir Percival*; one LCU; the SS *Atlantic Conveyor* and MV *British Wye*. Argentina additionally bombed the British tanker *Hercules*, which was not part of the Task Force. More ships and lives might have been lost: *Atrim*, *Brilliant*, *Broadsword* and *Sir Galahad* were all hit by bombs which failed to explode.

2   Murguizur, 'South Atlantic Conflict', p. 137.

3   Cable text and operational details from Argentine navy sources.

4   For example an American admiral who took part in US-Argentine naval exercises code-named Unitas and Ocean Venture '81 remarked to his opposite number, Rear-Admiral Horacio Zaratiegui, commander of the Southern Naval Region during the Falklands war (interviewed in Buenos Aires, 24 March 1983), that he saw the islands as 'two fantastic unsinkable aircraft-carriers'.

5   *Official Report*, 21 December 1982. A striking instance of the extent of US penetration is the location of the CIA's Buenos Aires station in the same office block that houses the Argentine High Command, in the Paseo Colón. At the time of the South Atlantic crisis, CIA operatives were in a position to monitor developments and discussions within the high command not only through their privileged access to Argentine senior officers but also through electronic eavesdropping.

6   Brazil also supplied aircraft – 12 Bandeirante reconnaissance planes – and Israel sent 22 Daggers. According to Galtieri, in his interview with Juan Bautista Jofre of 11 August 1982, reported in *Clarín*, 2 April 1983, the Israeli air force 'told me it had pilots available too . . .'

7   German Sopeña, 'Historia de Una Mediación Frustrada', *Siete Días*, 26 January 1983.

8   Félix Luna, 'Habla el Presidente del Peru', *Todo es Historia*, no. 191, April 1983.

9   'They could not possibly be described as "proposals".' Sir Nicholas Henderson, 'America and the Falklands', *Economist*, 12 November 1983, p. 55.

10 The following text is the authors' free translation of the original telephone transcript in Spanish.

11 Quoted in *Estrategia*, no. 71–72, Buenos Aires, September 1982.

12 From interviews with Costa Méndez in Buenos Aires on 13 and 19 April 1983.

13 Quoted in German Sopeña, 'Historia de Una Mediación Frustrada', *Siete Días*, 26 January 1983.

14 Authors' translation from Spanish original.

15 Phone interview with Dr Arias Stella in Miami, 10 June 1983.

16 Phone interview with Dr Arias Stella in New York, 8 June 1983.

17 Quoted by Andrew Wilson and Arthur Gavshon, *Observer*, 5 June 1983.

18   In his column in the *Daily Mirror* of 23 June 1983, Paul Foot quotes
     a statement by Prime Minister Ulloa in which he recalls that he told
     Haig late in the morning of 2 May that the Peruvian and Argentine
     leaderships reckoned that they had an agreement but that it might
     take 24 to 48 hours for the three Argentine commands to be
     consulted. In the meantime, could Haig make sure that the British
     took no hostile action? Haig said that he would do his best, but
     there was 'a strong government and a determined people over
     there'. Ulloa emphasized the importance of pressing the British for
     restraint. Haig promised that he would do his best.

19   Telephone interview on 17 September 1983.

20   Oscar Raúl Cardozo, Ricardo Kirschbaum, Eduardo van der
     Kooy, *Malvinas, La Trama Secreta* (Sudamericana – Planeta,
     Buenos Aires, 1983), p. 229.

21   Telephone interview with Dr Arias Stella, now Peru's ambassador
     to the UN, January 1984.

Chapter 6

1   *Belgrano* details from her former captain, Hector Bonzo, in tele-
     phone interviews on 3 June 1983.

2   'The *Belgrano*: I had no qualms sinking her', *Sunday Mirror*, 11
     September 1983.

3   'Why the *Belgrano* was doomed', *Sunday Times*, 5 June 1983.

4   Sir Nicholas Henderson, 'America and the Falklands', *Economist*,
     12 November 1983, p. 55.

5   Admiral Woodward, lecture to Royal United Services Institute, 20
     October 1982.

6   'World This Weekend', 30 January 1983.

7   Report in *La Semana*, Buenos Aires, 12 May 1982.

8   As reported by Captain Bonzo, Buenos Aires, 6 October 1983.

9   Quoted in *Casos*, no. 7, Buenos Aires, June 1982.

10 Ibid. Three weeks later they were still treating Pardo's lungs in a
     shore hospital. He had internal bleeding and severe inflammation
     from breathing toxic gases.

11 Telephone interview with Ugo Villareal of the Centre for Ex-
     Combatants in Buenos Aires, 6 January 1984.

12 Inaudi's account is quoted from *Revista 10*, no. 31, Buenos Aires,
     11 May 1982.

13 Henderson, 'America and the Falklands', p. 55.

14 *Official Report*, 4 May 1982, vol. 23, cols 29–30.

15 Ibid., 29 October 1982, vol. 33 col. 104.

Chapter 7

1   Sir Nicholas Henderson, 'America and the Falklands', *Economist*, 12 November 1983, p. 55.
2   Authors' translation from the recording of the press conference.
3   Henderson, 'America and the Falklands', p. 56.
4   Ibid., p. 55 (authors' emphasis).
5   Ibid.
6   Ibid., p. 56.
7   *Boletín del Centro Naval* no. 733, October–December 1982, Buenos Aires.
8   *The Falklands War* (1982), pp. 163–7.
9   Henderson, 'America and the Falklands'. Further quotes below are from the same source.
10 *The Falklands Campaign: The Lessons*, Cmnd. 8758 (December 1982), p. 10.
11 Henderson, 'America and the Falklands', p. 58.
12 Ibid., pp. 58, 59.
13 Dr J. C. Murguizur, 'The South Atlantic Conflict', *International Defense Review* 2 (1983), p. 138.

Chapter 8

1   'The Inside Story of Galtieri's Arrest', *Gente*, Buenos Aires, 14 April 1983, pp. 5–11.
2   Rattenbach gave a preliminary version of his Report to the Army C-in-C in mid-1983. The full Report was published late in 1983. The account given here is based on details leaked to the press and published in the Buenos Aires paper *La Voz*, 24 August 1983.
3   *Falklands Islands Review* (the Franks Report), Cmnd. 8787 (January 1983), para. 339 (emphasis added).
4   Reply to the Editor, *Daily Mirror*, 20 May 1983.
5   See note 18 of Chapter 5.
6   Lecture given at the Royal United Services Institute, London, 20 October 1982, and reprinted in the *RUSI Journal*, March 1983.
7   30 January 1983.
8   Interviewed at Brooks's Club, 22 November 1983.
9   *Guardian*, 4 June 1983.
10 Interviewed in Buenos Aires, 24 March 1983.
11 *Official Report*, 21 December 1982, col. 902.
12 Interviewed by Arthur Gavshon, *Observer*, 5 June 1983.
13 *Official Report*, vol. 44, no. 9, cols 500–03.
14 Ibid., 4 May 1982, vol. 23, cols 29–30.
15 Ibid., 5 May 1982, vol. 23, col. 156.

Chapter 9

1 Latin America Bureau, *Falklands/Malvinas. Whose Crisis?* (1982), pp. 106–7.

2 Sir Nicholas Henderson, 'America and the Falklands', *Economist*, 12 November 1983, pp. 52–3.

3 Anthony Barnett, *Iron Britannia* (1982), pp. 122–5.

4 Simon Jenkins, 'The Thatcher Style', *Economist*, 21 May 1983, p. 32.

5 Henderson, 'America and the Falklands', p. 54.

6 Ibid., p. 60.

7 Henderson, interviewed at Brooks's Club, 22 November 1983.

8 On 5 May, according to the Insight Team (*Falklands War* (1982), p. 182), a signal from *Hermes* announced that the Task Force was only to be kept operational for another month. The 5th would have made a feasible deadline for an Argentine response.

9 Henderson, Brooks's Club, 22 November 1983.

10 Our information from sources close to the Peruvian leadership is that Lord Thomas was in touch with Lima by telephone late that weekend.

11 Henderson, 'America and the Falklands', p. 55.

12 Ibid., p. 56.

13 The Nimrods carried AD 470 Marconi transceiver equipment. *Invincible* was the lead ship of NATO's anti-submarine warfare force. Broad-waveband transceivers enabled her to pick up Soviet signal traffic from air, sea and from land, even from far out in the north-west Atlantic.

14 Henderson, Brooks's Club, 22 November 1983.

15 Henderson, 'America and the Falklands', p. 56.

16 *The Falklands Campaign: The Lessons*, Cmnd. 8758 (December 1982), para. 211.

17 Philip Windsor (Reader in International Relations at LSE), 'Diplomatic Dimensions of the Falklands Crisis', *Millennium: Journal of International Studies*, vol. 12 no. 1, p. 88.

18 *The Times*, 21 July 1976.

19 Tables based on Gallup Public Opinion Polls.

20 Speech delivered at Cheltenham Race Course, 3 July 1982.

21 Quoted in Anthony Barnett, *Iron Britannia* (1982), p. 12.

22 *Latin American Times*, August 1983, no. 52.

23 According to *Jane's Fighting Ships, 1982–83*, four frigates being built for Argentina in West German yards were supplied with 2 Rolls Royce Olympus TM 3B gas turbines and 2 Rolls Royce Tyne RM 1C gas turbines; David Brown UK Ltd supplied gear systems and Hawker Siddeley the main engine controls. Decca supplied surface search and main radar navigational

equipment for 6 corvettes also built in West Germany for the Argentine navy.

24   This heavy water was at the centre of a complex transaction which began when the Americans sold it to Britain and West Germany for their own use. Before the Falklands war, both countries were trying to resell it to Argentina. Negotiations were suspended when the crisis flared. Then Britain turned over its share of ownership and control to West Germany, knowing that the negotiations with Argentina would be resumed after the conflict. See Rob Edwards' account, *New Statesman*, 18 November 1983.

25   Testimony to Subcommittee on Inter-American Affairs of the House Foreign Affairs Committee, 5 August 1982. Enders offered no statistics on Latin America's *domestic* casualties in the same period.

26   Reported in *The Times*, 18 November 1983.

27   Interviewed in Bahía Blanca, 11 April 1983.

28   Rattenbach Report, Article 756.

29   Ibid. Article 890.

Suggested Reading List

A   In English

1   Books

Anthony Barnett, *Iron Britannia* (London, Allison & Busby, 1982).

Patrick Bishop & John Witherow, *The Winter War* (London, Quartet Books, 1982).

The Falklands Campaign: The Lessons, Cmnd. 8758 (London, HMSO, December 1982).

Falkland Islands Review (The Franks Report), Cmnd. 8787 (London, HMSO, 1982).

Tam Dalyell, *One Man's Falklands* (London, Cecil Woolf, 1982).

—, *Thatcher's Torpedo* (London, Cecil Woolf, 1983).

Julius Goebel Jr, *The Struggle for the Falkland Islands: A Study in Legal and Diplomatic History* (New Haven, Yale University Press, 1927 & 1982; London, OUP, 1927).

Robert Harris, *Gotcha! The Media, the Government and the Falklands Crisis* (London, Faber & Faber, 1982).

Max Hastings and Simon Jenkins, *The Battle for the Falklands* (London, Pan Books, 1983).

House of Commons, HC 154, *The Future Defence of the Falkland Islands* (3rd Report of the Defence Committee, Session 1982–83), Minutes of the Proceedings of the Foreign Affairs Committee, Session 1982–83.

Sunday Times Insight Team, *The Falklands War* (London, Sphere, 1982).

International Institute for Strategic Studies, *Strategic Survey 1982–83* (London, 1983).

Jane's Fighting Ships, 1982–83 (London, 1982).

Latin America Bureau, *Falklands/Malvinas. Whose Crisis?* (London, 1982).

Stockholm International Peace Research Institute, *The Falklands/Malvinas Conflict* (Stockholm, SIPRI, 1983).

2   Articles and Periodicals

Malcolm Deas, 'Falklands Title Deeds', *London Review of Books*, 18 August–2 September 1982.

The Economist: all coverage from April 1982, and notably issues of 10 April, 1 & 8 May and 19 June 1982.

Lawrence Freedman (Professor of War Studies, King's College, London), 'The War of the Falkland Islands', *Foreign Affairs*, vol. 61 no. 1 (Autumn 1982).

Sir Nicholas Henderson, 'America and the Falklands', *The Economist*, 12 November 1983. (See Costa Mendez' reply, *Economist* 14 Jan. 1984.)

Adrian J. Hope, 'Sovereignty and Decolonization of the Malvinas/Falklands', *Boston College International and Comparative Law Review*, vol. 6 no. 2 (1983).

International Affairs, 'Falklands Retrospective', issue mainly devoted to the Falklands question, vol. 59 no. 3 (Summer 1983).

Millennium: Journal of International Studies, 'The Falklands Crisis: One Year Later', issue devoted to the Falklands question (see in particular Peter Beck's article), vol. 12 no. 1 (Spring 1983).

Martin Walker, 'The Giveaway Years', special supplement, pp. 11–14, *The Guardian*, 19 June 1982.

Admiral Sir John Woodward and Major General Sir Jeremy Moore, 'The Falklands Experience', lecture reprinted in *Royal United Services Institute Journal*, 20 October 1982.

B In Spanish

1 Books

Norberto O. Beladrich, *El Parlamento Suicida* (Buenos Aires, Ediciones De-Palma, 1980).

Carlos S. Brignone, *Los Destructores de la Economía* (B.A., Ediciones DePalma, 1980).

Cardozo, Kirschbaum and van der Kooy, *Malvinas, La Trama Secreta* (B.A., Sudamericana–Planeta, 1983).

Ambrosio Romero Carranza, *El Terrorismo en la Historia Universal y en la Argentina* (B.A., Ediciones DePalma, 1980).

Bonifacio del Carril, *La Crisis Argentina*. (B.A., Emecé, 1960).

—, *La Cuestión de las Malvinas* (B.A., Emecé, 1982).

—, *El Dominio de las Islas Malvinas* (B.A., Emecé, 1964).

Roberto García, *Patria Sindical versus Patria Socialista* (B.A., Ediciones De-Palma, 1980).

José Martínez de Hoz, *Bases para una Argentina Moderna* (B.A., 1981).

Armando Alonso Pineiro, *Crónica de la Subversión en la Argentina* (B.A., Ediciones DePalma, 1980).

Robert A. Potash, *El Ejército y La Política en la Argentina* (B.A., Editorial Sudamericana, 1982).

2 Articles and Periodicals

Ana Baron, 'Como y por que Hundimos al Belgrano' (interview with Captain Richard Hask, Commander of British Submarine Fleet in the South Atlantic), *Gente*, Buenos Aires, 14 April 1983.

Jorge Capsiski, 'Informe Secreto, Malvinas, Como, Por Que y Para Que', *Siete Días*, 30 March 1983.

Capitán Pablo Marcos Carballo, 'Dios y Los Halcones' (an account of all the Falklands missions flown by the Argentine air force), *Siete Días*, Buenos Aires, 1983).

Sergio Ciancaglini, 'El Arresto de Galtieri', *Gente*, Buenos Aires, 14 April 1983.

Capitán Jorge Luis Colombo (Super Etendard squadron leader), 'Operaciones de Aviones Navales Super Etendard en la Guerra de las Malvinas', *Boletín del Centro Naval*, Buenos Aires, no. 733 vol. C (October–December 1982).

Nicanor Costa Méndez, 'Islas Malvinas', *La Nación*, 1 & 2 September 1983.

Roque Escobar, 'Una Oportunidad Malograda por Nuestra Propia Ineptitud' (interview with Admiral Horacio Zaratiegui), *Siete Días*, 30 March 1983.

Estrategia (Special Edition on the Malvinas War), Buenos Aires, no. 71–2 (19 September 1982).

'La Historia Secreta del Arresto de Galtieri', *Gente*, 14 April 1983.

Félix Luna, 'Habla el Presidente del Peru', *Todo Es Historia*, Buenos Aires, no. 191 (April 1983).

'El Informe Atribuido Al General Rattenbach', *La Nación*, Buenos Aires, 24 August 1983.

La Nueva Provincia, Bahía Blanca, special editions on the Malvinas War, 2 April 1982 and 2 April 1983.

Doctora Giuliana Bossi de Rocca, 'La Soberanía Argentina en Las Islas Malvinas', *Boletín Informativo* no. 208 of the Organización Techint de Buenos Aires (October–December 1983).

German Sopcña, 'Historia de Una Mediación Frustrada', *Siete Días*, 26 January 1983.

'Por Que Se Perdio en las Malvinas, Borrador del Informe Final del General Rattenbach', *La Voz*, Buenos Aires, 24 August 1983.

Juan Bautista Yofre, 'A Un Año del Desembarco en las Malvinas' (three interviews with General Galtieri), *Clarín*, special supplement, 2 April 1983.

Index

Give them
the pleasure of choosing

Book Tokens can be bought
and exchanged at most
bookshops in Great Britain
and Ireland.

NEL BESTSELLERS

Orbit	*Thomas Block*	£1.95
The White Plague	*Frank Herbert*	£2.50
Shrine	*James Herbert*	£2.25
Christine	*Stephen King*	£2.50
The War Hound and theWorld's Pain	*Michael Moorcock*	£2.50
Spellbinder	*Harold Robbins*	£2.50
The Longest Day	*Cornelius Ryan*	£1.95
The Case of Lucy B.	*Lawrence Sanders*	£2.50
Acceptable Losses	*Irwin Shaw*	£1.95
Crabs's Moon	*Guy N. Smith*	£1.75
I, The Jury	*Mickey Spillane*	£1.25
The Seven Minutes	*Irving Wallace*	£2.25

All these books are available at your local bookshop or newsagent, or can be ordered direct from the publisher. Just tick the titles you want and fill in the form below.

NEL P.O. BOX 11, FALMOUTH TR10 9EN, CORNWALL

Postage Charge:

U.K. Customers 50p for the first book plus 20p for the second book and 14p for each additional book ordered to a maximum charge of £1.63.

B.F.P.O. & EIRE Customers 50p for the first book plus 20p for the second book and 14p for the next 7 books; thereafter 8p per book.

Overseas Customers 75p for the first book and 21p per copy for each additional book.

Please send cheque or postal order (no currency).

Name ....

Address ....

....

Title ....

While every effort is made to keep prices steady, it is sometimes necessary to increase prices at short notice. New English Library reserve the right to show on covers and charge new retail prices which may differ from those advertised in the text or elsewhere. (B)